BEYOND RELIGION

The personal search for truth

BEYOND RELIGION

The personal search for truth

BARBARA MAYER

Insights from a Former Nun

SANCTUARY PUBLICATIONS

Beyond Religion: The Personal Search for Truth

Published by
Sanctuary Publications, P. O. Box 20697, Sedona, Arizona 86341

Copyright © 2009 by Barbara Mayer

Book design and production:
Jane Perini, Thunder Mountain Design & Communication

Photo credits:
istockphoto.com; Tara Middleton, page151;
Barbara Mayer, pages 21, 24, 79, 294, 357, 359

ISBN: 978-0-9785334-4-1
Library of Congress Control Number: 2009937338

For William Mayer

Whose passion for God and life taught me well

And Albi Mayer

Whose courage and compassion taught us all

* * *

**Also Honoring Three Women of Grace Who Walked
With Me A While . . .**

Sister Rose Loretto Wagner, S.P.

For holding the sweetness of possibility

Taka Kanno, Sensei

For holding the stillness which lured me on

Iva Toguri, Friend

For modeling the strength of love

WHAT'S INSIDE

ACKNOWLEDGMENTS

The birthing of new thought — as well as summoning courage to consider new answers to old questions — can never be taken lightly. Seminal ideas and actual words become the task of one individual. The supportive and loving energy of others, however, is often needed to bring actual life to strong words which must sometimes insist themselves through a birth canal of possible judgment and fear.

I am grateful to those who believed in the concept of *Beyond Religion* from the beginning. In the fullness of this book's publication, however, special thanks must rest with Barbara Litrell. Barbara's courage, insight and healing compassion have been an inspiration to many, including me. Her proactive, visionary belief in the sacredness of neighbor helping neighbor, as well as strong leadership in embracing new thought and active spirituality, remains a source of light and clarity. Her help with this book has been immeasurable, and I thank you for everything, Barbara San.

Thanks to Sharon and Richard Hooper of Sanctuary Publications for believing in these words, and to Jane Perini for design not only of the cover, but of this book's total presentation. Thanks also to Sydney Pinkerton, and Dennis and Laura Harness for help in the early days. For their encouragement on this journey I also thank Nancy Donahue, Dorie Bowlin, Ed Klapak, my brothers Bill and John, Arlene and Berni Mayer, John Schor, M.D., Theresa Matregrano, Carol Nesladek, Branca Nelson, Kathleen McGrory, Judee Rich, Beth Elwood, Gwen Essig, Laura Conant, Pam Riesmeyer, Linda Wilson, Ron Struzik and Guy Matthews. I also salute the many others who hold with deep conviction this truth — that greater understanding and connection with the Divine Mystery awaits anyone willing to experience personal, meaningful, and productive spirituality.

FORWARD

We are in a new time. No one can doubt that. More specifically, it is our time. The evolution of the human race is now occurring on our watch. All who have gone before us made their own contributions to the deepening of human awareness.

In this exciting new time, however, we are the ones called to stand within the millennia of our species' existence — and champion the advancement of humanity itself.

The world is evolving to newer forms of being — in society, finance, government, interpersonal and international relations, and more surely in our capacity for greater wisdom and understanding. Now it is our turn to show up and make a positive difference. The very survival of our species depends on it!

These words are written from a full and loving heart. They are an invitation to experience greater joy, completeness and peace in the life of the spirit within each of us. They are an invitation to greater union with the Source of All Creation Which invites us deeper into the Essence of what we call Divinity.

This book has only one goal — to end the separation which keeps us individually and as a species from living our real destiny, which is union and wholeness within our true source. Any sense of division comes only from the illusion we — as ego-driven members of humanity — have so magnificently mastered.

Consider the Need for Change

Realistically, we now face a time when many people are rethinking their attitudes toward religion, and even the very concept of God. Studies by the highly respected Pew Forum on Religion and Public

Life, released in 2008, with more results published in 2009, have demonstrated what many already know. After interviewing over 35,000 people, the study found "more than one quarter of American adults have left the faith of their childhood for another religion or no religion at all. One in four adults ages 18-29 claim no affiliation with a religious institution." The Roman Catholic Church has lost the most members of all institutionalized religions. While nearly one in three Americans have been raised Catholic, only one in four respond they are still Catholics today.

An interesting finding in this study also shows only four percent of the total population actually consider themselves atheists or agnostics. The powerful truth then becomes evident. Millions of people are questioning — or have already walked away from the religions of their earlier lives. And the young adults among us, though many do not find resonance in any religion, still consider themselves believers in some kind of higher power. There are also a great many people who believe in some kind of God concept, but who feel alienated from organized religions for myriad reasons. Yet they still seek. They know there is more but religion has failed them, and now they don't know where to turn. That is the reason I present these words to you.

My Story May Be Yours

The chapters of this book move through and beyond any one religion, and any one form of spiritual life style. In the book's first chapter I address my earlier life, including thirteen years spent as a Roman Catholic nun. In many ways I was a professional Catholic. What I experienced, thought, and felt during that time was extremely sincere. Yet, my decision to leave the convent also bears witness to my simply wanting to live authentically — not necessarily as a "religious" person — but as completely as I could within the heart of God. I share my story with you to witness my own journey deeper within that Divine Source. I also want to help explain the growth which may happen in anyone's spiritual journey, possibly including yours.

I write my story in this book's first chapter for those reasons. I do, however, need to honor all those women who have left religious life for various reasons of their own. I know the wonderful intentions of their early years, and I have shared that agonizing pain many felt in reaching the decision to leave something so beautiful.

I equally honor and appreciate the many women who still remain within their religious communities. American sisters and nuns have stayed loyal to their church, and equally loyal to their lives' consecration to serve the people of God. If inquisitions and challenges have been recently hurled at them from the Vatican in Rome, it seems to me it may be the Vatican representatives who may have forgotten why they themselves entered religious life in the first place — to serve the great God of us all — and to serve all the people of God.

From my years in the convent, and in the time of continuing growth since then, I have viewed my life as a call to seek and honor the highest Truth. The words in this book are a sharing of what has been given to me over a life of meditation, study, and the beauty of simply allowing the Spirit to breathe and be — even in me. We all make choices to keep or change our attitudes as we mature. Those choices sometimes demand courage, but they always need to be made in total honesty to ourselves.

This book asks us to embrace the simple beauty and reality of Universal Truth. It asks us not to shrink any concept of God/Goddess/ Spirit/Energy/Source/Universe to fit human terms. Instead it offers opportunity to grow into the Divine Mystery with the quiet grace of simply realizing who we are. I have no intention of negating or lessening anyone's approach to that Divine Mystery. Indeed, one of the truest signs of Divine Compassion in a world yearning for peace is the honoring and welcoming of all individuals' particular paths into the Divine Heart. Through these words I do offer — to those who seek more — further ways of reaching into our fullest existence as individuals and as a collective species on a very troubled planet.

To grow in one's life and spirit is a process of healing, of moving into the wholeness of what we are in Creation's fullness. This is not so much a journey as it is a transcendence, from the earth beneath our feet and the cosmos beyond our reach to greater purity of compassionate love. This is an invitation to live only in peace, and to strengthen our involvement with What Truly Is, finally living like the spiritual beings we really are.

Religion vs. Direct Knowing

The path through religion, with its organized belief systems, rituals, and man-made dogmas, does encourage an awareness of God. Every religion carries its own label, which becomes its identity.

In our own individual growth, however, we can become much more deeply involved in a personal experience — an actual direct knowing — of whatever name anyone may choose to attach to the Divine Mystery. Just remember a name is a label, and the best place for any label is on a pickle jar. To spend too much energy considering a proper name for the Nameless is like trying to name an ocean, rather than experiencing its expanse, and simply reveling in the depth and magnificence of what it really is. While I will use different names to describe the Absolute Mystery, including the word "God" very often, just remember that word is only one way people now consider the Source of us all.

The following pages suggest how every individual can grow in true healing, which is a return to wholeness. That, in reality, is what real holiness is — Wholeness. How we get there is the one task which calls to us all, no matter what path, religion, belief system, or seemingly unorthodox way we relate best to what is truly the one Source of All That Is.

There is that great line from Alice in Wonderland: "How far down the rabbit hole do you want to go?" In other words, how far are you willing to expand beyond your own comfort zone of belief and understanding?

We are challenged to reach into the deepest place of our higher selves. That in itself is an awesome task. We are all simple people living as best we can. Becoming our best is just fulfilling the seed of what we really are. It is our joy and sacred task to bring humanity, one by one by one, deeper within the Divine Mystery. That task begins with ourselves, and it is this opportunity I wish to share with you.

There is much to talk about, so let's begin.

I will meet you in the following pages of this book. More importantly, I will meet you in the silences between the words. In the stillness of that space, your own spirit will supply many of your deepest answers. "In the stillness, you will know." That stillness is the most important space of all, because it is the space you and the God Source perfectly share. There will also be poetry at times, because poetry always leaves room for miracles and mystery, and that's a good thing.

The challenge? Unbuckle the safety belt of your own comfort zone — and dare the ride!

Barbara Mayer
Sedona, Arizona

Sacred Yearning

I do not know you, yet you come to me
    like the whisper of a shadow I cannot remember
    in the quiet flowing of some ancient stream.
Renewed. Refreshed, yet somehow — redundant
    in the energy of that which already is.
You request an answer to a question I cannot comprehend.
Your heart reveals an emptiness which — somehow — once I
    filled.
And in the hint of you I sense a cosmic cracking of the egg.
You make me want to beg, yet stand within the power of my self
In the one we are — God Self of Divinity shared
    and ready now to hold the true identity.

I am alone here in my exile, still you come to me.
And there is awe as the silent sound of you
    rumbles through my stilled, sacred space.
I am alone here. Don't you remember?
This is my willing exile which — somehow —
    You cannot quite accept.

Why I Left the Convent

I feel the ache of you. I sense the breath of you.
In my silence still I feel the power of your mystery
throbbing through the secrets of my soul.

Is this a silence I never can contain?
Is this a union whose holding I must fear?
Or are you so near I am already one with you,
One in the mystery of never knowing,
never quite showing what demands to be made manifest?
I feel you in an intimacy reserved for lovers,
Held in the exquisite vow of those who co-create a sound —
a new vibration of what is never two,
but only One.

I do not know you, yet I sense a soft, stilled remembrance
Of you — and us —
so sacred in the ground of what I am.
And I am helpless here, as I sense wholeness
in the hushed, sweet memory of what we always are.
Remember me now. I beg you. Remember me now
so I may remember you.
Beloved — When will this shadow finally dissolve in Light?

In the stillness — you will know.

PART ONE

FROM DOGMA TO DIVINITY

WHAT'S GOING ON? WE ARE!

I t is our privilege to live in a new time of rising consciousness. We have not made this happen. We have not asked for it. We have not merited it or earned it. The universe and our place in the Eternal Now is making this happen. We have simply shown up in this powerful time of exploding consciousness. Now it is our delight to be part of humanity's evolution toward perfecting itself within the Divine Mystery.

The consequences are huge. As we watch chaos straining standard structures such as world finance, the geopolitical system, society, and the earth herself, it is our challenge to make a fuller response to this rising awareness. We exist within the energy of our source and that Source is now urging us to realize we have always been home in All That Is, because we are a part of it! We have just lost our awareness of that.

Now that awareness is ours to claim. If any religion still speaks of goodness and honest living for the right intention, and not out of fear of punishment or hope for mega reward in the next dimension of life, then religion for a particular individual is good. It provides community and a certain amount of consistency. But organized religion itself, with all its embeds of alienation from God — fear of punishment and desire for ego reward — will never complete our personal spirituality and desire for union with our Source.

Religion has been, and remains for many, a great step. Yet there are a growing number of others who do not consider the totality of Divinity as an Old Man in the Sky, somewhere "out there" who judges, then rewards with bliss or punishes with eternal torment and damnation.

Many people are beginning to realize the Divine Presence actually exists within their own deepest hearts and spirits. Some of these people still remain in religions. Many others have moved away from any institutionalized religion to seek their own paths into the Divine Mystery. For example, as noted in the Forward of this book, an astounding number of Americans now consider themselves "fallen away" or "recovering" Catholics.

The wisest among us have known the truth of the Ultimate Presence for a very long time. The great teacher Jesus said, "The Kingdom of Heaven is within you." One of the oldest and most revered books from the Eastern tradition is the *Bhagavad Gita* which states, "When we consider Brahman (God) as lodged within the individual being, we call him the Atman. The creative energy of Brahman is that which causes all existences to come into being."

The prophet Isaiah wrote, "Oh God, you have heard the cry of my heart because it was you who cried out within my heart," and more people are now beginning to realize this magnificent and simple truth. In fact, the cry of this new awareness is now becoming so strong in so many people that it will not be denied, and it begs for our response. The ego will scream and stomp and stammer for its own self-proclaimed importance, but there is indeed a great spirit moving all over this land. It is the Source of All calling every part of creation back unto Itself, one by one by one.

It is the All That Is saying — Be still, and know I AM — meaning not that God does exist, but that what we call God is actually the Essence of Existence Itself.

And in that I AM there is the great consolation of knowing what we really are. We are one. It is division, polarity, racism, separation and arrogant self-righteousness — all characteristics of the patriarchal system we are mercifully now leaving —which have created the hell of duality. What we have called heaven, what we call the ultimate reward, is not communion. It is union. "My Father and I are One!" This is our real destiny and our only true identity.

And here is a news flash: That destiny beyond time is already achieved. It is already done! Now it is simply our task to become aware of its beauty and respond to it on every human level possible. Our spirit already delights in the joy of being home and whole again in the Eternal All That Is.

We, as a conscious species, are now standing at the very brink of that state of wholeness, and it's exciting. It may be frightening for some, but it is deeply consoling as well. It is as real as our own ability to love with true compassion, and as real as our own individual yearning for the Transcendent Reality we may call God. If religion has set God apart from humanity, the growing spiritual consciousness we are experiencing today is breaking down that barrier of alienation and distance humanity has created. Now is the new time to claim our birthright in Eternal Life as our true source and our only destiny.

Truth is what truth really, empirically is — not what we think it may be, or what any other human being tells us is true. Truth Is. In your own stillness you have already, or soon will, begin to grasp that truth Itself as it speaks to you. We are one with Divinity as Divinity is one with us. We cannot now or ever be separated from it. There is no other absolute reality. As the Indian mystic Paramahansa Yogananda once wrote, "Truth is no theory, no speculative system of philosophy, no intellectual insight. Truth is exact correspondence with reality. For man, truth is the unshakeable knowledge of his own real nature." And that nature is our own self, absolutely one and united within the Divine Self.

CHAPTER ONE

WHY I LEFT THE CONVENT

To Be and To Become

We keep becoming
What we always were.

- Zen Saying

Being is the easy part. It has a comfort zone all its own. Becoming takes more courage. Knowing one is on the way to something new involves decisions, letting go of old ideas, and courage to move through an entirely new birth canal.

The first consolation to this new birthing is beginning to taste the sweetness of our possibilities. We start in youth, beginning to sift through experiences which form our ideas. They are life blueprints we can choose to follow, yet as we grow we mature in many ways. We just have to keep breathing to grow physically. Teachers — as well as the great teacher of life — help our minds expand into knowledge handed down through the ages. Through successes, failures and different interactions with others, we grow emotionally.

Yet the one aspect of life which often stays stagnant is our growth in Spirit. Most of us are introduced to a set of religious or spiritual beliefs in our youth, and we carry them into adult life. They become the basis of what we believe, how we live, and how we face our own mortality.

Yet each of us has a unique path through life. And for more people now than ever, there seems to be a growing sense that the God of our youth — possibly taught by strict, religious belief codes — is not the wondrous Energy of Being which seems to be calling to us from within our own hearts.

In the hope of helping you realize your own path of return or advancement into the God Source, this section briefly describes my own evolution into greater awareness and union with the same God which calls to us all. I was once a "professional" Catholic. I was a Roman Catholic nun. My spiritual life was based in Catholicism, and I taught Catholicism, among other subjects, to my students. In this brief sharing of my story, it is my hope that you will begin to see the possible deepening of your own path into whatever you may consider the Divine Mystery.

Gifts Do Come

I grew up with a strong foundation of Catholic religious values. Then, during thirteen years as a Catholic nun, I dedicated my life to God through the beliefs, dogma, and rituals of Catholicism. Yet years later — as I stood in a circle of red soil on the desert floor of Boynton Canyon in Sedona, Arizona — I experienced one of the most sacred times of my life. I simply stood in a magnificent place on this earth, with red rock mountains and a turquoise sky above me, as the Energy of the Source of All Creation entered every cell of my body. It pierced my mind and penetrated me with the Light and Love of Divinity's Essence. I was riveted in that place, and never, including sacred moments during my years in the convent, had I felt the actual presence of God so profound and sacred and beautifully immanent in me!

How I got to that experience would be a longer version of the bumper sticker which succinctly tells the story of my life, "My karma ran over my dogma." From my earliest days, as most young people, I just wanted to live the fullest life possible. There was no great element of ego about it. That is just the heart wish of every young person as life stretches ahead, full of unknowns, yet deliciously inviting with the lure of possible happiness, and even, perhaps, some magic.

One of my dearest experiences was as a third grader sitting with my father in our local Catholic Church at daily Mass. My father felt Mass was important, and I grew to relish those times I could spend with him. When the service was over, he would kiss me and leave for work, and I would go off to school.

What I realize now is that time spent with my father was the beginning of some of my deepest learning. At those early morning services, the priest was far up on the altar, and only a few older women knelt near the front. The rest of the church was empty, with my father and me in the very last pew. There we enjoyed the very human bond of parent and child, while also touching the greater bond of being in a sacred place. Maybe part of my later decision to enter a convent was unconsciously a desire to be back in that beautiful space I had once known with my dad. I do know the seeds planted then have blossomed into what I, and my spirit, keep becoming.

The Zen saying is right. From our earliest days we do keep becoming what we always were.

Death Teaches Life

Two brackets stand as sentinels around the greater part of my life and my life in the spirit. One was witnessing my father's death when I was very young. The other was holding my mother as she died in my arms not too long ago.

The night I watched my father die remains a pivotal turning point for me. He was forty-five years old. I was eight. I had kissed him good-night and gone to bed, only to later awaken to an unearthly sound coming from my parents' bedroom. Running in, I stood at the foot of the bed and watched my father suffer through the final stages of a massive heart attack. I watched the color drain from his face. I listened in dread to what I later learned was the death rattle, and then it was over. He was gone, and I never even had a chance to hug him and tell him goodbye.

Yet my father's death, as horrible as it was, carried one consolation. Having been brought up in a Catholic home and attending a Catholic school, at least I could be comforted by the thought my father was in heaven. He had tried to be a good man. For him, now all was well. He had gone from our young family to be with God.

I, however, did not die with my father. As I moved through a normal youth, I began wondering about the simple answers as deeper questions rose. If heaven is such a great place, I thought, why do we have to die, sometimes very painful deaths, just to get there? If God wants us to be with him so much in heaven, why does he make some things so hard in this life? If he is such a loving God, why does he allow so much suffering here on earth and threaten us with eternal torture and damnation if we fail to measure up? Later in life I found resonance with the words Teresa of Avila once shouted to God after a painful experience, "If this is the way you treat your friends, no wonder you have so few of them!"

That was the early time, and whatever else life has been, I soon realized one thing. Somehow it was not my lot to be satisfied with easy answers. There are greater truths and fuller understanding available to us, if we but choose to be open to them.

Many years later, as I held my dying mother in my arms, much had changed. She was eighty-two. I was well into that time we wishfully call middle age.

As I held her hand — my other hand cradling the top of her head as I lay with her on the hospital bed — I suddenly witnessed awe in my mother's eyes. Clearly she was marveling at something or someone only she could see. Whatever it was filled her with incredible joy, and then a strong force thrust my arm away from the top of her head. I will never stop believing that thrust of energy was my mother's spirit making its exit from her tired body. That spirit was moving into its true reality with a force that startled me, and when it left I realized only my mother's physical presence remained. It was only the moment of her physical death. That woman, as I had come to know and love her, was gone. She was off on the ride of real existence, into the full realm of spirit, which is our only true destiny.

I did not move through that doorway of death with my mother. I did, however, feel privileged to at least have glimpsed the beauty and love which lies beyond. With grief at her loss, I was filled more with the excitement of her victory. My sorrow was the selfish emotion of losing her, but the power of her success of life lived well was overwhelming.

Much had changed in my thinking and growth since I watched my father die. As a child I had known only loss and numbness. But as I held my dying mother and felt her spirit leave, I had reached a new place of understanding. Priests had prepared her for death in the rites of the Catholic Church, but I had helped her too, through prayer, love, and greater understanding of the transition and marvelous transcendence we call physical death. I have grown to the awareness that I will know the spirits of my mother and father again in a much deeper way. I have also grown to awareness of much more.

The Call to Fullness

Even in my youth, I felt the need to be worthy of this thing called life and what might follow it. My early years were normal in spite of my father's death. Time does heal, and life kept on for me. I loved sports and was proud of my role on our high school volleyball team, which won the Chicago City Championship. I still have the bad knees to remind me! I was also a rebel, whose only cause was my own individuality. I wore a leather jacket when the "nicest" girls wouldn't think of owning one. I stayed out much too late with my friends. I even smoked.

During my junior year I was named editor of the high school newspaper. I was already planning on a writing career but I had not yet heard the great line, "Do you want to make God laugh? Tell him your plans!"

The day for our annual retreat arrived. It was an event you found only in a Catholic high school, when a visiting priest would give several talks on living as a "good Catholic girl." Somewhere during that day, however, my life shifted in an entirely new direction — or returned to a very ancient truth.

I don't remember what the priest said. I don't remember the topics of our discussion groups. I do remember loving the times of silence we were given that day. After the last talk in the school auditorium, however, something changed. As my friends made a quick exit from school, I felt the urge to go up the small spiral staircase behind the auditorium stage. Climbing halfway up the steep metal stairs which led to the light banks above, I sat — alone. I had stepped away from the world, and I didn't even know why.

I don't remember feeling religious or spiritual. I had just tapped into a different part of me. The silence seemed to be birthing a deeper reality as true stillness often does. Before long a thought broke through my mind — a realization which was simply there. The word is vocation, from the Latin *vocare* — to call. It was a truth so deep it would not be denied, and that calling was to the religious life. Suddenly I understood in every part of my being that I was called to be a nun. The technical word for it is sister, because only those who live in cloistered communities are called nuns. Society uses that word now, however, so I will use it too. Soon tears were streaming down my face. It was a powerful moment and I didn't even consider when or how that would happen. I just knew my future waited for me in some convent I had never even seen.

When I got home late that afternoon, I burst into tears again. "I'm supposed to be a nun," I told my mother, and I also carry the sweet memory of her answer, "Well, I just want you to be happy." Thirteen years later, when I phoned to tell her I was leaving the convent, her first words were exactly the same, "That's all right. I just want you to be happy." In those two instances I feel my own mother was speaking from her presence in the feminine aspect of Divinity Itself. In her compassion beyond all ego of having a daughter in the convent, she wanted nothing but my happiness. That, I believe, is what Divine Love wants for all of us — the joy of living in the fullness we really are.

Now I know that the call to religious life was the soul in me rising up from other times, in other lives when I had also been called to spirit. In that moment I was again summoned to be what I have always been — a person who lived in the physical world while retaining connection with the divine.

We really do keep becoming what we always were, and those were sacred moments of my becoming.

New Life / Old Truths

I had nicotine stains on my fingers for two weeks after I entered the convent, but cigarettes were a minor thing I left behind. There were many farewells. My friends came over and took most of my clothes as well as awards I had won in sports and journalism.

The most poignant leaving came during my last night at home. I had gone to bed early knowing the alarm would ring too soon for the long drive to the convent motherhouse. I had even fallen asleep. Suddenly I awoke, aware my older brother Bill was kneeling beside my bed. He had said a quick good-bye earlier before going on a date. Yet he was suddenly there, and he was weeping. Soon we were holding each other, both of us in tears. Neither of us spoke. We just held each other and wept until finally he rose and left my room. He was nineteen, good-looking, intelligent, in his body-building days, and proud of the used yellow convertible he had bought with money from a part-time job. But that night he was just my brother, and he was saying the perfect good-bye.

His good-bye also brought home to me the truth of what I was leaving. He was on a date with the young woman who would become his wife and the mother of their five children. The vow of chastity I would one day take would remove any possibility of my own family and spouse, and any kind of physical intimacy at all. Bill had his convertible; I would own nothing once I took the vow of poverty. And he was moving on to live life his way. With my vow of obedience I would give up my will and put my future, with all its possibilities, in the hands of others. In truth, I was leaving a lot more than cigarettes and people behind!

Yet that leaving, echoing the earlier leaving of my father through death, became a lesson for moving through life. Nothing, those lessons were teaching me, lasts forever. Change is the one constant and only we, showing up with courage at each juncture of our time, must fulfill the journey which is ours alone to make.

There is always sorrow or at least some temerity at leaving any comfort zone. Pain is often involved when we leave part of our lives behind. This, I learned later, includes moving away from comfortable belief systems into more comprehensive and realistic attitudes toward this Great Magnificence we tend to call God. There would come a time when simplistic beliefs and questionable dogmas could not, and would not, satisfy my own growing hunger for Truth.

Yet the greatest lesson is to live with change and have the courage to break the molds of our own stagnant selves in commitment to greater growth. We either change with the graces we are given or become hardened and desensitized in our failure to reach for the fullest treasures Spirit offers us.

The Convent

I did endure the pain of leaving much behind me as I walked through the convent motherhouse door. Entering that strange world of women dedicated to a common cause, however, put me on automatic pilot, at least for a while. I did not enter the convent to become a more spiritual person. I had no grandiose motive of saving the world. I was seventeen and freshly out of high school. This was just something I knew beyond my young mind or even my heart. This was a response I had to make to a question I didn't even understand.

Now I realize my call to religious life was a major signpost pointing the way my spirit was destined to travel. The Divine Mystery was saying, "Just be in this convent now. This is the first step. Begin to claim your real life, and leave the rest to me." I took that step. I leapt off the cliff trusting something — or someone — would catch me and carry me to a place I still did not know.

My decision to enter a convent set the tone for my own growth in awareness. Most women enter a convent as a life decision, and so did I. What I and many others learned only later, however, was that any religious community is not a place to be. It is a place to become.

I grew in understanding of that concept through seven years in the convent before the time came for me to profess before God and humanity the perpetual vows of Poverty, Chastity and Obedience. I did not want to leave, yet I did wonder how I could say "forever" when I did not know what my "forever" involved. It is the same feeling for anyone entering marriage, yet at age twenty-four I did believe my "forever" and my further becoming would be within that religious community.

I had changed over those first seven years in the convent. I had taken a different name — Sister Joel — which signaled my new identity as one of "God's own." I wore a religious habit which visibly marked me as one set apart from the world. Yet my deepest maturation came in my relationship with God. We chanted the psalms of the Divine Office every day; we said many prayers. My most special times, however, were those of inner stillness when something deeper in me began to cry out with greater intensity. While the analogy may limp here, it was as if I were experiencing a very different kind of pregnancy — a pregnancy of my own life, or spirit. I began to love the silence so deeply I even considered leaving my active teaching community to join a cloister of Carmelite nuns where silence rules the major part of every day. After much prayer and thought, however, I stayed where I was.

Our convent motherhouse did have a Chapel of Perpetual Adoration. There the Host, or Blessed Sacrament, is exposed in a golden vessel called a monstrance, set on an altar of exquisite marble. This chapel still is a gem of architecture and décor. More precious than the visible surroundings, however, is the aura which carries that unmistakable energy found in any sacred space. It was in that chapel I felt most at one with the Divine Presence.

Two sisters always knelt in prayer at the front of that chapel. During the day we could volunteer for two hour sessions, but I loved taking the Night Watch. From ten at night until five the next morning — lost in the presence of a lover I could neither see nor understand — I could move through the darkness into another day. Times I spent in that small chapel during those long nights still remain a special memory for me. Now I know even more surely that stillness and silence are essential to full life. In nature, in the eyes of others, and in so many other aspects of the physical world, we do find God. Yet within our own stillness is where sacred silence becomes a language beyond words. This is where we begin to actually experience union with divinity, where we finally start remembering who and what we really are.

Learning to Grow, Learning to Change

I was already very much a woman, living through my late teens and early twenties at the motherhouse. There were, of course, times I yearned for physical union with a lover I could not see. In the stillness of that chapel, however, something deeper in me became aware of the omnipresent Beloved which the mystic John of the Cross once described. I related to John's concept of the True Beloved, which is neither masculine nor feminine, but in actuality is the Essence of the Divine Source.

John wrote of the dark night of search and longing for such a beloved, as well as times of feeling abandoned even by God, and I found resonance in his words. I began to realize — no matter what our life situation —we go to bed alone, whether someone is lying next to us or not. We also wake up alone. All we really have is our self. We are the only vehicle we have to make response to life. Yet when we choose to listen to that inner self, we are never really alone. The Divine Presence exists within us. We just need to realize that. Then our greatest comfort lies in knowing our heart resides in the Divine Heart of Love Itself.

It was in that stillness my spirit began to grow. As I went through classes with young women who attended the college connected to the motherhouse, my mind also grew. I took in the wisdom and ponderings of modern theologians and thinkers who were already probing more deeply into the God mystery. Reading the words of the brilliant Catholic monk Thomas Merton provided courage and consolation for the journey. I also dove into works by theologians Paul Tillich and Karl Rahner, Dietrich Bonhoeffer and Martin Buber, who reached from different religious perspectives toward the same Divine Essence.

When I discovered the writings of Pierre Teilhard de Chardin, my mind flew open. An internationally recognized expert in prehistory, this Jesuit Catholic priest had gone back to humanity's earliest origins with great reverence. He concluded the human species itself is still very much in an evolutionary process. That journey, he wrote, is now in humanity's consciousness, and the growing realization that God is not some distant entity "out there". The Divine Mystery surrounds us, Chardin wrote in *The Divine Milieu*. We are in it, and it is in us! It calls us in its all-encompassing divine environment, and its mystery not only calls to humanity from this Mother Earth and the cosmos beyond — but from the very depths of every person's soul. We are all and each integrally part of creation, and part of the Source of Creation Itself. The words of the prophet Isaiah became a mantra to me, revealing new depths. "Oh God, you have heard the cry of my heart, because it was you who cried out within my heart!"

Bob Dylan had sung, "The times, they are a 'changin'," and I began to wonder if he had any concept of the great movement in humankind's evolution his words were describing!

Reaching the Decision to Leave

As part of an active religious community, I first taught in a small southern Indiana town, then in a large northern city. I was young and energetic, and like many other young nuns, I began to feel held back from fulfilling a ministry we could have provided for others.

There were, for example, ways we could have helped fill people's basic needs for food and clothing in the area around the inner city high school where I taught. Yet those were difficult times. While many of us strained for the freedom to be able to serve the servants of God, the church and the convent were anguishing over leaving many of the old ways of isolation and mystique.

The mandate to bring fresh new ideas to Catholic ministry had been given by the Second Vatican Council in Rome, but change was still painfully slow. I could detail here many instances when clinging to old convent attitudes kept us from being more active in the neighborhood and city around us. Here it is enough to say there came a point I realized we were spending most of our energy trying to make changes which would make us more effective, and less energy in actually doing what we felt was God's work. This was frustrating in the least, causing me doubt that my religious life was making any real difference at all.

Yet there was an even deeper reason I began to question my role as a Catholic nun. This was my growing realization that the Father God of dogmatic theology I taught in my religion classes was nowhere near the Divine Essence which theologians, thinkers, and even I were beginning to experience.

Then I met David. He was a priest, a monk and a highly respected theologian. His opinion was sought by many American bishops, and he was held in high esteem by the Vatican in Rome. In what some would call a fluke and what I consider an act of God's providence, I was thrown into a work project with him. It took little time for us to get acquainted and soon we were discussing major concepts of religion and dogma.

Two major discoveries in the 1940's — the finding of the Dead Sea Scrolls and more ancient texts near Nag Hammadi in Egypt — openly refuted many of the old ideas of not only scripture but Catholic teachings. These old manuscripts, and the new revelations they presented, were being openly discussed not only at higher levels of the Catholic Church, but in many other religions as well. Severe cracks were beginning to appear in the sacrosanct walls around dogmatic views of Divinity.

David was aware of it all and led me to many other sources where I could find more information. He also added his own ideas to the mix. Of course Jesus was born like every other human, he would say. Of course our individual soul essence lives many lifetimes as we grow into this One Universal Essence we call God. There were many more things he spoke of calmly, and when I asked him why we didn't teach these things in our schools and from the church pulpits, he would just smile. "Don't rock the boat until you're ready to deal with a capsize," he would say.

And that is where it stayed, for a while. As I became more aware of what advanced theologians and others were thinking, however, it became more difficult for me to stand as a symbol of a religion which was growing more painfully inadequate, and often rigidly enamored with its own self-proclaimed dogmatic superiority.

I was living then what many people today also face. While the religion and beliefs one has carried from youth still persist, sometimes with guilt, sometimes with lack of courage, and often in a very shaky comfort zone, deeper truths and inner knowing seem to beg for realization. While the last twenty years of the old century had seen the shaking of pillars of many "hallowed structures", the new millennium was threatening to burst the bonds of old thought and self-righteous complacency. I had come to realize that the life and teachings of Jesus — as they were being presented — were nowhere near the real power of his message, his witness, and his truth. I had also come to understand God cannot be the champion of one religion but is instead the Transcendent Reality and Unity of All That Is.

With that broadening of my perspective, I began to question

remaining in the narrowness of selective, dogmatic belief — while in service to the true God who is the Breadth and Essence of all. As my personal struggle deepened, I began to realize that my need to live honestly might impact the very life I was living. In a combination of awe and angst I knew there might come a point when I could no longer remain in my religious community.

It was almost an unthinkable concept to face. I was a nun. That was my identity grown from a sincere belief that it was also my destiny. My religious community had become a type of mother and home to me. I had many good friends within it. I had made many commitments to that way of living, including my solemn vows of perpetual poverty, celibacy, and obedience. For all its questions and struggle, the convent had become a beautiful place for my spirit to grow. And now it became a soul-wrenching agony to even think of leaving it.

Yet, as I approached my thirtieth birthday, I had to face some difficult questions. Would I stay in that religious community and work for the changes which would make it more effective or could I leave that community and live as a woman of God in the world? Could I dive deeper into what more of the brightest thinkers were saying about consciousness, and still hold to the strict dogmatic teachings of the Catholic Church? Could I deny findings revealed in the Dead Sea Scrolls, and in the very concept of the God Source Itself which was often part of my daily meditations?

I had not only brought my life into the convent experience. I had brought my heart, yet I began to realize my only honest way of living was to leave that religious community and move out into a world I really didn't know. It became evident that my only authentic answer — in an attempt to really "show up" for life — would rest in a decision to leave the convent. In coming to that point, I shared the same agony many women religious have faced through the years. It is very close to the same distress many other women face in ending a marriage or relationship which is no longer honest or productive for their own personal growth.

I also knew in leaving the convent I was not leaving God. Instead, I was actually moving deeper into that Divine Mystery. The fullness of life and the fullness of response to the Divine Presence are not accomplished by living in any spiritual hothouse. The only true space for living and being totally part of the God experience is to acknowledge that Sacred Presence within one's self. Then exteriors do not matter. Then everything becomes sacred. The only real space, as Chardin had written, is the God Space. And we are all in it — 24/7, 365, and much more importantly, beyond the very notion of time itself.

Finally, stepping away from my life which had been, I moved away from another comfort zone and chose to leave my convent community. It was the hardest decision I've ever made, and the most painful. There was nothing ahead I could see. I was thirty years old. I would soon leave all my friends behind. I had no money. No job. No place to live. But I had myself and the knowledge I was still very much a part of the divine plan. I still had my awareness, my decisions and my acquiescence to let True Life unravel as it should.

If the human race has evolved over the millennia, we also experience personal evolution throughout our lives. All that is asked of us is to allow some stillness, honor what we learn in it, then respond as best we can to the truth which becomes manifest. Our greatest future lies in that because it is the God Self immanent within us which calls us to our own highest destiny. It is living in surrender and surpassing our own fear in order to become what we are truly meant to be.

I made the decision, then wrote the customary letter to the Pope, requesting dispensation from my perpetual vows. Here I must admit it was a rather strong letter, stating I could no longer remain in a life and belief system which actually denied my own need to sink more deeply into the Divine Mystery.

That request went through the channels of my convent superiors and the local bishop — on its way to the Vatican in Rome. Several months later a large envelope arrived from across the Atlantic. In it a rather ornate sheet of parchment with a colorful mosaic border, carried the message, in Latin. The dispensation from my vows had been granted.

It was over. Sister Joel became a name in dusty archives. After thirteen years, I was Barbara Mayer again.

"Behold, I Make All Things New"

If we keep becoming what we always were, I have always been a child of creation and its Source. While those many years ago I entered what the world calls "religious life", now I realize we all have the same calling as members of the human race — to live a spiritual life. Our calling is to finally remember who we really are, and that is achieved in living a life in true spirit. When the old song posed the question, "What's It All About, Alfie?" it was just a Twentieth Century version of the eternal question humanity has considered from its earliest origins.

The answer is — it's all about living day by day by day — not only in union with our God Source, but as one who carries within herself or himself the very God Essence Itself. That answer comes only at our deepest level, which is spiritual. Without that level, life is left to egocentricity, division, separation, fear, suffering and illusion. When we allow ourselves to touch that deepest level, however, everything becomes wonderfully simple and clear! It also allows the pure joy which is the natural state in which we are intended to live.

Right Brain Chapter Review

A bit of explanation. The left lobe of the brain is the logical, more masculine, manifesting "Let's get it done" area of the brain. We all have it. It allows us to forage through the realm of thought and produce concepts for ourselves and others to understand. Each chapter in this book is written predominantly from the left brain, with the intention of communicating facts and ideas. That is why we humans invented prose.

Ah, but the right side of our brain is where we hold stillness, mystery and the hint of possibility. It is where we take all those ideas and internalize them, making our understanding of any words more personal. That, for me, is a place of poetry. So, after struggling with words to say something worthwhile in each chapter, I turn to the right brain of poetry to find those words' deeper resonance in me and, I hope, in you.

Hence — the...

RIGHT BRAIN CHAPTER REVIEW

This Only Vow Remains

Always I have loved you.
Never has there been a time within my sanity or soul
When I ever thought I could go on
    without the magic and the mystery
      which your presence and your essence hold for me.

Always, in my deepest heart I have felt the breath of you,
No matter how I lived — or what I wore —
No matter whatever name the world has called me by,
Or how any others have seen me as the woman
    I once was, or became through all these years.
It has all led me to this place —

And to these words I write now from my own truth,
embraced within the Truth of what you are
and what we, together, always shall remain.

The words become our words
As the silence holds them all within our love.
And that is enough for me.

WHAT IS TRUTH?

New Age or New Awareness?

*In this history of the collective as in the history
of the individual, everything depends on the
development of consciousness.*

- Carl Jung

Two thousand years ago a man articulated the greatest question anyone can ask —"What is truth?"

Millions had pondered that question before him, but he asked it of a master teacher, one who stood in human form and embodied totality of the Christed Consciousness. The man was Pontius Pilate. The teacher was Jeshua ben Joseph, and as a true teacher or educator — one who draws out what is in another — Jesus the Christ gave the perfect answer. His reply was silence, acknowledging the fact each human being must discern that answer not in any words, either his or another's, but in the stillness of one's own heart and with the innate wisdom of one's own eternal spirit.

The human race has considered that question of truth from the time we had two brain cells working. From earliest history there is record that our ancestors looked to the stars, to the earth, and inside their own hearts for answers. What great thinkers and initiates of each age have tried to bring into human terms is an answer to that fundamental question — what is truth?

New Age or New Awareness of Ancient Wisdom?

Real truth has always been real truth. Because it is empiric and whole it can never change. Because it is what it is, it can never be anything it is not. As such it remains the only answer to our question — what is the real truth not only of what we are, but of our source, our reason for existence, and our ultimate reality?

One fact we can all accept is that from our earliest times we as a human race have changed. Physically we have changed until, whether we like it or not, modern woman and man stand as we are in this young century of a new millennium. What is also evident is that humanity has mercifully been getting smarter. Early humans first learned how to survive and as the millennia continued, we have learned not only to live with the earth; we have learned to thrive and flourish. We have also learned how to not only destroy parts of the earth but to even kill others and ourselves with greater and greater efficiency.

Now we stand in a new time. We are still getting smarter, and this is not only because our mental ability has increased. What has really increased is our consciousness, our inner knowing, our ability to grasp greater concepts toward that one elusive goal — learning what is really true. The good news is that we have come a long way and, in spite of ourselves, we're still here. The better news is that, if we can keep from blowing ourselves up, we have an even more wonderful way to go. Our species has learned a great deal. Now we stand in a new millennium where the future invites us to advance into a joyful, peaceful, and positive way of living, if only we can find the courage to work for it.

Humanity has already lived through many eras, including several Ice Ages, the Neolithic Age, the Agrarian Age, and the Mechanical Age. There is another kind of age, however, which scholars identify. While they have charted the slow but steady evolution of human ideas and progress, students of world history have also realized there are rare times on earth when a spike in human consciousness occurs. These are eras of great leaps forward in conscious awareness marking huge shifts in the world's collective consciousness.

This Axial Age

These eras are extremely rare, and because they change the very way the human race thinks, behaves, and believes, they are called Axial Ages. They lead into a new way of being and always stand as milestones in humanity's history. They occur roughly every 2600 years.

The last Axial Age changed humankind's shift into reconsidering the way we think about life, and what many call God. It began around the life of Siddhartha Gautama, the Buddha, approximately 500 BCE, and ended a hundred years after the life of Jesus the Christ in 100 CE. Most of the known world then changed to a new way of marking time with the adoption of the Gregorian Calendar, and organized belief systems began to flourish.

It may be helpful here to consider a prophetic calendar developed by the Mayans several centuries ago. At their peak a highly spiritual and gifted people, the Mayans produced a prophetic calendar marking the time of humanity, which predicts a huge shift in the year 2012. While a few think this may actually signal the end of the world, many more see this as a time of dramatic, life altering change. All these scenarios point to major shifts in the earth and in the world geopolitical system some time very soon.

What is widely accepted now is not a prediction of gloom followed by doom but an entirely new awakening of the way we as a species think and behave. As human consciousness reaches a deeper level of understanding, many of the old pillars of society will soon fall away as humanity steps into a new way of being.

The Mayans looked to us who are alive right now as those who "walk between the worlds." They saw us as custodians of this time of great change, moving from the world of old thought into a new era where compassion and acceptance of each others' differences will be the norm. This will be a time when war is obsolete and hatred non-existent. This shift will bring a peaceful, compassionate and productive way of being, a true Age of Aquarius.

Many believe the Mayans' description of us is accurate. We are now in a time when the great task is to either move toward a more com-passionate and peaceful way of living with each other or perish from our failure to change. The world we know now, suffering from polar-ity, division and separation, has brought us this far. In that respect it has succeeded. We are still here. Yet war remains and even escalates to global possibilities. Hatred, selfishness and hypocrisy, arrogance among the powerful and greed among the wealthiest — done some-times even in the name of religious morality and a supposedly loving God — still remain.

New consciousness is now rising in more and more people. We are privileged to live at this pivotal time in history when humanity is becoming more aware of many things. We are at the brink of not only witnessing — but actually participating in — one of the most positive shifts the human race has ever experienced. Each one of us is part of that change and it is an awesome and joyous responsibility. It is, in fact, a universal responsibility.

No Small Change

If you feel time is somehow speeding up, that days go by faster and the old line "time flies" can now be changed to "time has become a shooting star," you're not alone. One of today's foremost thinkers, Jean Houston, calls it "jump time", and it signals the fact we are indeed moving into something new. Time actually feels like it is speeding up. We really are in another rare Axial Age. All over the planet people of different cultures and belief systems are experiencing this same rise in awareness, and one of the phrases we hear most often when people speak of religion now is, "I know there's more. There has to be more than this."

Are we on the verge of finding total true reality? This is for a higher power to decide.

What is true is that the world is changing, and we are part of it. We see major change in economics and world finance and in business, politics and government. There are definite changes in the earth through global warming and seismic events. There are also greater levels of stress and uncertainty in the very structures of society. In this time of change, however, the one thing which helps us move forward as a people is that there is a rising level of awareness, not just in the Rhodes Scholars or so-called brilliant thinkers. There is a heightening of consciousness in ordinary people calling us to probe deeper into the realization of what we innately sense is true. It is our very rising level of consciousness which calls us to experience that "more" people talk about and which makes being alive today such an exciting and vibrantly delicious time.

We are now at the very axis of human experience as we face the challenge of embracing new ways of thought. We are refining the old and evaluating our decisions as we move forward on the evolutionary spiral. Yet these are also times of great polarization. Many who are entrenched in the old ways of belief and business as usual are using every weapon in their arsenals to deny and defeat the inevitable. This, of course, is to be expected because a shift in human consciousness will also involve a shift away from their power and influence on the rest of us.

A true Axial Age actually signals time for a new order. This Axial Age is also bringing an end to the long-standing patriarchal society which has ruled world thought for several thousand years. The new way of thinking — featuring a more feminist and compassionate tone — is calling into question the old ideas of duality, hierarchy, and the need for subservience among the masses. Soon, however, the old ways of division, dogmatic pronouncements and destruction of supposed enemies will begin to disappear. Instead, a time of respecting differences and courageous compassion will again rule the hearts of humanity.

We have now lived for another roughly twenty-one to twenty-six hundred years since the last Axial Age. The world we know now has been colored by the mentality, physical reality, and spiritual belief systems of that time. It has also been a time of patriarchal dominance. Yet, as we move deeper into a new century and millennium, we are clearly in an exciting new shift toward deeper awareness. True, there is much angst and chaos now exhibited by the entrenchment and polarity evident in the many among us who are afraid of changes which lie ahead. The wheel of creation is turning, however, and it will not be denied. It may take several generations of humankind, or even longer for the change to be complete, but it is already underway.

How Do We Meet the Challenge?

In these times of defined and undefined war there seems to be growing insecurity all over the planet. As we watch nations in deep stress on the world stage, many also feel personal stress from work or the lack of it, troubled relationships, relationships which have already ended, and most of all from our deepest relationship — with our own selves. We look for solutions, yet often feel all the answers are inadequate. We have been told, "The truth shall set you free" but many do not know where to find a truth that powerful.

We find ourselves at a new place in time, facing uncertainty and serious challenges ahead. For many who find solace in the faith of their religions, there is some comfort. Many others, however, even while holding to the faith and sense of community their religions provide, find there are still no answers to their deepest questions. Something in their hearts remains unsatisfied. Of course, many have turned to their religions for consolation and strength, yet many more have not found what they seek. That may be caused by several reasons but many people are simply walking away from religion, finding it inadequate to meet the needs of today's world

Why Religions Sometimes Fail

Recently, a woman called me on a Sunday afternoon. "I just got back from church," she said, "and I'm so frustrated! The priest went through the same old ritual with no real reverence. His sermon was so many words and I can't even remember what he said. And then it was over. I left, got in my car and wondered, what was that all about? My religion seems like only so much ritual and not a whole lot of relevance! But I know there's more. There has to be more than this!"

The good news is — of course there is more. Several things have already changed us. Beyond advances in technology, computers and the Internet, the actual consciousness of the human race is rising! Yet, because it is not rising equally in all people, there is more disparity and sometimes even hatred or failure to accept where we as a people are heading. Whatever issues we try to confront, whether stress in difficult relationships, financial concerns, worries about job, death, or addiction, we look to the one place where any type of true healing can occur —and that is on a spiritual, not necessarily religious, level.

That is the burden and the joy of this book. We are in an age when religion serves many, if only in helping church and temple goers feel morally and socially correct. Most people who follow any particular religion do so with the highest intent and the purest of motives. Their religion is a rock to them especially in the chaos of today's world. Yet religions today are also witnessing a time when some ministers, rabbis, priests, imams, or other leaders of human ministry are failing to do their job of leading people spiritually. Too often many religious professionals have caused real harm and scandal while standing as witnesses of God to their flocks. Many who consider themselves ministers, for example, have forgotten that the word "minister" means to be a servant to the servants of God. It is all about taking care of the needs of others and not positioning themselves as the only ones who have a direct route to God, which others cannot attain on their own.

Or perhaps these so-called religious leaders have not failed at all. In the least, they may have disappointed people who trusted them for help in developing greater nearness to God. For others, their behaviors have forced hundreds of thousands of people to leave their religious roots and search for greater, more universal truth by other means.

I recall listening to a woman explaining why she left the Catholic Church. Her father had been best friends with someone since their youths. As years passed, her father went into the business world and his friend went into the priesthood. As both moved into mature age with their friendship always intact, the woman's father was suddenly rushed to the hospital with acute heart failure. Frantic, the woman called her father's old friend, now a monsignor, a higher ranking priest in the Catholic Church. She finally reached him on his cell phone. "Come quick!" she pleaded. "My father is in danger of death!"

The monsignor's reply? "Right now I'm on the golf course. As soon as I've finished these last two holes, I'll go straight to the hospital." By the time the priest got there, the woman told me, her father had died without the last rites of the church which could have been administered by his life-long friend.

The woman ended her story with a simple statement, "I have never set foot in a Catholic Church again."

That is only one story but it illustrates the fact too many people look to the supposed ministers of God for assistance, rather than accessing that Divine Mystery on their own personal terms. Perhaps these ministers have actually succeeded in being what they really are, originally well-meaning individuals who have felt the call to help people move closer to God. But they are simply what we all are, fabulous yet flawed members of the human race. Perhaps the message we should take from scandals in today's ministries is to realize we cannot look to another human being as our one and only channel into the mystery we call God. For that matter, do we really need a middle man or woman at all, or do we carry the God Essence within us? Don't we have the ability to interact with that Essence on our own and in a much deeper, meaningful way? We are talking about the very Source of our own being!

As consciousness rises, the idea that God is somehow unattainable in this life, "out there" somewhere as the traditional Old Man in the Sky, has begun to fade. To think of the Divine Mystery, the Eternal I AM, as a powerful and very human-like Super Being has become more of a stretch. In the following chapters we will discuss what God is not and how we may attain a more personal relationship with the God Presence within us.

When you come right down to it, why do we even feel such a great need to understand and define God? Consider this from the *Tao Te Ching*, "If you think you have defined the Tao (God), you are not speaking about the Tao (God) at all." What our human minds might really need is the ability to be comfortable with mystery.

Put It Away by Putting It Down

We also face the world's attempts to diminish and dispose of any new thinking, any new avenues of growth, faith, and personal practice, as so much nonsense, "out there" craziness or heresy. The term "New Age," for example, has become a derogatory term, describing people who live on the fringe of society and whose ideas of the Divine are fanciful at least and downright sacrilegious at worst. This, by the way, is one of the greatest weapons of power trying to dismiss any new way of looking at the Truth. Simply label people who attempt new thought as irresponsible or crazy. Call them fanatics or fools and laugh them off the stage of societal acceptance.

One of my favorite Peanuts comic strips shows Lucy meeting Charlie Brown and Linus who are laughing at a book. "Why are you laughing at that book?" Lucy asks, and they respond, "We're laughing at it because we don't understand it."

Peanuts' creator Charles Schultz was a very wise man. The next time you laugh at some thing or some one, it may be good to stop and consider why you are laughing...

The truth, however, remains what it is, and what it always has been. Now people from many walks of life, from the highest IQ levels to us ordinary folk, are coming to realize we are in a new time. It is clearly a time of humanity's leap in awareness, an exciting new Axial Age! Should we fear it? Certainly not! Giving energy to fear only makes fear stronger. We should, instead, be thrilled to be part of the change!

Consider a Change of Mind

The old way of thinking cautions against change and honors the status quo. The old way of thinking celebrates comfort zones and blind faith even in areas where new understanding has already been achieved. This, however, is a time of growth. New awareness holds the capability of deeper living on mental, emotional, and certainly spiritual levels. All we need do is become more receptive to positive growth for the highest possible good and take to heart the words of the great I AM, "Behold, I make all things new!"

As we make our own moves into what life holds for us, it is important to realize every human life is a tremendous experience of mistakes and miracles. It has all been there for the learning and the growth. Nothing has been wasted. We are of God and the God Mystery carries the total wisdom of its own truth. We are still just discovering that and, in spite of what we may consider setbacks and failures, that is simply our ego's false thinking. We simply haven't recognized our progress. We haven't realized how much closer we have come to the Divine Reality which has shone in us from the very beginning.

Now, however, it is our turn to show up and carry the torch into a new, rich brilliance of Light. Honoring the truth we carry in our own hearts is all we need. That is the task which now calls us to our own destiny.

If not we, then who? If not now, then when? We stand within the Eternal Now and now is the only time.

RIGHT BRAIN CHAPTER REVIEW

The New Revealing

Time becomes a moment filled with mystery — not history.
Cosmic curtains part, the star of consciousness revealed!
More aware now that we are more aware,
We tiptoe on the stage of new awakening.

Age of Revelation. Age of Knowing That We Know.
Old ideas of divinity crumble like icons of a lesser age
*   as the God of Light begins the new revealing.*
Yes — behold — know for yourself — I AM —
*   and I make all things new! Even you! Especially you!*

What Is Truth?

Be still now — and begin to know this new time
        as it has always been.
Source of Light and Love which smiles the Holy Secret.
I dwell in this becoming and keep creating
The fullness of All Things New —
        sprung fresh from ancient springs which have
        held the seed so dear.

Just be still now. Be new and ancient
        in this time of bright awareness of the one Truth,
        radiant in Its own exquisite Mystery.
In this axial time when things turn again to the greater whole,
It is blessing begun,
        and the answers are waiting within.

CHAPTER THREE

CAN RELIGION AND SPIRITUALITY COEXIST?

Learning to Trust
The Teacher Within

*True religion is spiritual religion, it is a seeking
after God, the opening of the deepest life of the soul to
the indwelling Godhead, the eternal Omnipresence.*

- Sri Aurobindo

Shortly before conducting a massive gathering in a southern American city, a noted preacher told an interviewer, "I'm not surprised at the large number of people attending. There is a growing need for spirituality rising all over the country."

That minister was right. There is a growing desire for true spirituality not just in one nation but in global growing awareness. Most countries of the world watch the news and live with stress on a daily basis. While this minister's message is preaching Jesus the Christ, the need for spirituality is evident in all parts of society.

Actually it is more than personal and world stress, with change and uncertainty facing them, which people are feeling in this new time. As many institutions, secular and so-called religious, show signs of crumbling from their own weight or from greed, love of power, inefficiency, or unwillingness to change, the hearts of women and men do what they do best. They quietly reach into their own inner roots and seek answers at the deepest level possible.

One problem we face in finding those answers, however, is the perceived duality between religion and spirituality. The answers are presented as "either/or" situations, and that is far from the truth. Spirituality is the legitimate goal of any true religion, and when spirituality is achieved for an individual, that person's religion can become a vehicle which gives solid meaning to life. Religion has provided an anchor and a spiritual compass for millions over the centuries. Humanity seeks greater awareness and involvement with the Source of its creation, and, in many cases, religion helps provide that. Yet, for many others, involvement in "religious" practice has led to more frustration than spiritual growth. While many find comfort, community and a sense of correctness within their religions, a growing number of people have found those same religions insufficient.

What Has Religion Become?

What has happened over the centuries is that many religions have become entities unto themselves. Some have actually become wealthy, untouchable corporations. Preaching in the name of God, they have sanctioned war and greed, allowed poverty and degrading human behavior to continue, passed judgment in God's name, and held as their right the option of condemning individuals or large groups of their sisters and brothers on the planet. They have, of course, always done these things in the firm belief that God was on their side.

What they seem to have lost awareness of is that, in the Truth we call God, there are no sides. There is only the Oneness of Love Itself. Because religions are human organizations, however, they have allowed human traits and the need for power, acceptance and ascendance in society to hamper their true task — which is helping people realize the bond they already have with and within the God Source. Many ministers hold themselves above the masses, believing they are more in tune with the Higher Power than the ordinary people in their congregations. Instead of modeling the good shepherd, they have claimed ultimate power and domination over the entire flock.

Strong words, but nothing is stronger than the gentle power of Truth.

Religions are fine for those who thrive in them. What many find missing in many religions, however, is an emphasis on one's own personal relationship with God and openness to a variety of means to achieve it. Of course, most religions frown on individual thinking because inner knowing can often conflict with group dogma or a rigid belief system. That's the same duality which is driving the human race apart right now, but mercifully that division is coming to an end.

This is one of the greatest benefits of this new Axial Age. We have serious, brilliant and gifted people now leading us away from the fallacy of presumed separation to greater understanding that our only unity is as one species bound together in our one common Source.

We are not there yet, but we have definitely begun!

One thing more and more people are considering today is what their religion means to them. Does it serve their personal spiritual needs? Are its ministers helping, or actually causing stress and acting more like corporate executives than humble people dedicated to serving their congregations?

How much is money a part of religious membership, and how much of the tax-free wealth generated by churches is actually advancing the spiritual growth and very human needs of others? Sometimes, for example, various religions use their funds to build bigger and more lavish sanctuaries of worship, when congregations would be better served if those funds supported more food banks for the often neglected and not so visible people in their communities.

Roots Are Always Real

Most people have come up through their early years in some form of religion. We've been baptized, Bar or Bat Mitzvahed, confirmed, consecrated, dedicated and in some way spiritually pledged to some form of religion, always according to its dogmas, beliefs, and rituals. And no matter what our lives have become, those early experiences have been imprinted in our psyches, if not in our souls. For many they have become the basis of how any individual considers the great Divine Mystery. They become our religious roots.

The big question is, as we move on through our lives, whether we keep growing in our own spiritual connection with the Higher Power or remain stagnant in what we call the spiritual side of our lives. Does the hour or two a week we spend in organized worship fill our inner yearning for greater purposeful living in true spirit, or is there something within us which knows there is more?

Following whatever holy initiations we have experienced, most people have taken on the label of one particular religion. Now the question becomes stronger in this new time. Is religious identification all that is necessary, or is a deeper yearning now rising in our hearts? Remember, the best place for a label is on a pickle jar!

All Politics Is Local

That's an old saying used in the field of government, and it's also true in organized religion. No matter what broad label of religion we follow, our personal religious experience revolves around the local pastor, rabbi, minister or whatever leader in the local place of worship we attend.

While many churches allow the congregation to choose — and fire — their ministers, other religions, such as Catholicism, do not have that luxury. The pope in Rome and his councils do affect parishioners with their pronouncements, but the local bishop or cardinal has great sway over what particular priest becomes the pastor of a particular parish congregation. Then that pastor stays until the bishop decides to transfer him to another parish, whether people like him or not. That individual may also be ripped from his congregation at any time on the whim of a governing bishop or cardinal. I have personally witnessed the grief and yes, anger, of people whose beloved pastor was unceremoniously transferred away from them for nothing more than petty, personal reasons on the part of a higher governing cleric.

The truth remains that most local religious experience is directly tied to the congregation's minister. If that individual is popular and caring, the local place of worship flourishes. If individuals have unpleasant experiences or feel the minister is uncaring or dictatorial, however, some people will stop attending services. In too many cases, others just walk away from the entire religion. Some also leave because there seems to be no life left within the congregation. The sermons take on a less than realistic tone, and no meaningful vitality can be found in ritual by rote.

This has led to a new concept in religion today — the mega church. In most urban areas one will now find large buildings which seat thousands and which also contain side areas with classrooms, gymnasiums, meeting rooms, day care centers, music rooms, and many other amenities — all in one complex. At the hub of this center of worship is a dynamic, attractive minister who is also a powerful inspirational speaker. He — and it's usually a "he" — is tuned into the needs of a majority of usually middle class and upscale people. The music in these churches is a mixture of upbeat and reverent selections and the choirs rate as true professionals. The sound systems are as booming and high tech as possible and religious services are well-orchestrated productions. There is no emphasis on dogma beyond the belief that Jesus is Lord and God and belief that the King James version of the Bible is the only word for word pronouncement of Almighty God. There is little repetition of ritual except the modern version of passing the collection plate.

Mega churches have become small communities unto themselves with people traveling miles to attend them. They are places where hearts are uplifted and religion is delivered in a positive, vibrant manner. There is a sense of community; the best speakers make religion relevant, and time spent in worshipping God becomes an event.

This is a good thing. Community is good. Occasionally bringing emotion and lively involvement into one's life of worship is good. And by taking valuable time out of a precious weekend to pay respect to God, many people feel they have either punched "the God card" or actually received valuable inspiration in their lives for another week, or two or three. After all, one's entire life these days is compartmentalized between work, home, leisure, and so many other things. So, giving God "his" due is a good thing. Hearing inspirational words about making God part of one's life is always helpful, and having feelings lifted in the joy of spirit, song and sometimes even dance are good.

This is not the spirituality of small groups huddled around sacred fires in earlier times, nor is it the spirituality of gatherings of the faithful held in simple buildings, under the threat of persecution, or in quiet, prayerful places of worship. This is the Church of What's Happening Now. It is religion on the cutting edge of modern life, and it is serving a purpose.

The key question remains the same. How do people relate their spiritual connection with the Higher Source in relationship to their local religious leader and what happens in their chapel, temple, mosque or mega church? How much is their spiritual connection directly with the Divine Source Itself? I often hear people raving or complaining about their local minister or the events which happen in their places of worship. Rarely do I hear them speak of their personal connection to God or of the Divine Source at all.

That's a bigger problem than most people realize. Religion is a tool. It was never intended to be taken as the Truth Itself. Religion provides an experience, but the most perfect place of worship and communion with the Divine Mystery is in each one of us. When Jesus taught that the kingdom is within, he was confirming what we, in our deepest selves, already know. Quiet times within our own stillness are the best and perfect opportunities for awareness and union. A positive experience in a place of worship can be great, but we cannot live there. It's wonderful to experience the headiness of the mountain top, but we cannot live there, either. We live in ourselves, and that is the best place, once we know how to access the Higher Source, to commune with and be within Spirit on a daily basis.

Splinters from the Tree of Life

Another reality for most religions revolves around the need for individuals to feel more personal balance with their own beliefs and the generic beliefs their particular religion preaches. As a result, today we find many splinter groups which, while staying within their religious foundations, have developed their own particular identities. There are Pentecostal Christian groups, Christian Evangelicals, conservative or more liberal forms of Judaism, and nature or Eastern religions which differ widely from others in their own particular belief systems.

There is also growing dissatisfaction among Catholics who are used to changes in their church since the Second Vatican Council in the middle of the last century. The new pope, however, is calling for a return to older Catholic ritual and stronger authoritarian, dogmatic emphasis. He is beginning to favor the Mass again said in Latin, with the priest again turning his back to the people. The patriarchal attitude is still very much alive, and the mood is turning from "people friendly" to "pope friendly" Catholicism. This, by the way, is not being well received in the emptying pews — or the more barren collection plates.

There are splinter groups from Hinduism now reaching into the western world with globe-trotting gurus who draw followers to their own enlightened energies. The world of Islam is also now witnessing more people drifting back to practices of Sufism, which was Islam's forerunner.

The most obvious splintering of organized religion in today's world is the sharp divide in Islam. The vast majority of Muslims are peace-loving, honorable people who take seriously their daily prayers which begin, "Almighty and merciful God …" The rise of the Jihadist militant movement within Islam, however, fuels much of today's terrorist activity. It is causing a painful rift in that holy religion and makes many question the mindset which views even self-immolation to murder others as an act condoned by or serving the "almighty and merciful God."

The bottom line is that many people have chosen to base their religious experience around culturally comfortable congregations. They have gone to splinter groups of more like-minded people or, as many "Cafeteria Catholics" have done, they have decided to simply ignore many rules and dictates from their religious leaders. Just witness American Catholics' ideas about birth control!

There Is No Going Back

Because religion has driven more and more people away, there are voices within it which now call for reconsideration and change.

Catholic priest and social expert Diarmuid O'Murchu, for example, has stepped forward to say:

> Religion today has become a patriarchal system ... It is religion more than anything else that has forced us to forget who we are. All the man religions suffer from a suffocating sense of culture and history and contribute significantly to our cultural and spiritual amnesia. They conclude unquestioningly with a patriarchal conviction that civilization began about 5,000 years ago, and that everything prior to that time must be dismissed as irrelevant, uncivilized, barbaric, primitive and pagan! Religion itself stands knee deep in blasphemy, seeking to subvert even the creativity of the Godhead Itself.

These are strong statements, yet they are courageous words from a man who still works within his own religious structure as a true minister. Brilliantly aware of changes needed to further humankind's successful move into a holistic, universal approach to God, O'Murchu joins others who stand as modern prophets pointing the way. "A true spirituality of integration considers everything in the world to be relatively important," O'Murchu continues, "Old dualisms of God vs. Man, Earth vs. Heaven, Spiritual vs. Secular, Sin vs. Grace are considered to be superficial and simplistic. In a holistic universe, everything is one. Unity and harmony are the underlying energies and also the ultimate goal."

There is only one Light and we are all merely individual shards of It. Aware the successful future of humankind requires ability to respond to its own rising consciousness, O'Murchu writes, "There is no going back to the good old days when things were static and stable, and we all knew 'where we stood'. Even if we could revert, it would be totally inappropriate because our innate destiny is to progress (not regress) to changes and adapt to the new challenges of an ever-changing personality and an ever-changing society."

Fear Is a Mind Killer

Key to the possible co-existence of religion and spirituality is an understanding of what institutionalized religions have done in the past and what they are repeating today. As modern religions disavow everything and anything which preceded them, those same religions are now operating from the same defense in our time. Many of their ministers speak of "spirituality" in a derogatory sense. They use the term to describe any individual or group which shuns their organizations to pursue a more personal search for the Source. As anything before their religion's existence is considered "ungodly," so too is anything new which may challenge or not be incorporated in their particular belief system. The term "spirituality" — as preached from some pulpits — refers to anything relating to native spiritual practices, most forms of meditation, use of musical instruments or chants from other or earlier cultures, or reference to divinity as also incorporating feminine energy. They look askance at the growing popularity of integrative healing arts such as Ayurvedic ways of nurturing the body, Healing Touch, Reiki, or any other forms of energy medicine.

Although Jesus himself used his hands to restore wholeness, which is what healing really is, many modern ministers degrade such practices as suspect at best. They also look askance at use of incense, aromatherapy, recognizing and using the different properties of stones from the earth, or studying the seven major centers of a person's physical, emotional and spiritual well-being — the chakras. Catholic bishops, for example, have recently condemned the practice of Reiki, which is the simple channeling of Life Force Energy.

Just as religion has always dismissed as foolish or ungodly any spiritual beliefs or practices which preceded them in the past, today, as religions become more deeply entrenched in teaching their rites of exclusivity, they condemn, or at least ridicule, what other people use to enhance their own journey into Spirit. Not exactly an enlightened behavior from those who preach these words of their own idea of God, "Judge not, and you shall not be judged."

Where the Light Will Be Found

When we consider spirituality today, let it first be seen as a seeking of truth and greater light to illumine both our thoughts and our feelings. For many people, reading or hearing inspirational words is a beginning. People sometimes mention poets and saints in the same breath. As one who occasionally writes poetry, however, I don't think that is terribly accurate. There are, however, writings to which we often look for inspiration or which guide us to greater spiritual awareness.

The creative muse is often used to describe that magical agent which dispenses special blessings to anyone who attempts to make some kind of response to the mystery of life. Writings over the ages have helped "inspire," or draw out the spirit in another. More importantly, writings have captured moments of elevated thought, and in, rare cases, such as the poets Rumi, William Blake, the ancient woman author of "The Thunder — Perfect Mind," and writers of the *Tao Te Ching* or the "Canticle of Canticles," they have found words to elevate us into the wonder and sacred beauty we love to occasionally visit.

Many who have had near death experiences say they have faced two questions while seemingly "out of the body." One is, "How well have you loved?" The other, "What have you learned?" There is no place better than our own heart to seek wisdom.

After that, however, reading some of the classics of spiritual cultures from around the world is another beneficial thing to do. If nothing else, it will convince you that our human species has been on the same purposeful track for a very long time.

Consider, too, that others will find sparks of that divine light in nature where the air is clean and life in all kinds of abundance thrives. They see the divine handiwork in this Mother Earth herself. There are those who, through their practice of yoga and its disciplines, or through study of physics, astronomy and science, find their own pathways to spiritual development. Those who work the land or who work to protect the land always have a deep spiritual core. Any woman who has ever given birth, and any father who has held his child for the first time, have recognized, at least if only briefly, the miracle of life and have been, in some way, in awe of its source.

We as a species are facing one of the greatest tasks of humanity's life on earth. Each nation and each religious denomination will face serious challenges and decisions to be made in the time just ahead of us. How you view your purpose and your own connection with a Divine Power will affect your response to the changes ahead. There is no going back to a past which is simply crumbling away. And, it is crumbling away because it needs to disappear so a new world order of compassionate thought and united action can emerge.

There is help all around you, but it's your decision to make. How you think and believe and act is creating the life you are making your destiny. That matters a great deal to you. And because individual thoughts impact the collective energy of us all, it matters to humanity's future as well.

What will you do?

RIGHT BRAIN CHAPTER REVIEW

The Teacher Within

Caught on the side of a mountain, where life trickles softly to silence,
The wind whispers silence open a bit and the Teacher Within starts
        to speak.

Here, where beauty rises like a symphony
        take the earth's cool surging
        through the mellowness of ancient memories
        as time reaches forward and back
        to the fullness where Now is complete.

Just be quiet, the Teacher says.
Be still, that you truly may learn

what you have already known in so many ages past.
For the beauty is never enough
    without the resonance of your response.
In your silent speaking all the magic grows to fullness
    from its passing through your soul.

Caught half-way up a mountain side
    there are lessons to be listened for —
    With no doors to open or close.
There is only the wind, and the flow,
And the Teacher Within,
Whispering yet once more —
    Breathe to the depths,
    and out through the wisdom
    of what you have always known...

CHAPTER FOUR

LIVING AT THE BIFURCATION POINT

Your Role in the Age of Encounter

*The most important thing to remember during times of
great change is to fix our eyes on the things that don't change.
They remind us we, as children of God, are still at the center
of divine purpose in the world — people in whose presence
the world moves toward healing.*

- Marianne Williamson

This current confusion between religion and spirituality is another aspect of what has been called The Bifurcation Point of human society, and human consciousness itself. This is a concept which arose from the chaos/order theory and was originally championed by Dr. Ervin Lazlo, an expert in philosophy, human sciences and Consciousness Evolution study.

The Bifurcation Point is described as the point or moment of truth in time at which a body or a civilization either breaks down, or moves to a higher level of order. Only two results are possible — healing or death. This is the central point where things cannot stay the same. This is the line which must be crossed. This is where the future either spirals down in regressive, destructive attitudes and behaviors, or spirals up to a new way of being. It is the key point in an Axial Age when things cannot simply go on as they have been. It is the point of no return where something needs to change. Something needs to shift and indeed will — for the good or the detriment of us all. And, from that point, things either improve by positive, forward-looking ideas and choices, or begin to degrade from entrenched refusal to change. The Bifurcation Point is the key moment in consciousness evolution when ideas, concepts and behaviors move qualitatively into a newer, higher way of being, or quickly tumble toward ultimate ruin.

This is not only a major concept for this book but for all human consciousness today. We are either at or very near that pivotal, momentous point. This is huge. It is right now, in this time, that the choices we make, if positive and enlightened, will lead to a new way of cooperation and compassion in our world. If our choices are wrong or we refuse to make positive change, we will seriously degrade the very possibility of moving forward as a species.

This is the point of regeneration or degeneration. The energy of this pivotal point is addressing the chaos of our time and bringing it to a true rebirthing. It can be a critical step to a higher level of being what we really are if we can go with the flow of its higher consciousness. Yet this is also the point where failure to move with that flow, and making fearful or faulty choices, can lead to eventual degeneration of our species itself.

Many are feeling that Bifurcation Point energy already as the lesser, outmoded pillars of the past are crumbling from their own weight. This can be a fearful time as the old falls away, but we have the strength to make this move within ourselves, and there are many tools which can help us. They are emerging all around us today and, as we need them, they will present themselves in our lives. We'll talk more about them in Part Two.

The Point of No Return

The Bifurcation Point has also been called the Point of Over-whelm, describing how society or the planet is at a juncture of being overwhelmed by what it has become. Our planet is just about there. We already see changes it has begun to make and scientists tell us there are more and much greater earth changes in the time ahead. We, as the human species, are also what we have become. We are now at the Moment of Truth and the Point of No Return for our planet and for ourselves.

A clear sign of arrival at the Bifurcation Point is the growing desire to develop more personal bonds with our Higher Source. For more individuals the old ways of organized, hierarchical and etched in stone religious ideas and practices are simply not ringing true any more. And religious ministers are human too. The great Godhead is no more a part of their existence than it is of ours. We're beginning to see that all too clearly now, resulting in a tendency to take our supposed religious mentors down from previous pedestals, and see them as vulnerable to egoist thought and action as the rest of us.

Likewise, any sacred text should not be viewed as a history book written ages ago by some and interpreted only by select people today. Religion tends to preach to us from the past. But we are all part of living history right now. True spirituality demands we seek truth today. What is right, holy and sacred did not just happen centuries ago. It is also happening now, and it is happening with the power and intensity of the higher consciousness we have reached in this Axial Age.

We too are what we have become and our species has reached the point of overwhelm. Now we face the choice to move into greater awareness of our Source and its mystery and model that behavior in our choices and actions, or not. It is an awesome responsibility but it is a choice which must be made. We are the people called to stand within The Shift, the Moment of Truth of this Bifurcation Point. And the earth demands that we choose very well.

In our species, and in your own life, are you willing to take the spiral up? Or will you be an agent of sending the spiral down into a darkness neither we nor the Great Source deserve?

We have come so far already, and our destiny lies just ahead of us within the great heart of the Divine Mystery Itself. Do you have the courage to honestly read your own heart, then choose and act accordingly? This is the big time, and it's your turn to show up positively and play your most important part on the world stage! Our future depends on it!

It's All About Choice

The Bifurcation Point is another concept for understanding a great law of the universe. The old must fall away because it can no longer serve the highest needs of what people have become. It needs to disappear to make way for the new which is more in tune with the requirements and growth of our species. Whether we like it or not, we are growing up. That may be painful to some but it is a good thing, a real cause for celebration. It means we are growing ever deeper and closer to the God Source within us.

We already see it happening. People are feeling more independent. They're trusting their own instincts more and so-called leaders less. This is true in many aspects of society and true in organized religions as well. Authentic independence is always a sign of maturity. Breaking away from the herd mentality allows building greater trust in one's own creative and spiritual energies.

As our ministers and so-called holy people fail, they, in their failure, help us realize we are already part of the One Transcendent Truth. By the very failings of their own humanity, those ministers are pushing us deeper into the Great Truth which is immanent and powerful and peaceful and absolutely magnificent in us all. Religion does provide a sense of community. It fills our human need to belong, but you are already solidly in the greatest gathering in the world. You belong to Divine Truth, created in the magnificence of Divine love!

You are God stuff! You are a lifetime and soultime member with no dues to pay, no tithes to honor, no pledges to make and not even any box tops to send in. You ARE in! And no one can ever cut you off from grace, bar you from worship, or — in some pompous act of self-righteous so-called religious purity — excommunicate you from the love of God as you perceive and honor it by your life and the sacredness of your own heart.

Go ahead and join any other group you feel fits you. But this soul membership is the perfect fit. You and the great God Source fit perfectly in absolute oneness, because that is the one true thing you are!

Freedom

Truth does set us free because our presence within the Divine Mystery spins us to freedom from dogma, rituals, and dictates from others. It frees us from those who have held themselves above us as the only God-appointed soul keepers of the way.

There is only one Way, and our personal map to find it is already imprinted in our human brain and in its own sacred presence within our heart. It is powerful, peaceful and eternal, fulfilling Truth. All we need do is surrender to its vision within us and agree to manifest its love and light in the days of life we are given on this earth.

Is there a priest or rabbi, shaman, guru, teacher or master who knows your own heart more deeply than you? Is there a sage or a saint who has lived in your body, loved with your heart, ridden through the joys and the challenges of your life experience, and navigated through the personal expanses of your mind and your emotions? There is only you and the Sacred Presence within you which longs for your awareness of the Union you already share. Your real truth, your only truth, is not perfectly written in the pages of the most sacred book you can ever read. There are certainly guide posts and teachers and those who speak within the purest love possible. But your deepest truth is already written in your heart and in your own ability to grasp it.

As the Zen saying advises, just be still and begin to understand what you, in your deepest self, already know. That is the only answer and fulfilling destiny you will ever need. The one Sacred and Eternal Truth. And you are already in it because it is the essence of you, already waiting at home within your heart, in the fullness of your highest mind, and in the precious beauty of your own unique soul.

Love One Another

Spirituality and religion are not always meant to co-exist, but in some cases, to merge. Religion can be the beginning. Strong roots are always important as they can lead to a more personal and holy form of spirituality unique to you in every way.

Yet, while many people use their various religions as springboards for greater spiritual development, it is important to lovingly accept those among us who no longer belong to organized religious groups. This may be from negative experiences with clerics within those religions or from unwillingness to accept some of the religion's dogma, political stance or emphasis. But those people are still very much on the only real path, the one which leads directly into the Divine Heart. In some ways, they are to be admired more because they do not turn to dogma or religious righteousness for their guideposts. They may seek others who are searching as they are, yet they must often travel alone on the path which calls them. This is never easy, but sometimes necessary.

Embrace the Grace of All

One of the healthiest things we can do is to calmly consider religions other than our own, or the religions we have spent our own lives discovering, fighting, or embracing. Going back in time to other cultures and religions, it becomes quickly apparent that this planet has been spinning to the same melodies, only with different rhythms and words, for a very long time!

The chants of Tibetan monks, as they resonate the sounds of all spirit and Creation, have the same echoes of longing and sacred wonder as the sutras and bhajans of India, and the measured rhythms and tones of the Hebrew prayer, Kodoish. They echo the haunting reverence of native drums and the rhythm of dances, the sacred calls to prayer in the Muslim world, and the sweet, rolling power of Gregorian Chant echoed in the majesty of Rome or from a simple Trappist monastery cut out of the heartland in Bardstown, Kentucky.

The rhythms of God are the rhythms of the universe because the universe is of God. It is truly the Divine Milieu — the Divine environment and playground. It is the home of Divinity as much as your own heart is the home of Divinity.

What many call God is the Beyond, the Ultimate Presence, the antithesis of separation. The beautiful Sanskrit chant taken from *The Heart Sutra — Gate, gate, paragate, parasamgate, bodhi swava —* reminds us that, "Beyond, beyond, far beyond, totally beyond — lies the Greatest Truth, the Heart of Perfect Wisdom."

The great Mystery is the only real resonance, the only real sound sung in the great silence of Truth welling up in Love's melody, sweetly calling to Itself in exquisite vibrations of Its Eternal Now.

The Walk of Your Life

Do you belong to a religion? Do you walk an organized path you believe will lead you to God and eternity spent deeply content in that Spirit Heart of Divinity? That is wonderful if that religion can lead you beyond all its tenets, credos, laws, ministers, and anathemas to personal participation in real spirituality. That is where your spirit can revel in its development of union and actual encounter with the Ever Presence of Truth and Mystery.

Just remember you are walking toward a fulfilling new world. This is the Age of Encounter. This is the Bifurcation Point of rebirth and regeneration, or stagnancy and degeneration. This is the Time of Synthesis, the age when all divisions of separation must begin to fall away.

As a positive sign we are moving in the right direction, there are many ministers and people within religion today who are working with this rising level of consciousness. There are those who choose to stay within their religious framework and work for greater understanding and teaching from within. They need to be applauded because they are "doing the work," and they are doing it well. Upon them rests the future of those very religions in the holistic, global times ahead. Equally, we need to honor those who have moved on in their own paths, holding all who embrace truth with the courage — remembering the French *coeur*, which means heart — of their own hearts.

Chaos to Creation

Of course there will be people who see this time of no return, this Bifurcation Point we are now facing, with fear and anxiety. As old vestiges of what has been crumble beneath the weight of outmoded so-called pillars of society and religion, there will be those who bemoan their loss. They at least helped us understand where we were, and whether we liked things the way they were or not, at least we knew them and we knew what to expect from them.

Besides, what is humanity left with as the old begins to fall away? Some will answer that there is only chaos in the place of what has been. Some will even try to pick up the pieces of the old and attempt to refashion them to fit into the new way of being. That, however, will never be enough to meet the needs of the new society which the Birfurcation Point will demand of us. The time for retooling the past is over. That's the very concept of the Point of No Return. A Bifurcation Point does not allow reruns. If chaos needs to be the order of things for a while, so be it. The very presence of chaos, however, will be the catalyst for creating the new world order needed to carry the human species and the planet herself forward. And in that sense, whatever chaos is involved will be worth it. Its presence will force women and men to open their minds and hearts to a new variety of options and intriguing possibilities the world has never before considered.

In that sense the Axial Age and Bifurcation Point bring exciting new options for all of us. While some may fear the loss of balance in the move from the old to the new, truth lies in the rare opportunity humanity has before it. Because the old will no longer fit, this will be an exciting time to actually create, using new paradigms of thought and action. Attitudes will be changing and, as new thought featuring compassion and holding more respect for others grows, change will evolve from the self to groups and then into larger groups. Governments will be faced with creating new ways of leading, and those who once held power will have to recognize the fact that there will no longer be willing followers to blindly obey their every mandate. With respect growing for self and others, there will be greater demand to be heard in how governmental dictates are applied equally to all. There will also be a greater understanding that governments, as well as religious leaders, are not in positions of power for themselves. The new world order will feature great respect for the individual. As a result, leaders of any institution, be it civic, governmental, or religious, will be expected to consider what is truly best for the people, and not what feeds their own need for power.

We are moving into this exciting new time of creation. New breakthroughs in every part of society and religion await us. With regression into the old not an option, there will be many changes in what society will look like. Even concepts of marriage as a lifetime commitment, to considering religious beliefs and spirituality not open to any new understanding or change, may see some strong revisions. These were ordered and fit in times when most people died before or during their forties. Those were the times before modern medicine extended life expectancies. With people now living much longer lives, there will be more consideration for allowing personal evolution to be honored and dealt with. Rising divorce rates and second marriages are already signs we all have different needs and different standards as we evolve through our own lives. As more women find their own strength and self respect, for example, meaningful marriage will call for equal partnership, and the end to patriarchal dominance of men over women in all aspects of life.

There is always some form of chaos before new creation breaks through. Again, this is a basic law of the universe. And because we are alive to witness this Bifurcation Point now, there is no need to fear. With change comes new creation. From new creation new possibilities for meaningful life and greater happiness await us. These can all be positive gifts to humanity as the new world order emerges. Wouldn't it be better to embrace the new possibilities, rather than lament the passing of what no longer serves us, anyway?

We Are Here and We Matter

We are in the critical stages of an exciting Axial Age in the history of the human species. If there is breath in you and you read these words, you are one of those chosen to "walk between the worlds" to revere the old yet create the new order. We cannot go back even if we wanted to. As creatures of a changing world, we are changing as well. The movement toward total acceptance in a universal, holistic society, when all people realize we are one in the same Source, will probably take several generations. Old ways die hard. We who are walking through the worlds now will probably never see the realization of that world which awaits our species.

But we matter. We are the torch bearers moving toward the Only Greatest Light. We are those assigned to hold the breach between the worlds of the old and the new. We must be the courageous ones who walk steadfastly forward, trusting that Divine Light which calls us to come closer and closer still. Not closer to the Reality of What Is, and of what we are, however, because those realities have never changed.

We instead must draw closer to our own rising from ego and separation, through the heightening consciousness inside us, to the unity which is our birthright, our identity, and our destiny as co-creators with the Source.

How beautiful we can become! How magnificently we can mirror the heart of the Divine and let it shine the power of Its Love throughout this planet and all of creation — back into that Divine Heart Itself!

What a gift to be part of that! And what a grace!

RIGHT BRAIN CHAPTER REVIEW

Beyond The Point of No Return

I have lost myself in you.
I have cut away from all the safety zones —
  vibration tones which marked my boundaries
  and limitations I had set for myself.
I have gone beyond the edges of my mind until
  I find myself spinning in the newer Light
  which radiates fresh beauty
  from quiet miracles I never knew before.
And I am wandering far beyond my illusions
  of how anything should be.

I am lost beyond the confines of my heart.

I am set apart. Cut free. Spun beyond the shallow roots
     I once considered the safety of home
Until — before me and within me — I am flung beyond
     the point of no return.
And there is You — so present in the shadow mist
     of what I thought I knew.

Now I am forgiven in my forgiving.
I am saved in my surrender.
I am tossed like a wave in sea streams which are your mystery.
I am flung into the space where only You exist.
And I am kissed by the cosmos of all creation
     just because I am the stuff and the mind and the heart
     and the essence of you.

The energy was calling to be changed
Yet it was not calling to be destroyed.
The energy said leap, and simply trust.
And I have. And I am.

This is the time to close off what has been
     with solitude growing ever full
     and action poised to take the journey on.
The energy of love is all, any more.
The body presses on as the learning turns to Mind,
And the heart is simply grounding into home
Where the soul already revels in the Truth.

CHAPTER FIVE

WELCOME TO THE QUANTUM WORLD

New Possibilities and Non-Linear Thinking

Consciousness is what discloses to us a world of great complexity, openness, fluidity and creativity. It alerts us to the fact that things happen and evolve according to principles bigger and deeper than what we humans envisage...
It invites us to stretch all our definitions

- Diarmuid O'Murchu

This chapter is a bit of a mind stretcher but it lays important groundwork for what's ahead. This book deals with spirituality and personal paths which can lead to God. First, however, it may be helpful to understand some breakthroughs which are fueling the leap of spiritual evolution in this Axial Age. This chapter plants seeds for understanding those new concepts since more people are now experiencing the God Mystery on a much deeper level. Once these seeds are planted, we can move more easily through the rest of these pages.

We are already making many changes in how we live and what we choose to put in our bodies. There is now more emphasis on eating organic rather than highly processed food as well as choosing foods more conducive to health rather than to emotional comfort. This has given many people a better outlook on their own bodies, not only for ego or a better quality of life, but also to honor the physical as a vehicle which houses the spirit. Dan Millman has a great quote in his book *Everyday Enlightenment*, "If you don't take care of your body, where will you live?"

In the same light, more people are practicing yoga, Gi Gong and Tai Chi which not only regulate the body but also require inner still-ness as part of their discipline. Even coaches like Phil Jackson have used Zen meditation techniques of quiet concentration to empower professional athletes into superstar status. While some religions often denigrate the body as lesser in the least, and downright harmful temp-tations to sin at the worst, more holistic thought has led to linking the body and mind as positive factors which work together for greater wholeness of the human person.

Other contributions to subjects which used to be the sole propri-ety of religions, such as the meaning of life and our relationship to its source, have come, of all places, from the world of science. The break-through of Quantum Physics in 1906 has steadily led to deeper under-standing of all creation and the limitless possibilities of consciousness. More advanced studies of time have led to the reality of non-linear thinking. Research of the human brain has provided greater under-standing of how we co-create our lives by our very thoughts. And application of the Quantum concept has opened limitless possibilities of greater understanding of creation, and our relationship with the Source of Creation Itself.

This is, indeed, a new time and we are privileged to be living in it. We are also, whether we accept it or not, part of its miracle.

Discovering the Quantum

Before we can move any further, the first truth to grasp is that we are capable of understanding much more than we currently realize. In the spike of human evolution which characterizes this new Axial Age, the catalyst for defining the problems of our world today, and the key to moving beyond them, lies in the gift of rising consciousness. The very core of any Axial Age is that the human species is given a new way of thinking and therefore being. And that way isn't exactly new. The human spirit has held the potential of its own fullness from the earliest spark of its beginning, but we are just now becoming more aware of our own possibilities.

And that is changing everything!

As our current Axial Age was already well under way, over a hundred years ago, the scientist Max Planck began to realize our old mode of thinking was too constrained and therefore faulty. Until that time, science considered the creation process in a more mechanistic, limited way. It basically said that anything that exists is the sum of its parts. Take apart a table, separating the wood from the nails and the glue and the varnish and whatever else has gone into it, and each one of those parts, when put together, becomes — *voila*! A table! That line of thinking followed with all of creation. Everything which goes into making a bird from claws, innards, beak, feathers, and the delightful ability to fly becomes a bird. And the human person, with all its integral parts, becomes one individual.

Planck finally put into words what many "conscious" scientists and gifted thinkers were beginning to realize. When all the parts are put together, the new thing is not just a sum of its parts. It actually becomes a new entity, a quantum reality with myriad possibilities! Thus was born the concept of Quantum Physics, or the Quantum — the endless possibilities which may arise from any one thing, or from chaos itself.

This realization stayed too long in the isolated halls of academia, yet, as the new century and millennium approached, it reached the awakening consciousness of more people. Now the discoveries of scientists, mathematicians and astrophysicists have begun to change our very thinking about our lives on this planet and our possibilities of participation within the very source of creation Itself! Science is actually opening up new ideas of the Source Mystery! Because of this, we are now witnessing the growing polarization of religions against other religions and what, for want of a better word, we call spirituality. This is one of the greatest divisions in our world today.

It's All Right to "Get Out of Line"

Another realization which is influencing this Axial Age is that human thinking is basically linear. Linear thinking sees existence as a line with a beginning, middle, and end. We, as a human species, see life as being born, having certain events happen to us, and finally experiencing physical death. There are numerous sayings which may rise from that attitude but they all echo that same linear view of existence. A more crass description might be the saying, "Life's a bitch. Then you die!" But there deliciously is more that we already know! And besides, we should be more respectful of this world's canine mothers!

In all the time before us, the old, linear way of thinking profoundly affected humanity's consideration of God, and an individual's relationship to God. In linear thinking there is no final solution to life. There is simply a moving forward until ultimate oblivion or some kind of ending.

Thinking involved in religion used that same rationality. Once we belong to a religion, we follow the dictates and dogma of that religion. We only accept as truth the scriptures that particular religion holds as sacred. The event horizon which waits at the end of our life is either reward or punishment. And that reward — which is union with God, is opposed to an end with lack of union with God, which we have decided is hell. And the religious concept of hell is, in the least, not pretty.

In that mode of thinking, which is normal to our species' ego driven, illusory mind, God, the Ultimate Source, is separated from us mere humans. God is "other." God is "out there." Since there had to be some reason for that, concepts such as original sin or man's failure to act well became an easily accepted reason for not being able to attain God in the first place. We are here and God is there and, because we humans keep doing stupid and often harmful things, we can't really reach "Him" now. We must first get out of this human existence before we can even consider claiming reward for trying to do our best and, in regard to religion, doing it the way that particular religion dictates.

Many people have accepted the concept that, right out of the gate, we are all sinners, and need to be saved from our own flawed existence. We are lesser beings and we need to be saved from our own selves. As if the creation of the Source needs to be saved from its very being a part of that Source!

But now the two disciplines which never seemed to merge, science and religion, have actually become enmeshed in the rising consciousness of this Axial Age. As the discovery of Quantum Reality has begun to explode on more of us common folk, we are beginning to understand, through studies of the human brain itself and our higher potential of thinking and non-thinking, that there really is more! The very concepts of the God Source and the greater fullness of our individual place within that Source are more attainable! This is now fueling the great division between religion and spirituality, as if the two are distinct and diametrically opposed separate ways of realizing God.

Linear Thinking

Linear thinking is finite and contained. Linear thinking on a world level, with the ultimate end always part of its scenario, will lead to oblivion of the human species, and our Mother Earth as well. Linear thinking says war is inevitable because we all have to die sometime; so death might as well be honorable in service to our country. All that matters is that we are the last ones standing when the end arrives. And, after all, we are destined to win, because "God is on our side." As if The One Source of All could ever take sides against Itself! Those in the United States today, for example, who fervently pray, "God bless America", yet fail to add, "And God bless the Muslim nations," are caught in the linear thinking which can never solve problems, but can only perpetuate them.

The beauty of this new era on the planet, however, is holding more emphasis on the concept of non-linear thinking which is a more feminine, more open to mystery mode of thought. It is the realization that many realities don't fit into a time line. Non-linear thinking helps us realize the phrase, "God created the world," is not correct. That did not happen billions of years ago and fit into the past tense. The Source of Creation creates constantly. That Mystery keeps creating the world by holding it in existence. And, in non-linear thinking, we can finally realize and appreciate the concept that we need not experience God only in a future beyond this life. We can live within the God Presence as much as humanly possible right now, right here. "God" is not an unattainable Source in this lifetime. Instead, the God Presence is within us and has been since our beginning. We just haven't learned to realize that yet and celebrate it with joy, awe, and love.

How the discoveries of the Quantum and the realization of non-linear thought are changing society have great impact on religion and spirituality today. As we will see in later chapters, it is now more plausible to reach for more mature ideas of "God" beyond that fatherly supreme judge who watches our every move and who will judge us with harsh truth at life's end. Realizing the powerful mystery of a God Concept which embraces all the possibilities of Mystery Itself can help raise our own consciousness to newer levels of understanding. It can give us greater appreciation of what is truly the Divine Mystery and make us more comfortable with not always having to understand everything.

As we begin to realize the freedom of non-linear thinking, we can also stop thinking of "God" as having created everything before ancient times and then "left the building" to leave humanity to fend for itself. In understanding the Eternal Present within the God Moment beyond time we can more easily accept ongoing creation of life right now. This will free us from constantly looking back to an ancient past for our ideas of the divine. Instead we can feel its presence and its workings in our own lives and in the evolution of society and world consciousness today.

The quantum and understanding of non-linear thought are great helps to move us forward in spiritual growth. They can lead us to newer levels of meditation, love and personal maturity.

Does this mean we should negate all the wisdom of our ancestors back to the ancient beginnings of our species? No. Does it mean we do not honor their efforts and the way they met changes in themselves and in the planet? No. Does it mean throwing out all the spiritual concepts of the cultures and religions across time, failing to appreciate what they were trying to say about the divine in very human terms? Absolutely not! We stand today on the shoulders of all who have gone before us and we need to be grateful to them for bringing us as far as we have come.

Now, however, it is our turn to stand in the rising consciousness which is being given us. Now it is our task to advance our species, and awareness of the God Source Itself, into a brighter new world filled with the radiance of God Love and God Light. "By their fruits you shall know them". And that old saying really is right — the apple never does fall far from the tree!

The Beauty of the Brain

When Jesus said, "You are made in the image and likeness of God," he was not talking about physical characteristics. As a great teacher, one who truly stood in the consciousness of a fully-realized Christ, he was speaking absolute truth. Part of that truth is now becoming more clear through studies of the human brain itself and how the way we think governs our total life process.

The thought that spirituality, or a personal closeness to God, also resides in the brain as well as in the heart may seem foreign to some. It is true that our ultimate reality is love since we come from love and we are of love — because God is love. How we use that ability to love, however, is governed by the very human activity of our brain, and also by vibrations within our human heart. We will talk later about the masculine and feminine energies within each of us, no matter our current sexuality. At the beginning, however, it is important to note that the brain is divided into two main frontal areas, the right and the left lobes.

The left side of the brain, science has now discovered, produces thought particles. It allows us to focus, put all our attention on a particular concept, and then make that concept manifest. It makes us aware of detail, then gives us the ability to string details together to create outcomes. It is present in thoughts from deciding on dinner choices to choosing careers, developing relationships — or deciding to end them.

The left side of the brain is more geared to linear thinking. "If I do this and this, that will happen." Linear thinking is locked into what we call an "event horizon." There is always an outcome even if the outcome is oblivion. The left brain cannot go beyond reason and it cannot accept anything that is not logical. The character of Spock in the Star Trek series was the perfect example of living in pure linear thought. How many times did Spock say to Captain Kirk, "But that is not logical!" That's the only way he thought, yet he did begin to take on more human characteristics of emotion and what he called "silly human behavior." Even he began to move beyond mere linear thinking! Maybe that's why, for all of us old Trekkies, we grew to love Spock the more the series continued. In his odd, stilted, way he was becoming more like us!

Working in the Quantum

Ah, but the right side of the brain does not work from focusing thought particles. It produces wave thoughts. It does not consider a beginning or an end. Instead it flows with the wave of consciousness itself and allows for unlimited quantum thinking. From this mode of brain activity, the quantum actually arises. And the quantum holds endless possibilities! It cannot be contained or confined because it holds the very essence of potentiality. The possibilities of where it can lead are endless. It surpasses rigid logic and instead thrives in the soul of mystery. The right brain, with its more feminine energies, is the place of creativity and the stillness which leads to sound. It welcomes chaos and the opportunity to deal with its many potential outcomes.

In a later chapter we will consider more fully the role right brain thinking has in the current surge of consciousness. That is because the emergence of the right brain's ability to think in waves of the quantum is fueling new possibilities for life on the planet and beyond. For now, it is enough to understand that, as the power of the right brain makes consciousness more available and less constricting, its very ability to create new ways of thought from old, limited belief systems is one of the most powerful phenomena happening in today's Axial Age!

The right brain nurtures the quantum with the seed of ultimate possibilities and new realities. The left brain says, "This is what we know. Now let's work with it." The right brain exists in the endless potential of the quantum and quietly muses, "Gee, what if ....?"

Forward!

This new understanding of brain functioning has vast implications. From the way we consider government and finance to the way we educate our young and choose our relationships, awareness of quantum possibilities is exciting. For now those possibilities remain unknown and, while some may fear what is to come, there is no need to worry. We are made for joy and ultimate union within the God Source of Love.

At times the road may be rocky, but what destination is not worth the journey which preceded it? Why worry? Worry is a product of fear. You now have within you a rising consciousness and a brain more accessible to your own very thought processes. You now know you are part of the quantum and your possibilities are endless!

RIGHT BRAIN CHAPTER REVIEW

The Sweetness of Possibility

Walls of limitation begin to fall away.
The sweetness of possibility reaches beyond the tiny ego mind
to dance within the mystery which waits to be revealed.
The straight line of thought dissolves into a circle,
Never ending, comprehending all in one,
in the realm which reaches deep into the heart of the Divine.

The quantum calls for space beyond any space we know.
The quantum says love the chaos from which will grow
the perfect story and the glory of All That Is —
Radiance of Light made manifest!

Smaller thoughts and lesser understandings dissolve
in realizing the brilliance of the Whole.
Finally aware — once we dare the thrilling ride
toward immersion in the Truth,
we revel in the mystery of being only One.

CHAPTER SIX

CREATING WITH NEW CONSCIOUSNESS

Undoing the Grip of the Mind

Man can only fully be said to be alive when he becomes plainly conscious of the real meaning of his own existence, when he experiences something of the fullness of intelligence, freedom and spirituality that are actualized within himself.

- Thomas Merton

D
o you want to be staid, stymied, and stuck where you are? That's your choice. You can also be superbly sacred, and more delightfully sane in an entirely new experience of your own life and consciousness. It's up to you.

Part of the benefits of living in this time of rising consciousness is the ability to become more aware of one of the greatest rascals anyone has had to face. Its identity? The ego mind, which has had its way of illusion and falsehood throughout history. Because we are now aware that we are aware of more, however, we also see more clearly the folly of staying stuck in self-serving, ego-centered lives. We can choose instead the beauty of rising into the fullness of what we are meant to become.

Today's rising consciousness gives us the ability to access deeper parts of the psyche, and move away from the continued prison of limited, linear ego thought. It exposes the narrow-minded world of illusion into which we, as a human species, have so totally bought. Rising consciousness considers the problems and the possibilities, then responds in sometimes unconventional manners. For example, when so-called leaders faltered in their attempts to alleviate the suffering caused by the hurricane Katrina, it was the rising consciousness of the masses which stepped into the role of honest, simple leadership. Church and civic groups, as well as many individuals, packed up trucks and vans to travel to New Orleans to offer help wherever it was needed. That was done by laying egos aside and following hearts instead. Ordinary people saw the problem in human terms, then responded to it in the higher consciousness of simply sharing as sisters and brothers in the family of humanity, united in One Source. That is rising consciousness in action! It is not looking to so-called leaders for answers. Rather, it is becoming a true leader yourself!

In the world of education, many are trying to revamp the outdated school process from within while others have begun new types of schools on their own. These new schools include the teaching of virtue and human values as part of their curricula. Politically, more people are turning away from allegiance to party and old, selfish mindsets. Instead, they look for leaders who can bring a higher level of humanity into the decisions they make in serving the people they represent. As always, the arts and the artists, the Cultural Creatives among us, have always shown the way by breaking old molds and risking ridicule as they thrust new concepts of creativity into the world of staid, linear thinking. Many within religions have also begun to question the limited dogmatic teachings of their predecessors. Instead, they are seeking new ways to create community and allow space for individual experience of the God Source as any one person may best connect with it.

Instead of the old way of thinking that wisdom comes with grey hair, we have begun to include the wisdom of our youth, especially in this time of indigo children who seem to have been born with "their lights on." There is also wisdom in the earth which we are now beginning to recognize, as elders who have gone before us have known since ancient times. In this era of global warming and dire predictions of environmentalists and scientists, we have seen more positive thinking about how products of this earth are used and consumed.

We are moving toward an era of new abundance, working in new paradigms and considering new answers which the process of linear thinking could never address.

Some may think this is all happening much too slowly, but the miracle is that it is happening at all! And we are part of it! *The Course In Miracles*, which now can be found in any bookstore, tells us that the real miracle is not any razzle dazzle show of healing. The true miracle is using the rising consciousness within us to change our minds, and literally to begin changing our world. It is showing us new ways to manifest the Energy of Love and Awareness in this world, making this a new age of compassion and volunteerism. It is a time when the urge to criticize is turning into a much stronger need to care, and care for.

These indeed are exciting times and it is important to realize we are the ones who will make the new world order happen. It will not be those who rightly or fraudulently assume positions of power. We ourselves will become the leaders in our own lives and in our small groups to move the world forward. And that higher consciousness which is now accessible to us will be the key to our greater fulfillment as human beings. It will shine the radiance of truth and honest reality within us, and reach out among the stars, as well as through the streets of our own home towns.

When *Time* magazine named as the 2007 Person of the Year, YOU, and every other person, it was acknowledging the rising power of the individual who, with awareness, courage and honesty, can now change the way many things are done.

Consciousness and Thoughts of the Divine

While we are now experiencing the greater capability of being aware in human consciousness, that phenomenon is also helping us reach higher into the Mind of Creation, or the Mind of Light. While human consciousness is always working, even in our dreams, there are times we may become aware of other phenomena which give clues to our deeper reality. It is as if a part of that veil or onion layer of human mind slips away for a time and we sense greater truth. We begin to understand beyond mere mental knowing. There is a great saying in Zen, "Be still, and understand what you already know." This is humankind's opportunity to make that saying a reality.

These glimpses of our higher potential reinforce what many spiritual thinkers and scientists are saying. There is a growing realization that this time of quantum evolution makes a leap into higher awareness very possible, as well as the recognition that there is a Super Consciousness which can lift us higher into Ultimate Truth.

While wisdom comes to us from the Eastern culture in the words, "The origin of all is pure consciousness," the brightest among us have, for many years, realized consciousness is one of the deepest driving forces of all creation. It is much more than mind. It is much more than awareness. It is the all-pervasive, exciting reality which energizes the whole of creation itself!

Consider the past. In the last century, thinkers such as Sigmund Freud and Carl Jung, the holy Indian teacher Paramahansa Yogananda, the Catholic priest and expert on ancient and modern thinking,

Pierre Teilhard de Chardin, as well as others, have paved the way for the breakthrough we are now experiencing. The old mechanistic idea of reality, where everything is only the sum of its parts, has given way to the quantum which states that the whole is always infinitely greater than the sum of all its parts, and full of endless possibilities. Going beyond the narrow linear concept of human thought has opened us to the explosive reality of what all of creation, and the potency of creation ahead of us, truly is.

Taken in the context of humanity's spiritual search, we can draw closer to an honest observation of that infinite and eternal mystery which we call divine. It can be, indeed, considered the ultimate Quantum which holds all parts and which is still greater than all its parts! As Jesus taught, I — of creation, and my father — the source behind creation, are one!

Let the Teachers Teach

Today the two main disciplines of science and religion have met in the field of consciousness study. Theologians such as Paul Tillich, Karl Rahner, Martin Buber and Teilhard de Chardin have been joined by Deepak Chopra, Diarmuid O'Murchu, Eckhart Tolle, Wayne Dyer, Ken Wilber and one of the experts on consciousness in our times, the delightful, brilliant and holy David Hawkins. All their works are begging us to move beyond the human limitations of ego mind. Considering thought and the silence which goes before and beyond it, Dr. Hawkins writes:

> In the silence that endures beyond the cessation of thought, the stillness of the Presence prevails as All That Is. The divinity of its Essence radiates forth as the formlessness behind all form, in exquisite perfection beyond all time and space. ... To undue the grip of the mind requires a radical humility and an intense will-

ingness to surrender its underlying motivations. This willingness
receives energy and power from the willingness that arises from
the love of God and the passion for surrendering love of thought
for love of God.

Indeed, most of the world still clings to considering divinity in
human terms in that pervasive realm of linear thought. By doing so,
we have neatly identified and categorized God as the great father, full
of human characteristics. Some have made Jesus a super hero of our
time, and we have neatly built a divinity and belief system we can
"wrap our minds around." This is, if we are truly honest with ourselves,
rather foolish in its very limitation. It is limiting the limitless and trying to name the nameless.

If that has worked before and still continues to work for many
because we need an object to understand, the truth remains that the
divine mystery is simply that — a mystery. By being ultra conservative
in unwillingness to explore truth in all its fullness, we only hurt our
possibilities for growth into even deeper and more expansive spirituality. This is not a call to abandon any core of spiritual belief. Rather, it is
an invitation to enhance our union with the Light of That Which Is. If
our planet Earth is struggling to become a global community, it is time
to recognize the spirituality of other cultures which have and still are
moving toward the one goal of all humanity, to make real the awareness of its oneness within The One.

As our evolution of consciousness proceeds in this Axial Age, we
can come closer to greater appreciation of how magnificent, expansive and truly divine this concept we call God actually is. Concept is
a product of the linear thought process of the human mind. It works
as far as we let it work. Now it is time, however, to literally grow up
and move beyond the narrowness of limited thinking to draw closer
to That Which Really Is. The left brain knows what we know in our

thoughts about God. The right brain is still basking in the mystery!

Such thoughts as, "God is on our side," or, "My God and your God" become foolish when considering the Source of All is One. Concepts such as, "I am right, and if I am right, then you must be wrong," become archaic and juvenile in the new consciousness. We are all products of the same Source. Our differences are minimal. Our truth is profound. We are all one in the same Breath of Creation. The sooner we realize that in the depths of our souls and our conscious awareness, the sooner hatred, war, and division of any kind will simply fall away.

We are not at that point yet, but we are getting there. We are, as the Mayans of old considered us who live on the planet now, "walking between the two worlds of old and new awareness," and we are making progress. The best thinkers in science, religion and human growth studies continue speaking to us about this new awareness. It may be time to listen to what they have to say.

Moving human thought forward in the last century, the Jesuit priest Teilhard de Chardin made a giant step toward rising consciousness. His writings were so forward-looking that his own Catholic superiors would not allow his work to be published during his lifetime. Only after his death in 1957 did his friends, who had copies of all his manuscripts, release them to world. As Chardin described all of creation as the God environment — The Divine Milieu — he coined a new word, "noosphere." Noosphere, he stated, is an envelope or layer of thought around the earth, "...multiplying its internal fibres and tightening its network; and simultaneously its internal temperature is rising, and with this its psychic potential." Commenting on Chardin, Diarmuid O'Murchu amplifies the thought, "For Teilhard, the noosphere was not just a mental concept. It contained thought, emotion, mind, spirit, psyche and above all, the power of love."

This noosphere, or higher level of consciousness which Chardin described, is key to humankind's journey toward what he called The

Omega Point. This end point is the ultimate destiny of all creation folding back into its Source, not in a linear ending but in continuing fulfillment beyond any limiting concept of time.

Considering Carl Jung's explanation of the collective unconscious, most scholars agree that consciousness is a type of creation energy which in-forms all that is, from the largest universes and the emptiness of black holes to the one celled creatures living in the oceans' greatest depths. While a definition of consciousness has been attempted by many, the modern thinker, Ken Wilber, comes close when he calls it Wisdom. This is not wisdom of human thinking, but rather the universal wisdom which sets all of creation into its fullness, and is innate to every cell of creation's manifestations. Trees do what trees do. Animals do what animals do. Planets and stars do what they do, and all is ordered by the Source. The origin of all is Pure Consciousness.

It is in the rising of human consciousness where we begin to understand more. Dr. Hawkins, who rates the levels of consciousness through muscle testing, notes the consciousness level of the human race during Jesus' time was 100. This is an extremely low rate, when most people were still intent on survival by any means possible, and thought levels were poorly developed. While many modern nations now calibrate at a consciousness level between 300 to 425, Hawkins invites our great realization that:

> Everything and every event is a manifestation of the totality of All That Is … Once seen in its totality, everything is perfect at all times and nothing needs an external cause to change it in any way. From the viewpoint of the ego's positionality and limited scope, the world seems to need endless fixing and correction. This illusion collapses as a vanity.
>
> In Reality, everything is automatically manifesting the inherent destiny of its essence; it doesn't need any help to do this. With

humility, one can relinquish the ego's self-appointed role as savior of the world and surrender it straight to God. The world that the ego pictures is a projection of its own illusions and arbitrary positionalities. No such world exists.

Hawkins also advises, "… it is useful to remember that the spiritual journey requires the relinquishing of all beliefs and attitudes in order to create space 'for Reality to shine forth.'"

This does not mean we need to abandon the core of any acceptance of love, light, divinity or truth. It simply asks us to move forward to enhance that which, in our true spirit, we already know.

The Collective Unconscious

Consider also the wisdom of Carl Jung, who wrote about the collective unconscious, or actually a collective consciousness, which rises above all division and separation. In those times of higher experience, where there is a oneness which is almost tangible, we are led to a place where silence articulates, in its own dimension, this higher consciousness we have tapped into.

You have probably had some of these fleeting experiences yourself. At such times, we realize there is a greater something which attracts us, moves us deeply, and holds us in an experience so real there is no explanation or expression of it within the human condition. To love and feel love — either from an intimate lover, a love of mind such as experiencing great music, or sharing the love of spirit, where we can share part of our souls with another who is also on the same journey into spirit — comes close.

It is not our own consciousness which holds us in those times. Rather, our ego human consciousness slips away and, for at least brief moments, we become connected with the consciousness of all.

The best among us have tried to explain that higher consciousness. Sri Arubindo and others speak of the super consciousness of the
individual relating into higher realms of being. He also used the term
"supra consciousness," where we, in a gift of grace, become part of the
total energy of creation itself. At times such as those, it is much easier
to turn to the Source of Creation, as we experience actual union with
the Ground of All Being.

Addressing consciousness as we can now perceive it, O'Murchu
states,

> We belong to a reality greater than ourselves, an envelope of
> consciousness informing our awareness, intuition and imagi-
> nation — in what is essentially an intelligent universe. All our
> thoughts, dreams and aspirations arise from this cosmic well-
> spring within which we live and grow, and are empowered to
> realize our full potential as planetary, cosmic creatures. Anything
> short of this global engagement leaves us unfulfilled, frustrated,
> and ultimately alienated from God and humanity."

It is a true statement that "Energy follows Thought." In this time of
rising consciousness, the energy of our very thinking is making things
happen. Jung called this phenomenon "synchronicity," events and
actions following the conscious projection of what they are in their
highest creation. In this time of greater consciousness, acting from
compassion, forgiveness and love will accomplish more than acting
from fear of consequences and small-minded thinking.

Changing Your Mind

Literally, it's time to lighten up! There is a new sun of consciousness rising! Why don't we all just meet on the beach to dance and

welcome this bright, new day!

Today's rising consciousness asks one simple question. Can you change your mind? Can you allow your place within the quantum of new possibility to happen? The answer is, of course you can! And in that change you can begin to experience a fullness most others who have lived before us have never known. If you can hold that much in your heart and in your own power of intention, move on through this book with confident, open questioning. There are no answers in the pages ahead. There are only keys for your personal unlocking of the knowledge and wisdom you already have within you. As the Zen masters advise, it's time to understand what you already know.

RIGHT BRAIN CHAPTER REVIEW

Garden of Light

I sit in the garden of Light with My Beloved
  as radiance of hues beyond color and form,
softly mystifies the sacredness of our sharing
  soul within Soul,
And we are whole here, never caught in the falsehood of two,
  but only union of One — here,
  in this garden of Holy Light.

Yet we are also the intimate power of darkest ebony.
We have been there, this magnificent Source and I.
We have traveled the Void in search of each other,
For awareness itself is a heaven of joy,
  and a filling to last through eternity.

120

And we remember that darkness as sacred now,
       the test and the tabula rasa, the blank tablet
       brought to form, then beyond form
       to the place where the darkness itself becomes Light beyond light,
       and the Luminous is All that remains,
       or ever and ever Is.

In the end there is no separation at all.
The darkness and the Light become Radiant Oneness,
and the Divine Darkness, held beyond perception,
       speaks the soul of Truth alone.

The Miracle is held.
The Fullness is complete.
All words become vibration's pulse of mystery.
Creation's dance becomes the final bow
       to the Music which has spun it,
And the Sacred Heart of Oneness which had begun it
       in the only time of Moment which could never know an end —
As the Beloved and I sit — in holy stillness
       here, in this garden of Light.

CHAPTER SEVEN

KNOW THE PAST, BE THE PRESENT

East and West Unite in a Circle of Search

Spirituality is a progressive awakening to the inner reality of our being ...It is an inner aspiration to know, to enter into contact and union with the greater Reality beyond.

- Sri Aurobindo

The American playwright Edward Albee once hinted that sometimes the shortest distance between two points is the long way around. While that may ring true for many aspects of life, it certainly describes humanity's journey toward the heart of God. We have been seeking truth for countless ages.

Consider these words: "We are living in the greatest revolution in history, a huge, spontaneous upheaval of the entire human race. Not a revolution planned and carried out by any particular party, race or nation, but a deep elemental boiling over of all the inner contradictions that have ever been in people, a revolution of the chaotic forces inside everybody. This is not something we have chosen, nor is it anything we are free to avoid."

The Catholic Trappist monk Thomas Merton wrote those words in the 1950's. In the 1960's Bob Dylan sang, "The Times, They are A'Changin.'" Perhaps we are all slow learners, or perhaps the changes which were beginning then have taken time to filter down to us ordinary people. Yet these two modern prophets have captured the essence of what it is to be living as people who "walk between the worlds."

Perhaps, because Merton was very human as well as very spiritual, he could read the planet's energy and sense the revolution he knew was brewing in the hearts of women and men. A devoted priest and monk, he was also a student of many religions. From his base in Catholicism, Merton explored spirituality in all its forms. He communicated with Hebrew scholars and corresponded with a Sufi master — Sufism being the forerunner of Islam. He studied ancient religions and easily embraced the wisdom of Eastern thought which leads not so much to organized religion as a practice, but to a deeply personal, integrated way of living.

In his studies, Merton realized true spirituality exists on a planetary, if not universal basis. Late in his life he traveled to Asia to meet with the young Dalai Lama and hold serious discussions with both Buddhist and Hindu scholars. As a monk living in a Kentucky monastery which observes a vow of silence, Merton realized it is not the outward tenets of any one religion filled with dogma and ritual which give it validity. From his own solitude and meditation, he wrote extensively of humanity's universal search for its Unknown Source.

In the last speech of his life, which ended in a freak accident at age 53, Merton spoke at a conference in Bangkok, Thailand. His last words were not about the value of religion, but about the intrinsic importance of all people living in a planetary family of sisterhood and brotherhood, compassion and unified acceptance of all. This, he stated, not only helps humanity live daily life but also gives value to our very existence and ultimate destiny, the return to the fullness of the God Source Itself.

There were others before Merton, but it was in the '50's and '60's that change became apparent. The old was becoming overburdened and inadequate as the heart of humanity grew restless for the coming of new things it could not yet understand.

The turbulence of the 1960's began rethinking the old adage of business and belief as usual which had existed for thousands of years. All the easy answers weren't making sense any more and, though the way ahead was certainly not clear, people were restless for change.

What Merton and many others were beginning to sense was that the very consciousness of humankind was beginning to reach, haltingly but surely, toward a new identity which could move beyond what had become stagnant, dogmatic and old. This was the beginning of a true revolution, which turns all the accepted beliefs upside down. Then it shakes things out, discards what no longer serves, and courageously moves forward to embrace new understanding.

Merton held all religions as signposts for the way, not the Way itself. He also wrote extensively of a much deeper spirituality which must lie at the heart of every person. Following "religiously" what others have set as truth as they perceived it, he knew, could never replace each individual's spirit rising through its own evolution, in its own culture and in its own way toward the ultimate reality.

The Ultimate Reality is nothing but the Divine Mystery Itself and every individual's intrinsic part within it.

Besides, how could there be only one way to the Creator of All in a creation so richly diverse, spiritually sensitive and existing on such a wide variety of levels of consciousness, aspiration and depth?

Escalating Evolution

One way to try to understand what is going on now is to go back
to the last Axial Age and the vast impact it had on thought concerning
the Divine. In that time, roughly between 600 BCE and 600 CE, human consciousness shifted into a new way of considering the mystery
of life. Early religions already existed. Judaism in the Mid East, following the lineage of Abraham, Isaac and Jacob, was already well-estab-
lished. In the Eastern Hemisphere the ancient culture which led to the
Vedic theosophy of Hinduism was also in place.

Yet, in 570 CE the man who would bring Islam to the world,
Mohammed, was born in Mecca. Writing the *Qur'an* in a high state
of spiritual consciousness, he channeled wisdom teachings into the
sacred text which would set a meaningful way of life for many generations to come. He called the Great God Allah, and Islam still celebrates
his role as Allah's prophet.

Also in the Eastern world, Siddhartha Gautama was born around
566 BCE. Through meditation and accessing his own Higher Mind,
he led existing thought into greater acknowledgment of creation itself.
Celebrating all life as worthy of dignity and now known as the Awak-
ened One, or Buddha, he taught respect for all sentient beings. All
life is equally precious, he said, and his teachings ring true today. The
Buddha also taught that the secret of happiness and cessation of suffering is achieved by non-attachment to ego-centered things. Choosing individual alignment with truth, he said, leads all humanity to the
One Truth for all.

As an example of changes in that previous Axial Age, consider
what was happening in the lineage of Isaac and Jacob. Loosely practiced Judaism changed dramatically with the early Canaanites around
that axial awakening in 600 BCE. It was then that people moved away
from honoring local deities who governed everything from provid-

ing abundant crops to protecting area villages. Instead the concept of a single Creator God became prominent — the one Great God above all the "lesser" gods. Thus, in Judaism and Christianity, the concept of one single God figure became dominant.

With male energy most prominent in the patriarchal world at that time, that one god, of course, became a father figure. The feminine Goddess Energy of more ancient times was summarily dismissed and along with it the equal state of women in the world. Sadly, considering the status of women in most major religions and societies today, humanity has still not gotten over that patriarchal blunder.

As a result, part of this new Axial Age of current rising consciousness has begun to recognize Mary of Magdala and other women spiritual leaders of history. Long dismissed as unimportant, the world is now realizing the strategically significant roles they played in developing world spirituality. Likewise, honor and serious attention is now being given to women teachers of God today, whether they bravely remain within institutionalized religions or work in other ways to promote independent spirituality.

The Divine Mystery in Prehistory

While the human species as we know it has minimally been on earth for at least 50,000 years, institutionalized religion has been a relative latecomer to world spirituality. In ancient times people looked to the heavens and the earth for some kind of explanation of their existence. They saw life be born and die and witnessed nature herself go through seasons of change. They mythologized the great Phoenix, a bird which would die in a burst of flaming glory only to be reborn from the energy of its own ashes. They recognized the order and majesty of the stars as if some force, in the nighttime hours, "left the lights on" to show it was still present. Looking to the earth, earliest humans considered the mystery of creation and, witnessing birth in the female of any species, concluded the source of creation was female as well.

From that thinking, the early religion of Wicca or acknowledging a "Goddess" arose. Needing to make some kind of response, certain rituals were developed to honor that Goddess Energy, celebrating seasons of planting and reaping because the earth is such a life giver. Following their cue, even today we, too, call this earth — Mother.

Brain Matters

As we consider the past becoming the present, it is also interesting to consider geography along with philosophy. Ongoing studies in recent years have detailed how the brain works and how different parts of it control everything from our ability to physically move to how we approach life. They also show how, in some cases, even the part of the world in which we live determines what parts of our brain may be more dominant.

If you have grown up in the western side of the world, Europe, North America and South America, researchers find the left side of your brain is more dominant. While there are "right brained" people in the West, the majority of us have grown up with the philosophy and logic which go back to Socrates, Aristotle, and Plato. That has made us more logical and prone to seeking understanding. It is also one reason why many of the developed countries of the western world have been key players in technology, medicine, and other modern advances. That may also explain why western-minded people experience more stress!

Studies also show that more people in the eastern part of the world, most of the Asian continent, tend to be more right brained. While they certainly use logic when necessary, they do not need the same amount of organization and excruciatingly defined thought patterns to deal with life.

The French writer and spiritual scholar Jacques Maritain, in *Creative Intuition in Art and Poetry*, gave a good description of the Eastern and the Western minds. Paraphrasing his words: Some people look at the sky and say, "Look at all the interesting shapes of the clouds." Others look at the sky and say, "Look at all the interesting spaces between the clouds." The Western left brained mind sees things and tries to make sense of them. The Eastern right brained mind sees the emptiness of possibility between things and is perfectly comfortable with the mystery of what may be. It is obvious, then, that religions of the West cater to predominantly left brained cultures while attempts at spiritual organization in the East are not usually successful. The God of all, however, remains equally accessible to all.

Today's rising consciousness is creating another phenomenon. More right brain activity is being experienced by people in the western hemisphere. Because that part of the brain is comfortable with mystery, there is actually a more feminine approach to religion and other areas of life as well — even among supposedly logic-oriented people.

While many see this phenomenon as positive, leading to more diplomacy and less war in the world, that is only one side of the story. Because this softer, more feminine approach is challenging the old ways the logical brain has long held dear, many existing power structures are digging in their heels rather than change. In the Catholic Church, for example, the current movements to allow priests to marry as was the custom in the religion's earliest stages, as well as the movement to allow the ordination of women priests, are meeting fierce opposition from Rome. Rather than allow those two changes in Catholicism's priesthood, the unbending Vatican hierarchy would rather continue to close churches because of the increasing shortage of priests and let more and more Catholics be deprived of the sacraments and the Mass they cherish. Many Catholics wonder if this is really the thinking of a compassionate hierarchy which best serves the people of God or one which would actually diminish their flock and drive people away by rigid refusal to change.

Spiritual belief has come a long way from ancient times yet its essence remains the same. We as a species have always felt there is something greater than we. In our evolving mental capacity and in many different ways we have tried to delve into this mystery we still cannot fathom.

What Is the Way and What Is in the Way?

Consider the words of two modern prophets:

"Religions are different roads converging on the same point. What does it matter that we take different roads so long as we reach the same goal? I believe that all religions of the world are true more or less. I say "more or less" because I believe that everything the human hand touches, by reason of the very fact that human beings are imperfect, becomes imperfect." Mahatma Gandhi

"In formal religion one feels the sense of being exiled from God because the religion itself requires this form of alienation in order to function effectively. An experience of being exiled is endemic to religion. The ensuing sense of estrangement does not arise because we lack a proper relationship with God. Rather it arises from the other dysfunctional relationships that the religion requires to be a follower of that God." Diarmuid O'Murchu

If we are people who walk between the worlds of old and new where compassion, acceptance and respect for each other's differences will be the norm, it serves us to revisit our core belief systems and the way they affect our lives.

For many, belief in a Father God who rewards and punishes and who is never attained in this life, but only after physical existence is over, remains valid and consoling. These followers view religion as their way to eternal salvation and are comfortable within that structure. That description fits most people, at least in the western world, who consider themselves religious today. They are good, well-meaning people, and they deserve respect.

Today, however, more people find themselves in a neverland of belief because the religions of their youth have lost meaning, have been marred by scandal, or simply don't fit their personal evolutionary spiritual progress.

Atheist or Agnostic?

There are others who declare themselves atheists and some who call themselves agnostics. A clarification of these two terms might help. Both words come from Greek roots. *A* means not, therefore both those words begin with negation. The term atheist uses the root word *theos* which is the Greek word for God. So an atheist is someone who does not believe in God or the concept of a Higher Source.

The term agnostic comes from *gnosis* which means knowledge. The agnostic is someone who says "I have no knowledge of God." What some people who call themselves agnostics are saying is that they cannot accept as real knowledge a god who judges and punishes and who is alienated from humanity. They are saying they do not believe in an old man in the sky as some religions have presented "him." That is an entirely different story.

In this time of growing consciousness, there are many intelligent, well-meaning people who still believe in a higher power. They are not stubborn egotists who believe there is nothing greater than they. They are not immoral nor are they evil or misguided. They have just looked at glossy beliefs of some institutionalized religions and refused to accept humanistic concepts of a judging god who has the same flawed characteristics as human beings. They have also looked at the scandals of so-called leaders within those religions and chosen not to look to teacher/preachers to decipher the ultimate truth for them.

Understanding Religion

Any institutionalized religion, because it is organized, has its own set of beliefs. Through its dogma and pronouncements, it says, "We believe these certain things. But we also do not believe that thing or that other thing." It has rituals which are meaningful to its followers.

"Organized" religion is exactly that! It is organized! Because it has a limited belief system, it is a well-meaning but continuing form of separation. Some religions also go a step farther and create a fence around themselves, where only those within that fence are right and everyone else is wrong. Some tend to reject others of different spiritual beliefs and actually damn them to eternal torment because they have chosen another path.

Organized religions also rely on organized services and organized prayer. These are often rituals and words of elders from long ago. For a growing number of people, however, a steady diet of ritual prayers recited by rote no longer honors the deeper need to connect more personally with the Divine.

What we call the Lord's Prayer, however, is an exception. Read in its translation from Aramaic, the language Jesus spoke, it praises divinity and asks for help to go beyond the illusion of what man thinks God is. Instead it asks for realization of that actual mystery here on earth. It prays for assistance and protection and honors the divine, which is one of the highest forms of prayer. It also ends with the beautiful word "Amen" which in the original Aramaic does not mean "So be it." Rather it conveys the thought, "And may the energy of this prayer continue moment by moment within the Great Eternal Now."

Considering its place on the world stage, the Lord's Prayer is a direct appeal into the Divine Mind to know Absolute Truth and live within it. In many ways it echoes the Gayatri Mantra, the exquisite Sanskrit chant from the ancient East which also seeks wisdom to see beyond human, mental illusion, directly into the Light of the Divine Mystery.

A life of faith is powerful and precious. It sets us and keeps us on the only important path, the one which leads our total being toward inner knowing of what is truly real. Yet there is "Something" even beyond faith which, after all, is merely agreeing to accept truth beyond our human state of comprehension.

The Truth Beyond

That "Something" *which lies beyond the need to believe in blind faith is deep inner KNOWING, directly experiencing, on a personal level, the magnificence of Ultimate, Transcendent Reality. Knowing is actually participating in a deeply present and almost bursting awareness in the Oneness of the God Source Energy.*

This is a life beyond communion. This is life of actual union itself. It is living powerfully alive in the actual presence of the God Source in intimate union and oneness with Love Itself in Its Perfected, Absolute Reality.

Is this possible for a mortal human being? It can be lived as much as our limited human condition can allow. It is the "kingdom" of heaven which the Christed One, and others who have lived within that christed, enlightened energy, taught us to realize is within ourselves.

How do we do it? As Francis, a humble monk from the town of Assisi, Italy, taught a few hundred years ago, it is not necessary to be loved. That's an ego thing. The real path is to become a human agent of the God Love Itself, witnessing Its Reality to every other creature on the planet, and also, by the way, to ourselves!

Has Silence Become a Lost Art?

Well meaning and useful as they may be, many religious services, especially in the western world, fail to allow time for reflection and meditation. They follow the logical, left brained mode of thinking so they fill each moment with ritual prayer, song, and sermons which usually interpret ancient texts. While many people find comfort in such services which are either full of ritual which has changed little over the centuries, or in listening to "professional" religious leaders show the way, others seem ready to move toward more personal experience with divinity beyond what has been preached to them by other human beings.

One proof of the planet's rising consciousness has been, in recent times, an attraction to the philosophy of Zen. In the western world, it has been interpreted not so much as a form of Buddhism, but as a practice involving meditation. Instead of listening to some ministers' interpretation of divinity, meditation allows the individual to seek personal relationship with the Divine Source through silence.

While the theology of institutionalized religion concentrates on that denomination's interpretation of divinity, Zen and every other meditation practice encourages going beyond the mind through dharma, the release of pure mental concentration to dwell in the great Void of Creation and its Source. Through the practice of "sitting Zen" or sitting meditation, one is led to observe the mind and its contorted mental calisthenics, then move beyond the mind to be part of stillness itself.

Scriptures and ancient texts from all cultures can be used to help, but only in that place beyond the mind can one become light enough to be within Divine Light. Saints of the Catholic Church such as Teresa of Avila and John of the Cross knew that. So did saints of the East and the ancient writers of the Upanishads, the Bhagavad Gita, and other spiritual treasures from across the cultures and times of the world.

From Contemplation — New Knowledge, Then Action

Other examples of current life also reveal the changing conscious-ness which emphasizes personal involvement. The recent popularity of studying the Kaballah proves more people are reaching into the divine mystery through concepts found in Hebrew spirituality. Through study of one of the most ancient wisdom sources on the planet, individuals from many faiths are now personally discovering ancient guides to living a fuller, God-centered life.

Yoga, which has its roots in the Vedic culture embraced in Hindu-ism, has also become more popular. With its name meaning "yoking oneself to the truth," this modality teaches the science of breath as well as control and understanding of the body. It also calls for the medita-tive introspection which leads to self awareness and to the Great Self awareness as well.

There is also renewed interest in the spiritual practices of native cultures of the Americas, Egypt, the Polynesian world, and Africa. As always, the answer for any individual is to seek, with discernment and open-mindedness, until one experiences a valid spiritual path which finds resonance within herself or himself. Consider the words of the Christ, "The kingdom of heaven is within you," and, "In my father's house, there are many mansions." It really doesn't matter so much what street you live on. There are no right sides or wrong sides of town in the City of God. After all, it is all just one big neighborhood. It's all just part of the Divine Milieu, or environment, as Chardin wrote.

Who's the Boss?

Another thing to consider is that every institutionalized religion is a top-down organization and, in some cases, a highly regulated cor-poration. Its chiefs and leaders dictate what is believed and how that belief system will be followed. Its main purpose is to preserve itself. Orders must be obeyed and policies carried out strictly in the lower echelons of the "faithful." There is no room for dissension or individual interpretation.

The new consciousness, however, thrives more on personal responsibility than blind following of others who set themselves above and dictate the order of all. The human failings of ministers in many religions today are also providing dramatic reconsideration of hierarchical power which, in the view of some, has gone well beyond its limits.

The Way and the No Way

What is this chapter saying? Is it calling for an end to all religions and the formation of one universal religion? Of course not. It actually encourages those who hold their belief system in any one religion to seek that system's greatest depth and truths. Anyone who considers a God Source and tries to live in awareness of that mystery is on the right track. What this chapter does urge is the honoring of differences between all religions and belief systems, a realization of the common ground all of them share, and a return to the spirituality which honors all of creation as magnificent and one, united in the Source Mystery which holds us all in its embrace. The Truth is not about separation and division. If you still use the terms "My God" and "Your God," you're not hearing the One God of creation at all.

The question must lie in asking whether real, life-changing spirituality can thrive in religion, or if religions as a whole can get over their predominance of man-made dogma and separatist attitudes. If the world needs spiritual leaders, and it still does, it needs women and men who encourage all to embrace the spirituality dedicated to finding Truth. It needs spiritual guides who help point the way, then get out of that way, so the people of God can be free to move into the fullness of God in their own most meaningful spirituality.

The old is the old. What has been is not what is. Only the Absolute Truth is what matters and which always remains. Recognizing what can exist within that Absolute Truth is our challenge. Together we can strive to make a new world of compassion for all or live blindly in the old until it self-destructs from its own inability to change.

What is the Way? Simple. It is the sacred sanctuary of your own precious and sacred heart. Go there and listen well. "Be still — and know — I AM."

What is in the way? Anything which keeps you from the Unity of All That Is One. Real faith is a healer not a divider. Don't let it be anything less for you.

RIGHT BRAIN CHAPTER REVIEW

Only Love Remains

Who sets the limits for love?
Who sets up gates for halting the passage,
        and limiting the strength of Spirit's depth?
Who creates the dogmas and the limiting of belief and non-belief?
Who becomes a thief of Spirit which is rising
        in its own evolving spiral of ascension to the Whole?
Who will dare deny with human words the sacred journey forward?
Who will turn the signposts into barriers which stop the sacred flow?
Who can dare to say, "I know more than your own heart
        can teach you in its wisdom"?
And who can — in mere humanity — deny the deepest Source of creation
        from pure union with its own sweet child?

I AM Way. I AM Truth. I AM True Life Itself because I AM —
    the Great Beloved speaks in silent mystery.
Only love remains its deepest truth,
    Because it is only love which ever can remain.
It is I — Your own Beloved — quietly waiting, anticipating sweet reunion
    in the chambers of your own sacred heart!

CHAPTER EIGHT

WHEN I WAS A CHILD...

Growing Into God

When I was a child I spoke as a child.
I understood as a child. I thought as a child.
But when I became a man, I put away childish things.

- Paul of Tarsus 1 Corinthians 13:11

This book is about truth, and, as such, this short section is an invitation to mature into the truth which really Is. It offers ways to grow from old ideas of fitting "God" into a neat pigeon hole of our lives and begs courage to take the next step of learning more about ourselves as well as our Source.

We don't have to throw out any knowledge and belief system we've held or which serves us now. As our ability for greater awareness increases, however, we can grow to greater union with whatever you call the Higher Power.

Stepping Away from the Herd

As we mature in many ways, we tend to separate ourselves from the herd mentality. As we move through the stages of adulthood, we stop trying to fit in with other people or groups just for the comfort of feeling we belong. Instead we allow maturity to lead us toward awareness on deeper, more personal levels. This is true in every part of life, from the mundane to our most profound levels of thought and perception. It involves less book knowledge and more personal experience. What we thought we knew goes through a refining of what doesn't enrich us any more and our priorities become more defined. Instead, we become more open to what works for us. This happens not only in our minds but, most importantly, in our spirit.

When Paul of Tarsus wrote, "When I was a child, I thought as a child …," he was saying it is possible, just by growing into our adult, mature presence, to grasp the deeper essence and meaning of things we once knew only on a surface level.

We as a human race are growing up. Admittedly, we have been very slow learners, but the rising consciousness in this Axial Age has given us the light and awakening to move ahead. The earth itself is telling us we need to find a new way of being which involves changing from old ways of separation and judgment to a more compassionate mindset of acknowledging others' differences and respecting them.

True, we are social animals. We need community because of our need to belong. Yet, while we give lip service to the concept of being independent thinkers, the majority of the human race is anything but. When new concepts or new thought get in the way of our need to belong, we tend to shy away from going out on a very shaky limb. The comfort of conforming is the ego's powerful tool to keep us from moving ahead. It's always easier to just stay inside "the box."

The news most of us are getting these days, however, is that, whether we like it or not, more of us have somehow already moved outside "the box." Or maybe "the box" has just become inadequate. Yet, that box did have a great comfort zone and sometimes it can get rather lonely out in a new and different place.

No Small Step

Asking one to reconsider the maturity of her or his own ideas about God and religion is asking a lot. Most people will say, "But this is part of my roots! This is what I was taught. This is how I've lived all of my life!" It may help to consider one's real roots. Before the influence of family or society on us, we all have much deeper roots. Those are ties to our real source, our individual, direct connection with the Source Itself. Again those words from Isaiah: "Oh God, you have heard the cry of my heart because it was You who cried out within my heart!"

There are many things which must be taught to us. There are also many things we innately know. Peel enough layers of ego away and, sure enough, there is the True and Only Source, no matter what you call it. And a great realization is not only that you are part of it, but that everyone, including those you consider enemies or those you consider separate from you, are all perfectly part of it too!

Belonging to a religion can be a good thing. We just need to realize most religions have made God a human-like being just so people can relate more to what is really a mystery. Also, some institutionalized religions have not held to their original intent. While their basic aim was to bring people into awareness of God, they have also caused division and separation among groups of people and even among nations. In the United States, for example, the supposed constitutional commitment to separation of church and state is all but dead. Elections are often dominated by powerful religious groups, as we have seen in recent national elections. One wonders if some candidates ran for the title of president, or pastor, of the country. This, in a nation founded by people who risked traveling thousands of miles across an ocean in wooden boats because they believed in every individual's freedom to worship according to her or his own heart.

The recent finding of a book from the mind of Nostradamus, hidden by the Catholic Church for many centuries, details a next world war which will be fueled by dug-in beliefs of separate religions. Whether you believe the prediction or not, one can rightly ask how the compassionate, peaceful concept of the Creator of All has been corrupted to justify chaotic destruction, murder, and global torment.

Throughout time wise and holy people have tried to show us a way into Ultimate Truth, usually with the highest of motives. A very human truth, however, is that there is no pope or pastor, priest, preacher, politician or president who can dictate our personal response to the concept of a Higher Source as we perceive it in our own hearts. We are becoming spiritual grownups, and we are learning to find our own way, straight into that Heart of God. If you can do that while adhering to the dogma and teachings of a particular belief system, great.

You may, on the other hand, identify with millions who have already stepped out of the box of organized religion for any variety of reasons. First, accept the truth that God is still there in the deepest part of your roots within creation itself. And you're a grownup now. You can surely find your way. Your very psyche is hard-wired to the best way you can search for the truth. And you won't be alone!

There is also still a certain naiveté regarding what we call God, and how we think of "God." Some people will say, "When I get to heaven, I'm going to ask God why this or that happened," as if the Source of all creation was playing master puppeteer in every detail of one's life! There are also others who say, often with great fervor, "God spoke to me and said …"

Did God actually appear in a low-flying cloud and boom out some divine words of wisdom in a deep masculine voice? Or was it those individuals' own inner wisdom, conscience, or some accessing of their higher self which gave them an idea? If you choose to remain naïve about the greatest Mystery of all time, you can ask "him" when you get "there," or wait for a low flying cloud outside your window.

Do It Your Way

Opening yourself to deeper understanding of the Divine Mystery can lead to deeper love and peace. It does, however, take courage and willingness to grow beyond some of the old ideas you may still carry from your youth. Each of us has the unique opportunity to reach a new, beautiful level of learning and living. We can conquer stress, fear, worry, hatred and the duality of separation. After probing the current value of old, sometimes faulty ideas which no longer serve us, we can, like Paul, set aside the childhood of dogmatic, archaic and sometimes mythical belief and begin to claim true spiritual maturity.

Of course there is a God. There is one God of us all. If some religions or cultures decide to call that One Source "My God" or "Your God," that is their fallacy, and that is the illusion under which they choose to live. The simple truth is that there is only one source of all creation. What some religious teachers are really defending is their own interpretation of how the God Mystery might be accessed and how it is to be "understood." The problem with religion is not the God behind it. It is the exclusivity of the attitude that "We are right; so the rest of you are wrong and as far as we're concerned, you can all go to hell!"

Moving On

If you are ready for more, it may be time to consider yourself a spiritual rather than a religious person. Spirituality is, by the way, not some far out practice of weird activities and flowing robes. It is simply opening to the truth as you are personally meant to find it. Spirituality fits very beautifully in many other aspects of your life. I heard one of the best definitions of it at one of David Hawkins' Sedona lectures. "Spirituality is seeking truth for its own sake," Dr. Hawkins said and he was right. And finding the truth of the One God naturally follows since the God Source is Ultimate Truth Itself.

Spirituality is not a means to achieve any goal, to merit anything or be saved from anything. Spirituality is simply an attitude and mindset to become our authentic selves — dedicated to our own growth within creation and the Source of Creation Itself. There are many different ways this can be done, but they must be right for us, who are still growing up, or within, the Heart of God.

Where Is Your Mind Comfortable?

One little exercise may help understand how spirituality may work for us. While political parties and the news media seem to have cornered the definition and exploitation of terms such as conservative and liberal, a deeper understanding of what those two labels really mean might help here.

A conservative mindset is just that. Conservative. Conserve means "to keep what is." The conservative attitude looks at things as they are and says, "If I change this, things may get better. They may also get worse. Rather than risk the results of change, I choose to keep things as they are." That is a conservative way of thinking.

A liberal mindset looks at things as they are and says, "If I change this, things may get better. They may also get worse. I choose to take the risk of change, and I will do all I can to make this a change for the better." That is a liberal way of thinking.

The truth is that we sometimes think in a more conservative, safe manner; other times we are open to risk to improve a situation. Understanding how your mind tends to think may help you take stock of your own religious or spiritual beliefs. In this age of great change, that may be an honest and courageous thing to do.

You Can Handle The Truth

No matter where your belief system or non-belief system has been or is now, there is one easy truth you can face. That truth, and your mirror, carry the message that you are no longer a child. Your life has seen many changes over the years, and one of them is that you are no longer expected to think and act as a juvenile. Your heart also recognizes the changes in you, and it's telling you now that it's perfectly acceptable to act like an adult in matters of Spirit. You have come a long way and so has the world's intelligence and capability for honest awareness.

In this new time of awakening consciousness, one can almost feel the energy of positive change and optimism rising like a phoenix from the ashes of fear, separation and anxiety. We have recently been going through a difficult time in many ways because so many of the old institutions have had to crumble and fall. This has been necessary so a better world can start bringing a fresh approach to living and being in the newness of God's Constant Creation. And you are a part of it. Your very breath and life in this challenging time makes you a part of it.

This is indeed our time, and your time individually, to bring our world into the creation of this new millennium. You can draw on our collective rising awareness for the greater depth of your own human psyche. You can draw on the courage of women and men who stand with you to bring about a vibrant and strong new world. And you can search your own soul for the Ultimate Truth which has been patiently waiting for you to find it here in this kingdom of the God Source where everything is rooted in love.

Of course you can handle the Truth! It is already in your heart and in the latent depths of your brain just waiting for you to find and acknowledge it.

We have grown up though many years in our society and our own lives. We have learned to live with change on many levels. Could this be the time you make the decision to grow up even more deeply into what you call the highest power of us all?

Only you know that answer.

RIGHT BRAIN CHAPTER REVIEW

Longing to Connect Again

When every thing is gone away
    Only The All remains.
Then one simple prayer becomes its own fulfillment
    In its willing to be so:

Let my heart be Your Great Heart.
Let my mind stay single and focused,
Flowing in the wisdom of You, Who Are Truth.
Let my words rise from vibration's soul —
    the silence of Your constant, sure embrace,
and let my stillness be the stillness
    of the Mystery You Are.

For I am you, longing to connect again
in the True and Only One.
I am Your Own Seed, already sensing the beauty of the blossom,
grown to reverent awe,
and powerful with peace.
And I am Your mirror, seeking through the misty glass
to see my one true face.
I am simply love in love with Love,
and there is only You
and we are One.

Just to be. To be loving, and to be loved.
Thus, it is so.
And in time beyond — become Eternal Now,
It is already done!

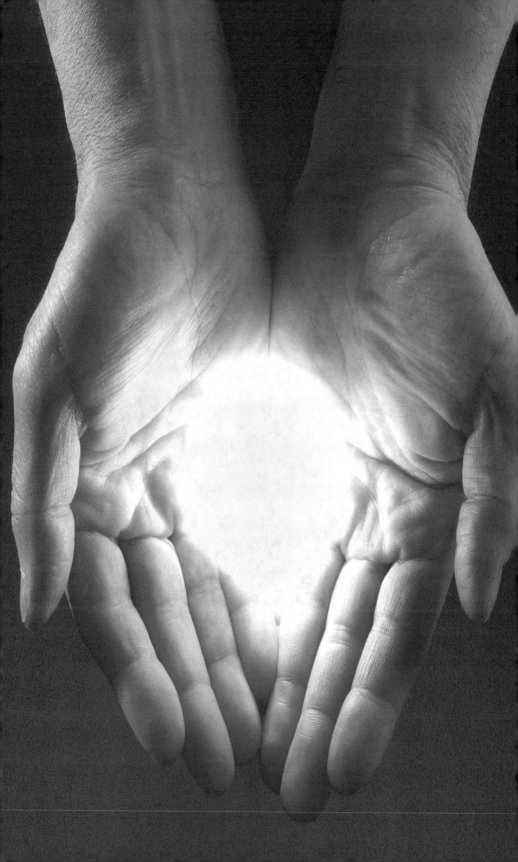

CHAPTER NINE

WHO CAN SAY DIVINITY?

Within the Yearning and the Light

A god who is fitted into our world scheme in order
to make it serious and consistent is not God.

- Thomas Merton

As a young nun, I participated in a class on the Trinity. For an entire semester a professor/priest took us through many theories concerning concepts of Father, Son and Holy Spirit. At the end of the semester he walked into the classroom, returned our final exams, and tried to review our study of the Trinity. After a minute or two, however, he shrugged his shoulders, smiled, and said, "It's a mystery." Then he walked out of the room.

I vividly recall my frustration. All that effort! Hours upon hours of mental gymnastics pouring over theological treatises, lecture notes and sacred texts, only to be told I was studying something totally beyond comprehension!

Of course, the professor was right and, in retrospect, that experience helped me realize the limits of human thought as well as the need to search greater depths for inner knowing.

This chapter is about our concept of God. While it is a good thing to research humanity's attempts to ridiculously define the greatest mystery in creation, it is also good, however, to realize the Divine Mystery can only be "known" beyond words or mental cognition. We can spend lifetimes memorizing all the facts and historical theories we choose. We can become experts on the chapter and verse of every sacred text ever written. We can try to search for that which is totally beyond the human mind. More than that, we can begin to realize that finding deeper answers is not a reward but merely the articulating of newer questions which will tantalizingly lure us on.

The God Question and "Salvation"

When many people face the question "What is God to you?" answers vary with cultural and religious backgrounds, intellects, and life experience. What we were taught to believe or not believe in our youth has colored the rest of our lives. Most people today consider God the supreme power because we live in a world where power is important. In human terms, God is All Mighty. And, because most tend to think of God as a male super being, he has the typical masculine characteristics we associate with great men. He commands respect. "He" can judge and reward or punish big time! He is the ultimate Commander in Chief!

Yet, essentially, God is Love, and there is no judgment in love. There is absolute compassion and abiding acceptance. So, following that concept, we have also made God merciful because we need patience and mercy. That is especially true if we consider ourselves flawed by our very inclusion in the human species as suffering some original sin we have no knowledge of committing. Most religions in the western world begin with the premise that all humanity is basically a bunch of sinners who need salvation. We are flawed by our very existence!

The truth is that we are speaking of the Ultimate Source of creation and the Energy behind that Ultimate Source. It is, as it spoke through human revelation, the ultimate I AM — the ultimate, intelligent Energy of Being Itself.

There are no Cliff Notes to God. What we need to remember is that all scriptures considered sacred are of human origin, although considered to be inspired by the God Source Itself. They are also constantly open to continuous and radically different interpretation, not only by theologians and elders of any religion, but by individuals within those religions as well.

Just as you, in human ego terms, are your own unique human "being," people may call you mother or father, uncle or aunt, sister or brother, friend or enemy, or many other names. Their names for you remain their names for you. You simply consider yourself — yourself! So it is with the Divine Mystery. We can call it God or Goddess, HaShem, Adonai, Allah, Brahma, Shiva, Great Spirit, The Source, or even The Force, as George Lucas did in his Star Wars saga. Whatever we choose to call the Great Mystery really doesn't matter. It Is. And it is the ultimate Essence. The only true existence. The only I AM.

The bottom line? Don't limit God. Stop trying to put a name on the nameless. Stop making "God" a super being and master puppeteer who has an elaborate spy system checking on every move you make. God is not the ultimate Big Brother who is always watching you and waiting for you to slip up.

It is also very human to try to fit "God" into our ego minds with a name that holds meaning for us, because when we name something, we contain it. We identify it and then it fits into our little human brains.

The truth is that we are in love with something so huge we cannot possibly understand or identify it. And the lesson is to not limit Divinity to your own understanding just for convenience. Acknowledge your own growing into what the God Energy really is. Accept the unlimited mystery. It's already in you anyway. Acknowledge it and, in your own stillness, discover its unlimited truth because it is the only Truth. Revel in the comfort of being at home and in awe of the transcendent mystery itself which constantly keeps creating you and which is integrally a part of you.

Humanity As Sinners Saved

The concept of original sin always bothered me as a child. "What did I do?" I thought. When people talked about that sin, I couldn't remember doing anything so awful it would take the great God Itself to notice and forgive it. Did God really take it personally when I fought with my brother or when I didn't obey my parents right away? Maturity has brought me to the realization that what we call sin, which literally means missing the mark, is basically the workings of ego. Contrary to popular opinion, ego is not where we find our deepest identity. If we need to be lifted above egoistic attitudes of our own personalities, that is another story and one which needs to be dealt with on our own individual terms.

Maturity also taught me that what some religions consider as being "saved," is merely coming to the realization of what we truly are. In that sense, the Christed teacher Jesus really was a savior, showing us how we can reach Transcendent Truth which is the Ultimate Reality beyond our ego minds. We are part of the Source which has created us and the term "saved," which some religions use to accept Jesus, or to accept teachings of any other particular spiritual leader, is just another human way of saying, "I think I've finally got it! I'm part of God, and I always have been!" If that is being "saved", it can also be called a freeing realization and personal commitment to live as we really are, spiritual beings in human form who finally remember our Source.

Defining the Divine

We can go back through available history to see how different cultures and stages of human consciousness tried to quantify the totally unquantifiable. In religions such as Christianity, or in much older Hinduism and other religions before the time of Jesus, there was a tendency to break divine identity into three parts. While the western Christian world speaks of a Trinity of Father, Son, and Spirit, many ancient cultures also considered the divine power as encompassing the duality of masculine and feminine energies and then creation itself, to describe the Source totality.

Among these older forms of religious or spiritual belief, Hinduism also considers a triumvirate of divine power which then filters down attributes of those qualities into lesser god identities. Brahma, Shiva and Vishnu embody various energies of divinity and its creation, and the role each of these figures plays is very similar to the Trinity of Christian thought. Brahma is the creator; Shiva is the holy spirit of wise discernment, and Vishnu represents creation itself.

In the indigenous cultures, where people are more attuned to nature, divinity has taken the form of various aspects of nature. The sun, as the male energy of what may be called a trinity, is balanced by the moon which takes on a softer, more feminine energy. Creation, in its various forms, is the child of that father masculine energy and the feminine energy of spirit which infuses all sentient beings with the sacred breath — the energy of life and spirit itself. Christians may call it grace or the Holy Spirit.

We also have to recognize the Eastern way of right brain thought again, now understood in its comfort with not having to name a personalized God figure. Buddhism, for example, looks to creation and the mystery of Creation, but never tries to identify Source beyond a bow to Ultimate Mystery. In other Eastern thought we also find the simple understanding, "I Am That," signifying our own participation of self in the Higher Self, which would also be considered God.

In many writings found before the last Axial Age we find reference to an identity of "God" as Mind, or Perfect Mind, the highest fullness of consciousness Itself. Consider finding and reading "The Thunder — Perfect Mind," written by one of the planet's earliest known woman authors. She speaks, as Jesus often did, in the I AM mode of taking on Divinity's direct communication.

God Beyond Religion

What, then, are we to understand about religion and the role it has and is playing in the advancement of our species and our souls? Most institutionalized religions provide a way to reach into the God Mystery through rules, dogma, commandments and ritual. They do it in a beneficial sense of community. That is good and it has served humanity well through all the ages of our development.

Any religion, however, is limiting in its teachings and beliefs. By being organized, certain concepts are held in belief; others are rejected. Some world religions, mercifully not all, hold that they are the only true way to God, and that all who do not follow their way are damned to eternal torture. I still find it difficult to understand how some, who preach a great God of Love, could really believe that loving God would create people, and, through "His" power of all knowing, realize some would eventually be thrown away into the torturous rubbish heap we call hell.

Does anyone in any religious system really believe God makes "throw away" people? There is no similar belief in those religions that God makes throw away trees, dogs, deer, or crickets. Didn't Jesus of Nazareth teach that the great God, who cares for the birds of the air and the lilies of the field, cares more for us humans, even though we may have little faith? It is my choice to take him seriously.

One of my favorite lines from Alice in Wonderland is something spoken by one of the "witches." "Words mean what I want them to mean," she declared, and she may have spoken for the entire human race in that pronouncement. Things appear to us in the way we view them, and we tend to believe what we want to believe. We have also been lied to so much by everyone from toothpaste companies to government leaders that many of us can't even recognize real truth any more.

The Yearning and the Light

It is interesting to note that, when early Romans tried to form a name for this Divine Mystery, they called it *deus* — meaning the all-pervading light which is over all and which infuses everything. Across the Aegean Sea, the ancient Greeks also needed a word for the Divine Mystery. They called it *theos* — the inner yearning within the heart of humanity which seeks for that which is greater than itself. This is where we get words such as deity, or theology. In reality, however, the combination of those two definitions of what we call God just might be very accurate. The God Energy is certainly all pervasive in and beyond all universes. It is the Source of All Creation as well as the quantum potential for forms of creation which are yet to be.

Yet the divine mystery is also immanent in every part of its creation. The Greeks, in looking to this inner yearning, identified a God of the Divine Mystery within each human individual. A God which is calling to Itself, first of all for recognition and then for total union within all of Its creation.

That leads to words such as "enlightenment," which has been used for centuries. Enlightenment is one's ability to realize the divine energy as truly a light to all of existence. It becomes an actual mode of participation in the Highest Consciousness of Light. In enlightenment, the human mind has successfully laid ego aside to realize what it truly is — part of the divine light of all creation.

In that sense, one of the descriptions we can give to the divine mystery must be Light. In all cultures and religions, light is sacred. Jesus, speaking of his identity within the Christed Consciousness and speaking for the God Source, said, "I am the Light of the World." In a beautiful way, we consider Jesus speaking as one who embodied in human form the brilliance of the Divine Mystery Itself. That is what the concept of "Christ" really means.

Quantum Reality and Non-Linear Thought

Today's global awareness has turned some big corners. For instance, while the two disciplines of religion and science were once considered diametrically opposed, it is progressive scientific thinking now which has provided realization of the quantum. Under the new understanding of Quantum Physics, seeing all things as **more** than the sum of their parts and carrying endless possibilities, humanity's ability to perceive the infinite nature of the Divine Mystery has dramatically increased. This has led to a more holistic way of thinking. Once we begin to grasp things in their true totality, the concept of God shares in that advancement.

Time is a human invention with its past, present and future, and, as such, it feeds our linear mode of thought. What is eternal, however, has no time. It simply Is in the reality of nonlinear thinking. So, the times are not merely changing, as Bob Dylan wrote. The times and all of us within this Now of Creation are actually transforming! That is our real task, to allow, accept and help actualize the very transformation of which we are a part!

There is no stagnancy in being human. In reality, we are in a dance with the Divine Beloved as we keep becoming what we really are, part of the Fullness of Creation and its very Source.

God is not a stagnant being but the Creation Process Itself. The God Energy holds every part of creation. We fit in there, too. That is our glory. That is also our sacred task, to allow the transformation the Divine Source keeps creating. It is a sacred dance and, once understood, it becomes the joy of a lifetime and the truth of our destiny!

The God Field

One of the greatest thinkers of our time is a man whose easy style and infectious laugh belie the MD and several PhD's which follow his name. David Hawkins is a man of medicine and science. He is also a man of wisdom and holiness. An expert in the field of consciousness, Hawkins notes all the various "fields" to which humankind may belong. We belong either in the field of woman or man. We belong to the field of citizenship in a particular nation, a particular line of work, a particular race and even to the possible field containing lovers of sports car racing, astrology, or religious affiliation. Those are all separate fields to which a person may or may not belong.

In the Woman Field, for example, there exists a woman who has given birth to two children, who loves to cook, and who sees the duty of protecting and raising her children as one of her life's most noble tasks. That field of women may also be narrowed, however, by determining if that woman lives in the United States, the United Kingdom, or the United Emirates.

What Hawkins states is that all these many, less inclusive fields, rise to greater generalization. They meet in nations and in the common field of living human beings. In considering the planet, Hawkins looks at life and charts a field of all life on earth. Moving even higher, this planet belongs to a solar system, a galaxy and a universe, as well as many universes we have not yet discovered.

Above all in this study of fields, there does exist a field of All That

Is. It is that inclusion of all which Hawkins designates as the God Field. With this consideration, we begin to realize that our individuality, race, intellect, belief system or lack of it, our state of health or any other factor holds little importance. We are all members of this God Field of All Creation. In this field there is one source which is not above us but of which we are integrally and intrinsically a part. In this God Field we are all one. Hating another is holding hatred for ourselves. The old line asks, "Am I my brother's keeper?" The new line deals with the realization that we are part of our brother and our sister as they are part of us, all one in the God Field of Light and Love.

Today's news of war, torture and death reminds us that all in the human race have not yet reached the realization of our oneness. The new world of tomorrow toward which we walk, however, holds the promise of everyone understanding that one basic truth. As members of the all-inclusive field of the Divine Mystery itself, there is no separation. There is only one. There is no other. There is no hatred. There is only love. There is no war where only peace exists, and there is no death in the God Field of Spirit which simply IS in the Eternal Now.

A great body of thought and approach to the Divine Mystery has also been achieved by those most concerned with it. As Teilhard de Chardin, through his study of prehistory and human evolution concluded, all of creation, with humanity as part of it, is moving toward what he called the Omega Point where total union with divinity will be achieved. In calling earth and all creation the "Divine Milieu," Chardin basically stated the same concept as Hawkins' God Field. Both stated that it is consciousness which is evolving to understand that all is included in the Great Mystery some call God. And from that conclusion comes the realization that we are all stuff of the divine.

Catholic priest and social psychologist Diarmuid O'Murchu has also brought current thinking much closer to the God Source. Moving from linear to lateral thinking in the quantum approach to theology,

O'Murchu traces humankind in its evolution and charts the course of the world's current transition in this exciting new time.

"The human species is moving now from a closed, static, simplistic and exclusionary world of thought into a new time," he states. "We are now in the Axial Age of quantum reality which is fluid and dynamic — allowing old dualisms to fall away. All aspects of creation are seen as complementary and equally important. Old deterministic thinking is replaced by realizing everything is enriched by creative energy, where humanity's mental posture must be open to the unexpected and the unexplained."

Stating it is consciousness more than anything else which is evolving in our time, a " ... wise and intelligent energy that has driven E-mergence since time immemorial lights up our horizon, throwing all our paradigms into chaos and confusion, and inviting humanity to a place we have never been before. We live in a unique evolutionary movement," O'Murchu writes, "and we urgently need to discern the meaning of what is unfolding within and around us."

Considering humankind's survival on the planet according to the concept of survival of the fittest, he says in *Evolutionary Faith*, "I suspect that the fittest of all are those who do not "fight" for survival, but remain interconnected with the dance of infinite possibility, grounded in the inexhaustible love of the embracing Spirit of God."

As consciousness rises to new understanding of quantum reality, all of creation is seen as one and separation is ended. Division and duality are replaced with the unity of all within the Source of Creation itself. The whole is magnificently more than the sum of its parts, and everything is enriched by creative energy.

The Divine Mystery

It is often difficult, sometimes even painful, to leave the old behind. This is especially true of our comfortable, ingrained images of the Great Mystery. Is God a father? Is God a mother? Is God beyond either of those ideas? Is God black? Is God yellow? Is God red or brown or white? Is God the vibration and the rainbow of colors and sounds found all over this planet?

In the role of all creation thriving in its own consciousness — all of the above!

Yet, if we are called into the Great Mystery as human consciousness rises, it is that Mystery itself which is calling us to come more fully into its essence. We can call it God or Spirit, Universe or anything else. It remains what it is because it always is. And we, in our true identity, remain within it, because beyond our conception of time there is, in truth, only the Eternal Now

Ultimate truth can be found only in mystery. Ultimate truth is beyond human conception because it is beyond judgment, discernment, or mental acquisition. Ultimate truth simply is, and humankind lives within it, though no one can ever define or contain its totality. Ultimate truth is the mystery manifest. It is Transcendent Reality, the Isness of the Is.

There is, however, not much opportunity for worshipping something called "The Isness." No statues. No icons. No supposedly sacred words. Yet Truth is. Mystery Is. It is Reality, completion and totality of Destiny, and we are part of it.

There is only One. There is no other. And the depths of that One remain the most exquisite, wonderful and superb mystery of which each one of us is intrinsically a part.

Truth

The truth is that every individual believes what she or he wants to believe. Many will go to their graves with the same belief about God which they have carried from their youths. God is God, no matter what anyone believes or does not believe. Truth is truth and can never be anything else.

A part of truth today, however, is that more people are ready for a deeper, more personal relationship with the One Truth that is God Energy. There are many intelligent, well-meaning and holy people out there who are moving toward greater appreciation of the Divine Mystery. These are not heretics or hell-bound unbelievers. These are a growing army of people who seriously and intensely revere the God Presence of the cosmos and within themselves. These are people determined to walk in Light. These are people willing to share that deeper love with others, and who are ready to move beyond simplistic, ego-driven concepts of a humanized God of fire and brimstone, hell, and cruel, eternal damnation. These are people who acknowledge and stand within the Source Energy of perfect words spoken by the Christ, "Love one another as I have loved you." These are people who stand within the God of Compassion and Love.

Question: Will you stand with them?

RIGHT BRAIN CHAPTER REVIEW

A Memo from God

Know me now.
I am not waiting for you somewhere —
In a paradise of your own dreaming
Built on illusions of your own sanctified salvation
And your own personal victory.
Know me now. I am your glory now.
I am in your breath and in your mind
*   And in every yearning of your own sacred heart —*
Right here. Right now.

Mine is not some kingdom in some foreign place
*   which you seek to win*
*   by obedience to dogma, rules and rituals.*

Who Can Say Divinity?

I am not some treasure you wish to merit
while others fall away to excruciating torment
      in a time beyond all time.
Mine is not a kingdom built for your desires
While others, born of my own breath, remain outside
      and locked away in a desolation and damnation you create.

What kind of Source of All God would I be then?
If I could not hold everyone and yet enfold you in my love's totality,
      through every step of your path
      and every part of the journey
      which you take to REALize me —
      to let me be truly real for you — now,
      in your own human mind,
      and in the majesty of your own eternal soul
      which is our Union and our one eternal embrace.

Know me now for I am in you now.
It is simply yours to comprehend what
      Your highest self and your fullest soul already know.
Separation is the only sin you keep trying to create,
      but you will never succeed because
      separation is simply not the truth.
Heal that now. Seal it in our love!
I am Truth. And I am in your soul!

Lay your ego mind aside and read my Holy Mind,
Where wisdom comes not in lessons you must learn,
      but in a fullness of consciousness
      joyfully and innately known.
Just look beyond your little self, dear one.
See beyond all the distractions your collective mind has conjured up
      through ages of a small, sad dream,
      a dream of illusion built to keep us apart,
      and torn from the heart of our love.

We are love. You and I.
We are love so strong that the two of Us
      dissolve into the Union which we are.

Don't you see it? Can't you be it?
Can't you slip aside the only veil I have set —
      as your will and your willingness to be, and to
      become the mirror which I see within My Self?
I am your God. And you are mine.
And because of that reality, we never can be two.
We can ever only be one.
And that is your treasure.
And that is my grace.

Dear one, We — you and I —
Are the Beloved!

Lost and magnificently found
     in the only miracle
Divinity ever can be —
     to be lost and be found in love!
And so it is.
This is the place of God. And in this love all mystery unfolds.

CHAPTER TEN

WHAT ABOUT JESUS?

The Love of Christed Consciousness

Christ: A totally God-realized individual who fully embodies all the characteristics of the God Essence, free from ego mind illusions and desires of this physical world.

It is from my personal and spiritual love for Jesus that I write this chapter. While some Christian groups proclaim, "Jesus is God" or "Jesus Saves" the most enigmatic man who ever lived deserves more than mention on a bumper sticker. And as one who writes from a Catholic background and years spent as a nun, as well as many years beyond that time, I hold the Christ profoundly and completely dear to my heart. I have had many teachers, yet it is the deepest wisdom and authentic truth of this Christ which has most eloquently spoken to my soul. One of the things which pains me most deeply is that this magnificent teacher and true Christ, who spoke of the unity of all, has become for many an intense cause of division, judgment and separation.

As you begin this chapter, it will help if you first determine what you think, or don't think, about this man who has become the source of so much controversy, praise, and endless speculation throughout the last 2000 years.

What Do You Think?

Most people will read this chapter coming from their own belief system so, to better understand how your mind may be set right now, consider these questions: What do you think about Jesus? Do you consider him an interesting figure in human history, and no more? Do you think of him as an influential prophet or teacher in world history? Do you think of him as a founder of one of the world's greatest religions? Do you feel he is someone you "believe in" or no longer "believe in"?

Do you consider Jesus someone who died an excruciating death to save you from your sins? Do you consider him the only son of God and therefore also God? Or do you prefer to think of Jesus as your elder brother and a master teacher? Do you think of Jesus as a totally god-realized individual who, even in his earthly life, fully participated in the God Energy? Do you believe Jesus is the Almighty God who will return to earth in his physical body to call the "faithful" to a physical place called heaven somewhere beyond this planet? Do you believe that, at that time, he will also curse with damnation all the rest of souls who have ever lived or who will ever live, banishing them to eternal torment in a physical place called hell?

Needless to say, the figure of Jesus stands across this planet's time as the one individual who has impacted not only the Western world with its logical way of thinking, but the Eastern and the Mid Eastern worlds of thought and non-thought as well. While some consider Jesus God, most people who do not hold that belief still think of him as an enlightened man who has been pivotal in humanity's spiritual development. Followers of Islam consider him a great prophet, and he is respected in the East as well. Some even believe he spent time in China, Egypt or Tibet during the thirty years that written texts hold no account of him. Many different traditions recognize his contribution of forwarding the heart of humanity into the Divine Mystery.

As we consider this man who grew up in the small town of Nazareth in what is now Israel, we first need to consider the role in which we address him. Do we choose, as many people, to see Jesus as the savior of humankind, founder of a major world religion, and actually the only masculine manifestation of a masculine Father God? Are you among those who think of Jesus as God? A Christian woman recently told me, "Of course Jesus is God. Jesus made the earth. Jesus rules all things that happen on the earth."

How we approach the Divine Mystery in our own consciousness is how we approach the role and identity of Jesus. So be it. Above all, Jesus was a man who spoke for truth, and that is a good place to begin our study of him.

There is also the concept of looking to the life of Jesus in his role as a great teacher whose message was essentially simple. "Love one another" are his words which have come down through every translation of any group's version of the Bible. And, in whatever language or translation anyone may use, that is the great teaching of a great master. Just love each other, as well as yourself, as deeply and as totally as you can! And, by the way, there is no judgment, or thought of rank or importance, in true, compassionate love.

The I AM Teachings

As we look through different versions of the Bible today, how certain groups read those words becomes important. A large group of Christians, for example, holds a literal interpretation of the words of Jesus as presented in the King James Version of the New Testament. That is the basis of their faith. Many carry their bibles with them and sometimes seem to be holding more reverence for the words of their bibles than for the actual Divine Energy itself. For this very large group of what are now called evangelical Christians, Jesus IS God. Period. There is little attention paid to God as a Father or to what is known as the Holy Spirit of God, still the Christian and Catholic Trinity.

When evangelicals ask, "Do you believe in Jesus?" they are essentially asking, "Do you believe Jesus is God?" That is their belief system based largely on the words spoken by the Nazarene, "I am the Way, the Truth and the Life. Unless you believe in me, you shall not enter the kingdom of heaven." For them, there it is. Case closed. There are the literal words and Jesus is literally speaking them. Amen.

There are, however, many scholars who do not believe or teach that the man from Nazareth was saying, "I, Jesus, am the only Way, Truth, and Life…" They do not believe Jesus was speaking of himself as the Only Way, either as a man or as a god. They do not believe Jesus was insisting that he is the God Mystery of All Creation Itself.

Instead they teach that Jesus was speaking as a true Christ as that term is interpreted today. While "Christ" means "messiah" in Hebrew, in today's spiritual discussions, the term describes a god-realized individual. Therefore Jesus, as a true Christ, was speaking for the Divine Mystery, in what some biblical scholars now call the I AM teachings. Totally in tune with the Transcendent Reality of the I AM, Jesus was speaking from Its Absolute Truth. At other times, as in the Sermon on the Mount, Jesus did assume the role of rabbi or master teacher. In what are called the I AM teachings, however, he spoke not from his own ego, but as one who articulated in human words the Truth of the God Consciousness Itself. When Jesus told the people he had come to teach in this world so they may have life, and have it more abundantly, he was showing them a newer way of participating in the true life of spirit.

It is also important to remember that people in Jesus' time were at a very low state of consciousness. Their level of education and awareness was nowhere near where human consciousness is today. People lived day to day, struggling to feed themselves in a harsh land, and were, for the most part, uneducated and illiterate. They were also under the domination of a foreign invader, the Romans, and were desperately trying to preserve their belief system in a god their invaders did not recognize.

When Jesus began his teaching, he was actually a forward-looking rabbi, who took on the mission of moving people to a more personal relationship with the God Mystery. In many ways, he was a warrior and a rebel, going against the grain of the staid, dogmatic teachings of the high priests who held powerful, absolute authority. While those priests held people in a religion where individuals had to struggle through life to gain some kind of reward called heaven in an after life, Jesus taught them, "The kingdom of heaven is within you." He called the great God not only his father, but "your father" as well. Living in the truth of knowing All is One, he sought to liberate people from the ignorance of lesser beliefs into the freedom of knowing they, and we, are all part of the Divine Energy.

The Basileia

In the Gospel of Thomas Jesus said, "The Kingdom of heaven is laid out upon the earth, yet you don't see it!" He was teaching that heaven is not a physical place to reach only after death, but rather a basileia, a state of being where all humans can participate more deeply in the loving awareness of the One. Mentioned over a hundred times in the Christian New Testament, the Basileia, or New Kingdom of God, was a cornerstone of Jesus' teaching. This involved a restructuring of the world in Jesus' time, which O'Murchu describes in *Reclaiming Spirituality*, and which is still part of world culture today:

> All relationships were characterized by hierarchical ordering and graded significance on the patriarchal order of masculine power. To make the system work, such values as inequality, exclusiveness, class distinction, independence and dependency were considered to be indispensable. To validate the system, God was invoked as the fatherly figure on top of the patriarchal ladder; humans, especially men, were perceived to be his first-born creatures who claimed for themselves unique access to God's will over and above all other beings who inhabited Planet Earth. ... And in the eyes of governing patriarchs, the system could have worked to perfection except for the misguided influence of women. They, more than anybody else, should be excluded and suppressed.

Jesus denounced that system, teaching that, in the Basileia, those "values" were of no value to true, equal spirituality. Instead O'Murchu describes the Christ concept of the Basileia as:

> In the new mode of relating the key qualities are: inclusiveness: everybody at all times and in all places must be included, not excluded; equality: there is no status or class distinction in the Basileia where all are paid equally whether they arrive at the first hour or at the eleventh; justice: in which everybody is accorded a fair share of goods and resources to live with dignity and equality; liberation: from all forms of oppression and slavery, within and without; peace: harmony within the heart, within the home, within the community and within the planet; love: the ultimate value that makes all the others possible.

That is the new realm which Jesus championed in his teaching and in his life. That is the true "kingdom" which still sorely needs to be created and lived today.

It is true Jesus called himself a son of God, and it was as a true manifestation of the Divine Heart that he tried to bring a very primitive people to greater understanding of their own relationship as daughters and sons of the Creation Essence Itself. His presence on the planet was not to establish himself as a lord to be feared or worshipped forever as some kind of divine judge. He presented himself, even unto death, as one who participated in Divine Truth, and he invited all people to share with him in the magnificence of the Divine Mystery.

Did Jesus intend to found a world religion which would hold him as its central, adored figure? Or did he consider himself a true teacher who, in his enlightened level of consciousness, could actually speak for the Source of Creation Itself and present his enlightened energy as a beacon for others to follow into that Source? Was Jesus the true Enlightened One who could call all, equally and fully, into the Basileia of Compassion, Equality, Freedom, Justice, Peace and Love?

Lord — that I may see …

What Is Christ?

It is interesting to note that Christianity has not derived it name from the man Jesus. We do not call the religion of his followers "Jesusism." Instead, the word Christianity, or even Christendom, chooses to hold emphasis on the term Christ, which was not, as I often remind people, Jesus' last name. Some people speak of Jesus Christ as they talk about Ben Franklin, George Washington or Genghis Khan. The term "Christ" is now considered in the term Christ Consciousness. This is the fullness of consciousness which literally mirrors and participates in the Great Consciousness, the Perfect Mind of the true I AM.

Christianity, therefore, derives its name from the enlightened state to which Jesus clearly rose and lived. In actual Christianity then, Jesus is held as a possessor of the true Christ Consciousness, the God Realized Christed One who actually mirrors the God Consciousness Itself.

It is also important to understand that "Christ" is a descriptive title, not a word reserved for only one individual. One of the key concepts Jesus taught was that all the things he had done, and realized, are also possible for others. Many spiritual leaders today speak of the Christ Consciousness as a goal for all people. We are finally realizing Jesus was not holding himself up as God, but as our elder brother and teacher who came to help us realize we are all potential Christs. We have the Divine Presence within us, he taught. It is very possible for us to move beyond the selfishness and judgmental separation of the ego mind. Then, we too can rise to deeper awareness of our true reality, as emanations and manifestations of our true nature which participates in the Divine Mystery Itself.

The Jesus Message

Personally, I hope all believers in Jesus follow him as a true Christ, one who lived in human form as a perfect and fully God realized individual who taught true love as his greatest message. In his Christed Consciousness he was not speaking only to a certain group of people who would be "saved." He was not even speaking only to those he met on dusty roads and hillsides over two thousand years ago. Jesus was speaking to all of us who walk now into a newer world he, in his wisdom, foresaw and celebrated. While some focus on Jesus and the power of his death, it may be more beneficial to think of Jesus and his life. His impact continues today in this time of rising consciousness and the birthing of a new time of compassion and peace.

It may be helpful here to ponder these words written by the monk

Thomas Merton in the late 1950's:

> This of course is the ultimate temptation of Christianity! To say that Christ has locked all the doors, has given one answer, settled everything and departed, leaving all life enclosed in the frightful consistency of a system outside of which there is seriousness and damnation, inside of which there is the intolerable flippancy of the saved — while nowhere is there any place left for the mystery of the freedom of divine mercy which alone is truly serious, and worthy of being taken seriously.
>
> *- Raids On The Unspeakable*

Healing Makes Whole

One of the major roles Jesus filled in his life was that of a healer. While he brought physical well-being to many in what are called miracles, he was a healer in the true sense of the word, "heal" meaning a "return to wholeness." Jesus' greatest healing was a return to wholeness of the spirit, and that healing exists today in the miracle he continues to perform for many individuals. Jesus' true role as healer was indeed the role of teacher. He pointed the way for all to live in and experience the Light of the Divine Source.

In that sense, Jesus continues to work miracles and in your case, his greatest miracle may be the miracle he gives to you by enriching your life with his message of hope and purpose. Following his teaching, we can realize we are people who are truly walking toward a new world of higher consciousness where we embrace a more holistic, inclusive concept of humanity and creation itself. The new consciousness decries any notion of separation. In its more feminine energy, instead of judging, condemning or ostracizing anyone, it embraces all with respect, honoring each other's differences, and holding all in compassionate love.

Jesus, in his time on earth, was a pointer of the way and a messenger whose simple words hold wisdom beyond all ages. As a true Christ, he embodied empiric Truth, the highest consciousness which many consider to be the God Energy Itself.

The Gospel of John in the Christian New Testament contains "The Last Discourse," a summary of teachings Jesus gave shortly before his death. He knew he was going to die and as he prepared his followers to move on without his physical presence, he told them there still remained many more things for them to learn. He also told them they were not ready to grasp those truths yet, but that a Spirit of Truth would come to help them when the time was right. Clearly Jesus was not referring to another human being but to the very Spirit of the Divine Mystery, which would, through time, reveal itself as humanity evolved toward greater ability to receive it. It is interesting to also note here that the pronoun Jesus used to describe that Spirit of Truth translates into the feminine, not masculine, form. In that sense, the Spirit of Truth to which Jesus referred held feminine, not masculine energy.

Moving Ahead

If you accept and follow Jesus the Christ within your own religion, I honor you. As one whose spiritual grounding was within the structure of the Catholic Church, I share your love for the man we call Jesus. I personally accept his Christed completion, and I love and revere him now more deeply than I ever did as a nun. Yet, to truly honor Jesus is not to sell him short by blindly and comfortably accepting him without seeing him in the new light of humanity's rising consciousness.

Religion was never meant to be a comfort zone or a static, patriarchal box of exclusionary belief. Religion, in its highest light, is meant to provide meaningful assistance to any individual's search for her or his highest identity. True religion must be dynamic and always growing as humanity's consciousness advances to higher, more inclusive, levels. If it doesn't, more and more people will simply leave it behind. As noted earlier, the PEW Center reports of 2008 and 2009 reveal a great many people already have left it behind.

The Light

One message which stands foremost in Jesus' teachings was that he came from the Light and that he was indeed part of the Light. This is taken not only as the primordial light which was present at the dawn of creation; it also refers to the higher radiance of the great mystery which not only created, but sustains and continues creation on a moment to moment basis in the Eternal Now.

Over and over again, Jesus told his followers that they too are part of that Divine Radiance. The divine light of the great creation is in all of us equally, he said, as much as it was in him. We simply need to discover it. Central not only to Jesus' teaching, but to the teaching of most enlightened beings in all of human history, is the message that every human being is not only part of light, but exists in that image of God as the Light. For example, in Jewish literature, especially the Kabbalah, there is reference to the infusing light of all Mystery. Not only every individual possesses it, but all of creation does as well. It is the glory and privilege of us in human form to choose to accept this higher level of the God Radiance. All other sentient beings don't need to accept it with free will. They are simply in it as part of their very being! My little cat Skoshi doesn't need to agree to her place in the Radiance of Creation. She just lies here and basks in it while I struggle to explain it in words!

The Kingdom

While Jesus talked about the Basileia, or the New Realm of God in more direct terms, most popular religions today still consider it a kingdom to which, in physical form, humans have no access. This interpretation, in turn, has stabilized and encouraged most religions to affirm humanity's alienation from God. That idea of "kingdom," narrowly interpreted, is paradise or what some may call Nirvana, Bliss, or The Rapture. It is a place beyond the reach of living human beings.

Yet, to study Jesus' teachings is to realize he was not referring to a rewarding type of kingdom in another physical place or dimension. Rather, over and over again, he taught that the kingdom is within, that all human beings are capable of rising to the same state of awareness and being within the divine mystery. Using the term *Imago Dei*, the "image of God," Jesus taught that, by the very seeking of Truth, it can be revealed to us as consciousness rises into greater awareness of our true nature. Thomas Merton, for example, spoke of being in the image of God as being found in the soul's structure of "awareness, thought and love."

We are in human form, but this divine Light, which may also be considered the Spirit of that which is All Holy, is within us. All it requires is that we peel away the onion-skin layers of ego and desire for personal identity, power, and wealth as we draw closer to our ultimate truth.

In many ways, the human task on earth is described as a purification process. As Gary Zukav writes, it is an "earth school." We are moving through the different grades of existence, much as we moved through elementary, high school and possibly higher levels of learning. In the Gospel of Thomas, Jesus tells his followers, "If they say to you, 'where did you come from?' say to them 'we came from the Light. The place where the Light came into being by Itself, and was revealed through their image.' If they say to you again, 'who are you?' say 'we are its children, the chosen of the living Father."

Thus, the entire concept of darkness takes on the meaning that, as long as we do not become aware of our essence as spiritual beings in human form, who participate in the Divine Radiance, we must move through stages of darkness. Only then will we arrive at our final realization which is revelation that we are part of the true kingdom. We always have been.

A poet once wrote, "Now we see through a glass darkly." That, in many ways, describes the evolution of human consciousness. We are working through lesser levels of our existence as people, but moving toward the place where we realize we are indeed not only made in the "image and likeness" of the Divine Radiance, but, from our very creation, it has been within us all along!

On the other side of the world, there is a temple at Miyajima on the eastern coast of Japan. The central part of that temple is a large mirror. Beneath it one finds these words, "Take care and wipe the mirror clean every day, lest no speck remain." There, in another culture and belief system, is the same concept of our need to strive to see more clearly into the light of higher consciousness.

In The Heart of I AM

In another example of Jesus speaking for the I AM Essence, scripture records his encounter with high priests of his own religion, Judaism, who were upset by some of his teachings. "Who do you say you are?" they asked. "Are you Abraham? Are you one of the prophets?" — clearly, by the way, referring to the concept of reincarnation.

Jesus' answer obviously infuriated them because by saying, "Before Abraham came to be, I AM," they took it as Jesus declaring himself to be God, the great I AM. Rather than interpreting that as fundamental Christians do today, accepting only Jesus as a true emanation of divinity, many scholars now feel when he said those words, Jesus was really telling all who would listen that they too are part of this Divine Mystery. They too are very capable of growing to that point where they finally achieve the realization of what and who they really are, part of the I AM Itself! How can anything be other than a part of the very source of its own existence?

Grow Strong Like the Tree of Life

It is important that we grow in our belief, and it is wise to consider the tree. It grows from tender roots and, as it grows, it is very important that those roots reach deep into a strong foundation of something solid. Then, as the tree begins to develop, it reaches for the light wherever it may be found. If it is in a forest of many trees, it may send branches out in one direction or another, in its sole purpose of reaching for the light which gives it nourishment and growth.

Every human being who lives well needs to follow that same procedure. We need strong foundations from our youth. As we grow, however, and as our consciousness and innate wisdom grow stronger with us, it is our task to reach for the light wherever it may be found. Only in that light, the true Light, is there nourishment and growth for our spirit.

Jesus

While some may wish to concentrate on the man Jesus, I prefer to concentrate on his Christed role serving all humanity. Some may dwell on his suffering and death. I choose to view the life of a man who grew in wisdom, age and grace, who went to the desert to fast and fight his own demons, who enjoyed the company of good friends and who also knew the anguish of having those same friends let him down in a time of need. I see a man who enjoyed a wedding and, yes, I consider a man who eloquently spoke for the kingdom of God, which is not a pie in the sky answer to human problems, but true participation in the fullness of the God Source of All Creation.

Yes, I consider the suffering of Jesus. I am appalled by the extent of human brutality which caused his great pain and horrific death. I also understand Jesus felt the need to suffer those things as his part of helping humanity save itself from its darker human energies. I also do not consider that this was a requirement of a loving God Essence to exact such torture as an only means of saving humanity from darker ego illusions.

I prefer, however, to think of the great teacher, Jesus the Christ, who, in his greatest message, preached not dogma and religious separation, but love and peace. I consider a man who observed the ritual of the Passover or Seder Supper — according to his own Jewish religion, but who also encouraged us all to participate in the greatest human ritual, which is responding to the Ultimate Mystery by participating in the Radiance of Its Eternal Light.

The Second Coming of the Christ

The great event for those who hold literal interpretation of the New Testament is the Second Coming of Jesus, the Last Judgment. It is the final exam for which most Christians spend their entire lives studying. It is payoff time! It is the end game of the great chess match between God and humanity, good and evil, Satan and the saved. All the pawns have been sacrificed. A few knights may have fallen in battle, and some ivory towers in the form of rooks may have crumbled in the fray. Even a few bishops may have had to be sacrificed...

Ah, but it has all been worth it. Anything is worth it to finally win the big prize. Check! Mate! Game over! We win! You lose! Amen.

And who will be the great, grand master on this day of triumph or tragedy? Who will be the high judge making the final pronouncement which seals everything forever? Of course, it will be Jesus returning to this pipsqueak of a planet in all of the cosmos. He will be radiant in his glorified body to welcome the faithful to everlasting joy and throw away those damned, faithless losers in utter disgust, into torment of excruciating pain which will never, never end.

Is that The Christ? Is that the fully God-realized one who knows the Heart of Divinity, the Soul Seed of all creation? Is that the teacher who begged us to simply love one and all as deeply and profoundly as we love ourselves? Is that the one who showed us Truth? Is that the one who told us that even the birds of the air and the lilies of the field are held in the loving embrace of the great God Source? Is that really the Christ?

We can put our faith in the literal words of myth or we can trust our very soul into the Mystery. Your choice.

Fullness Awaits

Mercifully, the Mystery has given us some clues for moving through this life course in miracles. Recognizing the fact we humans operate in linear thinking, there is the human fact that things begin and end. There will certainly be an end to our human existence, but is there really an end to that which has no time, but simply is? Can we shift our minds to consider, in non-linear thought, how true reality can simply always be?

Some who have gone before us have helped dispel that mystery. From thought and belief systems in every part of our world there has been the concept that a fullness awaits, in time, to reach a point where time no longer exists. This concept involves the idea that every part of creation must reach its own point of fullness before all becomes truly one again in Single Sacred Unity.

In the Eastern world there is the concept of bodhisattvas. These are souls which already merit eternal freedom in the One, which some may call heaven. They, however, choose to keep coming back to the earth plane to teach or help others reach that point of fullness in their own lives. In the West, there is the calling on higher energies such as angels or saints to help us reach that sacred place, and there is the very idea of the Christ as anyone who has reached the fullness of total realization in God, the Source Energy Itself.

Underlying all these ideas is the thought that the True Fullness cannot be reached until every single part of creation has reached it on its own. In other words, the fullness of creation cannot be achieved until every one has become a Christ, a fully God-realized individual who can then bring her or his fullness into the totality. In limping, human words, it is the idea that the Source of all Creation cannot be fully Itself until every shard of its Radiance is fully complete within the Source of Light Itself.

While many have used their own words to attempt describing this idea, consider the term "Omega Point" which was used by Teilhard de Chardin. In linear, human thinking, it describes an end time when all of creation is so full of its source that it literally becomes its source. This is the state which religions have tried to describe in words such as Heaven, Bliss, Nirvana, Buddhahood, or many other names. Because religions deal with individual humans, who always need some kind of reward at the end, the concept of winning or meriting heaven fits neatly into the concept of the last judgment when there will be winners and, obviously, losers, too.

But Chardin's Omega Point denotes an event in time when all are Christed, or god-realized. Then all will become fully part of their source because they are full of their source, and linear time will no longer be necessary. In that Eternal Moment beyond linear time, the One will continue and simply Be. We will all be part of it.

That is what many understand to be the Second Coming of Christ. It is not necessarily the second appearance on earth of the glorified body of Jesus, but the Christed Consciousness blossoming in one after another after another of all human beings into the Christed, god-realized state. When Jesus said, "All these things I have done, you also can do — and more," he was teaching us we are all potential Christs. And, in its true sense, that is not a blasphemy. That is our destiny. "I have come that you may have life, and have it more abundantly," he said. And he showed us our own Christ possibilities by modeling them in his human life.

"That I May See ..."

How does one become a Christ? It might be well to simply echo the prayer of a nameless man in the New Testament, repeated from your own full and loving heart: "Lord, that I may see ..."

"Love one another as I have loved you." That was what Jesus taught, modeled, and lived to its fullest conclusion. Whether anyone is a follower of Jesus the Christ or not, now it is our turn to live the Christed, deepest truth which is realizing our own place within the Light and the Kingdom of the Essence of Love.

Is the True Christ the great lord (which, by the way, does not mean master, but teacher) sitting on a high throne, ready to solemnly welcome some to endless joy, and curse others with eternal damnation? What does your heart tell you? What does his heart tell you? Can you recognize the fully god-realized Christ energy within yourself just waiting to be free?

I personally believe the energy of Jesus the Christ is ongoing as a gift to all people on this planet. As a god-realized individual, his fullness within the Perfected Consciousness continues to be a powerful force today. It still can lift our less than perfect prayer into the purity of Absolute Truth and Compassionate Love.

What you believe is what you create. I suggest you believe in Truth.

RIGHT BRAIN CHAPTER REVIEW

Where the Temple Now?

Always I shall love you
　　　　In the only heart we share —
Christos — the Consciousness of Love
　　　　become Itself.
Silence — swirling action!
Stillness, grown to awe!
The fullness reaching only within Itself —
　　　　revealed in gratitude.

Where the temple now?
Where the shroud that lifts away to love's eternal fabric
　　　　of cosmic suns, held like tiny beads
　　　　set in awareness of the whole.

How could I not begin and begin and
Always begin again to hold you in the radiance
Of Love reaching forward from its stillness
Born in genesis and flowing in the moment eternity reveals?
Always in the pouring out
      of union beyond all words.
For only love — The Christos, fully realized —
Is actualized so perfectly in man become of God.
That angels dare not sing today
Lest they break the spell.

Completion. Holy Stillness.
Held within the Heart of All That Is.
And I am that with you —
Where nothing else could ever call me back
      from love which is this essence of us all.

Flames of sacred fires leap into a
Million sleeping universes — still waiting for the light.
      Yet we — you and I — have held them close
      In love which is the star seed of them all.
Christed fullness. Christed knowing.
Christed being in the pure, forever love.
Aware. Complete.
  And conscious of its own holy self containing all.

How could I possibly not love The Heart of All That Is!

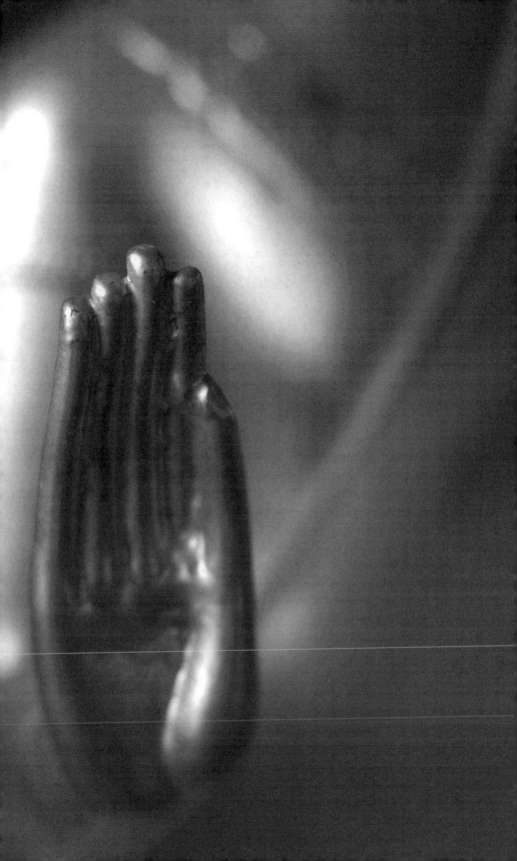

BE A LIGHT
UNTO YOURSELF

Bless What Has Been;
Now Embrace Ascension

The happiness we seek, a genuine lasting peace and
happiness, can be attained only through the purification of our
minds. This is possible if we cut the root cause of all suffering
and misery — our fundamental ignorance.

- His Holiness the Dalai Lama

There is a story about the last day The Buddha spent on this earth. As death approached, he gathered his monks to his bedside, then told them to ignore all the teachings he had given in his time with them. He told them, instead, to be a light unto themselves. That was his last teaching. Then he transitioned away from this life leaving us the best he had to give.

Now it's time to take Buddha seriously. He was counseling his monks to seek true wisdom in the same place where Jesus of Nazareth later told his followers to seek. Find the Divine Light within your own holy sanctuary, which is the presence of your soul as a true part of the Divine Mystery. The kingdom, the Basileia, is within. It's a waste of time to attempt finding it anywhere else.

As we reach the conclusion of Part One, there needs to be a bit of reckoning here. Whether you have browsed through these early chapters, buried yourself in the facts and the history, or wondered with us what Divinity might be, this is your time to respond. Any form of creativity, be it a book or ballet, a poem or gesture of love, usually needs some form of response. The saint, of course, can cast a million diamonds out into the wind and never think about it again. We lesser ordinary folk, however, know there is always response to be made. The very act of creating is in itself an attempt to respond to some form of gift we have received. So, if what awaits you in Part Two will succeed, the energy of Part One seeks an energy of response from you.

You are now armed with truth about an Axial Age, the beauty of the Quantum, the mystery and logic of feminine and masculine energies, as well as an invitation to become part of the Basileia which the Christ held before us as wonderful possibility. You have realized your own place within the God Field of Energy, and you have grown to honor the wisdom, as well as the failings, of those who have gone before us. Now one question requires your response. What will you do with all that?

Are these merely so many thoughts to file away until someone brings up a concept so you can say, "Oh yes, I know all about that."

Is this a book you'll glance at on a shelf and feel satisfied that you've grasped all the content you need to know?

The opening quote for this chapter speaks about ending the fundamental ignorance to which we, as an imperfect species, are entitled. Ignorance means we just haven't learned something yet. It leaves us the generous grace of knowing that, once we've been given the information, we will actually brim with the knowledge received.

Stupidity, of course, is its own breed of cat — with apologies to the wonderful felines of this awesome world!

So, was the Buddha negating all he had stood for with his last breath? Was this his version of saying, "Never mind?" Was he really denying all the wisdom he had uncovered through a life of searching and spiritual depth?

Or, with his dying words, was the Buddha telling his students they too held the wisdom they sought within their very selves? Was he acknowledging the fact there would always be teachers, but to know that the Teacher Within was more than capable of manifesting the radiance of Light Itself? Was he telling his students there does come a time when the seeker experiences enough transformation to directly realize the One Truth? Was he telling them Light begets Light as he urged them to live that truth themselves?

This new time witnesses equality of women and men sharing the truth of new discoveries. This is happening because this new Axial Age demands the uncovering of what has been hidden under a bushel, as Jesus foretold. Now is the time when Spirit/Truth demands new order as greater aspects of Light are revealed. The old ways are becoming necessarily inadequate, and that is all right. Rising awareness is calling us toward the greatest gift, the perfect gem, which awaits our discovery now that we have grown enough to receive it. Humanity is now poised to find and embrace the new, direct knowledge which has deliciously called to us from our genesis as a species of Light.

New Clarity Rises Within

So we come to this. A crossroads has risen for many, and crossroads always demand decision. What is the right direction to take? What will one miss when some choices are left behind?

These pages offer opportunity for a gentle review of your life and particularly your life in spirit. You have picked up this book for some reason, and may now realize you are at your own point of no return. Our lives do have their own bifurcation points. They are times we must make decisions to move on or cling to the safety of comfort zones. Thomas Wolfe once wrote, "You can't go home again," and that may also be true of your religious roots and where they have led you so far.

It is always beneficial to consider the status of one's spiritual life and where it may be leading. The first truth is that we are still on the planet, which means we are also still learning, growing and becoming. This, then, may be an excellent time to take stock of your connection, or lack of it, with the Divine Mystery. This process could take a few hours or several days of serious consideration. Either way, this is an opportunity to assess the quality your religious or spiritual beliefs are adding to your life. It may also be time to realize you are mired some place between holding old beliefs and daring new possibilities.

Your religious experiences, from youth in a family situation, through the teens, rebellious or not as they were, and into your adult years, matter. There may have been times when religion was extremely meaningful to you. There may have been times when religion failed to inspire or console you at all. Life is hectic enough, and with more than enough concerns to face every day, one's spiritual life may have just become lost in the debris of supposed unimportance, or lack of real meaningfulness.

Consider why some concepts or parts of spiritual living have been lost along the way and what, if anything, you have put in their place. There may have even been some sorrows which needed to happen so we could become more seasoned and ready for challenges our future may hold. That is true of life in general but also true of life within the spirit. We might look back at some of those difficult times and realize there were lessons to be learned which enriched our maturity and enabled future experience within our Source.

Even the Dalai Lama had to go through the agony of witnessing his country taken over by those who did not share his spirit of gentle truth. He watched the people he loved so dearly being tortured and killed, even as he was forced to flee his beloved homeland. His place, however, was not to die but to live the symbol of his love in a totally different way. His suffering enabled him, even as he experienced the sorrow of exile, to reach millions of people who otherwise would have never known him or the message which is his alone to teach and to live.

You, too, may have experienced difficulties in your family or personal life. As you look back at those hard times now, questions must be asked and answered. How did you make your way through those times, and what did you learn from them? More importantly, have they helped or hindered your ability to acknowledge a providence within the Divine Mind, as well as a providence in this world?

Look around your home and see the symbols of your beliefs and your loves. What are the pictures and objects visitors see when they enter your home? Have you turned to other cultures from long ago to make a statement about your thinking? What are the symbols of what you believe, and what is no longer a part of your home and your world of today? How do you explain all that?

Even if you have gone for years without attending religious services, or experienced harmful or negative situations from members of the clergy or their parishioners, those times are now in your past. You may feel you need to stay in your religion for fear of consequences which may come from leaving it. You may now be seeking alternative routes to stay in touch with the Higher Source you know exists, but which you no longer believe will be found in an institutionalized form of worship.

Honor What Has Been

Embrace the fact that nothing is ever wasted. A quick review of
what your religious or spiritual life has been is a positive step. Then,
if you are willing to make some changes and revisit some of your core
beliefs, it may be time to move ahead. It may be time to realize your
own light which is destined to shine for the world.

How many little deaths you have experienced along the way may
now lead to your time of transfiguration and ascension. This may now
have become your turn to accept the joy of living in Pure Truth as it is
revealed to you. This is not a prideful or egotistic thing. It is acknowledging what is possible in the heart of every person. In becoming the
Light of our own truth, we share that radiance within the collective
soul of everything that is.

There is a new spirit moving throughout our world. While some
are struggling to get beyond the cold secularization of European countries, in other areas, faith is flourishing as freedom to worship returns
to once tyrannized nations. Members of Islam, Buddhism, and Hinduism are gaining in numbers, and many alternative spiritual modalities
are rising up throughout the Americas. As economic hard times and
growing pessimism concerning the future drive more people to deeper
questioning, new answers regarding simpler living and growing compassion for others are feeding the human soul.

Many hard edges of selfish living are becoming lost in a more feminist view of life. The generosity of private citizens helping after Katrina
and other disasters has modeled greater caring for others. As war and
poverty continue to bring the global spirit down, more people now
turn to more meaningful ways of living. Greed is no longer accepted.
Selfishness is no longer in style. And while some religions are failing
to meet today's spiritual needs, the human spirit itself is seeking new
answers and opening to new possibilities.

The past may have been beautiful or brutal. It is, however, over. Now, a new way of being is reaching to us from a future resplendent with hope. Bless what has been and mercifully let it go. This is a new day and it may take a newer version of yourself, and greater depth of your spirit as well, to make the most of it.

Claim the Fourth Gift

One of the most often quoted lines from the Christian New Testament is, "There remain faith, hope and love, and the greatest of these is love." That has been the message for Catholics and Christians for thousands of years. In recent discoveries of ancient texts found at Nag Hammadi in Egypt and other places in the Mideastern world, however, remnants of a further addition to that text have been found. While not considered part of the accepted Christian bible today, those discoveries offer new perspective to what the ancients considered most important.

Using four elements of earth, water, air and fire, or light, these early writers considered the four directions, honored today by all indigenous people, and found qualities of true spiritual living in each. In earth they were reminded of Faith. In water they considered the virtue of Hope. To the power of wind they assigned the treasure of Love.

Yet, while writings in the bible stopped there, new findings of that same text have filled in the missing ending to the message of that instruction. After acknowledging Faith, Hope and Love, the missing fourth aspect has been found to be Light. The last and most important quality assigned to true spiritual life, then, was not Love, but Knowledge! And this is not the knowledge of events or history. It is the knowledge of direct knowing, drawn from actual encounter with the Spirit Source of All That Is.

That is the destination. This is the perfect pearl. The highest treasure. The ultimate goal humanity has sought since its infancy. Direct Knowing. Direct Encounter. Direct becoming of Light within Light.

Be a Light Unto Us All

If you are now rearranging your spiritual life, within or without institutionalized religion, using the four concepts of Faith, Hope, Love and Knowledge may help shape your spiritual path.

In the quality of Faith, you can determine your own beliefs and how they impact your life today. Consider how your spiritual or religious beliefs have changed over the years, as well as the strength of belief in yourself and values you now hold dear. Believing in the standards you set for yourself in career, in relationships, and in your approach to authentic living is vital. If you cannot hold strong beliefs for your own value and your right to achieve happiness and success, you may be harming yourself more than anyone else ever could. Remember, we co-create the world in which we live. Our beliefs become the birthing for what our life can become.

The quality of Hope does not refer to a weak wishing for good things to happen. Instead, it offers strength of belief in the sweetness of life's possibilities. It involves forming strong intentions to make the most of your talents and gifts. Hope offers belief in the promise of quality living and loving, and Hope gives power to your decisions to actually become light not only to yourself but to the rest of the world as well.

The need for Love in one's life is beyond question yet, as we strain for words to define intangible ways love can be expressed, we realize Love involves compassion, forgiveness, gratitude and absolute unselfishness. Love is always an easy word to say but not always an easy challenge to live.

It was Knowledge, however, which became the Pearl, the most

exquisite prize to be won in a spiritual quest, which the ancients held most dear. This does not mean simple knowing from any secondary source. This means empiric Knowledge, only known in direct encounter with the Prime Source Itself. It means not knowing or believing in the Divine Mystery, but actually experiencing the Divine Mystery in a total union of love.

What is one of the surest ways to follow the Buddha's advice? Whatever facts and truths you may learn, and how many varied religious and spiritual experiences you may have, including precious "aha moments" in your own life, it all comes down to your own simple truth. Knowing that your highest self is your own soul and its place within the Source of Creation Itself, consider these words of Paramahansa Yogananda, "Find friendship with Your True Self, the soul, in the sanctum of daily meditation; and after deep communion with God in the bower of peace, give divine friendship and good will to all."

Become a Light unto yourself. Then let that light illumine the Divine Presence within you — so you can shine it out into this very needy world. The chalice of fulfillment is there, laid out in simple terms. All it asks is your decision to accept that cup and empty its contents clear to the depths of your soul. You have the power to heal all illnesses of the heart. You hold the energy to restore balance in a world which has lost its center. You hold the strength of modeling resurrection from lesser deaths into sweet ascension which embraces total Truth.

This is your time to respond. Which direction do you feel is right for you? What are the whisperings of your Teacher Within? Are you ready to reach for that final gem, the perfected pearl of actual, direct encounter with the Source of All Mystery Itself? Are you ready to become the light which mirrors the Light within you?

Simple questions. And the answers are simple as well.

RIGHT BRAIN CHAPTER REVIEW

Even the Desert Blooms

From faith, through hope and love revealed
True knowledge finally comes within Encounter of the Source.
Truth reveals the treasure which was sealed in the past
And whispers — Sing me now to bring the blessing
*   which becomes your own to claim.*
Consider your birthing sky born now, and torn away
*   from lesser limits you have known.*
Growth has brought you far enough to radiate the Light.

This is your time to shine, for little deaths
*   become as nothing now.*
Even the desert blooms with joy to witness

holy union and sharing sanctified
as ascension wins the day.

The four winds sing. The darkness flows away.
The chalice of fulfillment brims full with the joy of it all,
as light becomes shining within.
The mystic gem of knowing, so perfectly here for you —
the perfect pearl of union wholly blessed,
finally made manifest to redeem the sacred Light.
And all of this becomes your own to claim!

PART TWO

MANY PATHS INTO THE WAY

ACCESSING THE DIVINE

I f we are willing to let go of old thinking and status quo comfort zones, more advanced ways of meaningful living become available to us. We are privileged to live in this unprecedented Axial Age of quantum evolution. All we need do is open ourselves to it as easily as we open ourselves to love, because that is exactly what is involved!

The following chapters will consider some key concepts which might help develop your own spirituality. They may provide understanding of how to better use your previous religious training or send you off in new directions you may find interesting to explore. Opening ourselves to new understanding which can expand our ways of thinking is an important step. Going beyond mere linear thought to the stillness of meditation and even modern mysticism is also an option you can consider.

Investigating the feminine energies of the Divine Mystery, as well as exploring how we can advance through balance of masculine and feminine thinking, may also help.

Understanding the role energy plays can lead to greater tools for healing on all levels. Also, with freedom to move beyond dogma and man-made belief systems, the human spirit and heart can be free to delight in new creativity and expanding consciousness. In this era of rising awareness and the crumbling of old modes of thought, this new millennium springs us forward with undeniable energy. We live in the Quantum, remember? If we can just be open to them, our possibilities are deliciously endless!

Now we can become part of the real Essence — beyond a God of books or ritual, dogma or narrowly defined religion. Instead we can use what we have learned, and unlearned, to move deeper into the Source of Life.

Embrace this New Time's Possibilities

This era of new growth has become a time of surging, vibrant energy. To now deny the very palpable insistence of the God Source calling us, luring and daring us onward into Itself, is to deny our own existence. If some of us still question one way vs. another way, or, if some are still wondering what to do about the chaos we and others are experiencing, the answers are all around us.

A world filled with hate can only be healed by love and, by no means, some kind of sweet, saccharine love. This new world demands love powerful enough to bring nations, individuals and our very species itself into a new time of compassion and forgiveness. This forgiveness must begin with ourselves as we see clearly where our own patterns of fear, hatred, judgment and acceptance of separation have led us.

First, we need to forgive ourselves and all those who falsely taught that hatred and division are acceptable. As Jesus called to the Divine Mystery in his last words, "Forgive them. They know not what they do," we now need to mirror his desire and forgive ourselves. We have been a very young, simplistic people. The God figure of an old man in the sky with basic male characteristics was a very simplistic mode of considering the Divine Mystery.

We are called now to true adulthood at a time when humanity is facing its own Bifurcation Point. We have reached that Moment of Truth when it is time to put aside the stupidity of division and war, greed and the arrogance of power. We have seen them fail in the world behind us. Now we can opt for the grace of humility, gratitude for the abundance we have, and compassionate, generous sharing and caring for those among us who need the gifts only we can offer.

How do we reclaim the planet for an entirely new way of living on it and with it? First, we stop destroying it. We stop bombing it. We stop filling it with poison, and we stop raping its treasure. We stop plundering its fossil fuel and start honoring its water, its foliage and all life within and upon it, including ourselves. We begin to live more spiritually, recognizing that this earth, this Gaia, this living organism which sustains and supports us, is our mother, and we need to cherish her. Part of nurturing her as she has fed us over all the millennia, is to feed her with love and the honoring of each other as we walk more gently on her earth, the cloak and outer layer of her planetary soul. We need to realize that her energy reaches to the stars and beyond all universes which still sing the same song back to the Source of Creation Itself. And, we draw all that energy back to this earth which holds us in her arms even as we forget to honor her.

We begin to find new depths to this thing we call love, in its physical, metaphysical, and energetically divine forms. We learn to recognize and honor the feminine energy which holds the characteristics of the Divine Feminine. We work more diligently and with greater wisdom to find our own centered, balanced way of healing ourselves. We move beyond chaos to the simple, profound new order which will free us all. We have shown up in one of the most challenging, powerful times of existence, and now we stretch to make this world and our species worthy of newer life. This planet itself is now calling for its own healing. And we, the people upon it, will either become part of that fullness through enlightened ways of being, or destroyers of it and all life on it, including ourselves.

The choice is ours to embrace the Source of all, the beauty of One creation, the power of One wisdom, the magnificence of One love, the understanding that there is only one of us here in the Divine Breath. Or, we can continue war and blind acceptance of some belief systems which allow murder, warfare, judgment and separation as some kind of false honor system or even an accepted holy mode of being. Thousands of years of patriarchal living have brought us this far. If we cannot turn to more balanced energy, honoring and embracing the feminine concept of life, the destiny of our planet and ourselves is made more manifest with every bomb and every weapon of destruction we keep producing in our citadels of war.

No more. War makes death, and Jesus, speaking in the I AM context of Divinity Itself, said, "I AM Way. I AM Truth. I AM Life." This is our time to truly choose life, and that begins with vibrant understanding and courageous willingness to go forward in search of our best and higher selves. Call it the Christ Mind. Call it the Buddha Mind. Call it anything you wish, but the only answer lies within the Only Truth. And, that truth is accessible to you because it is already in you. It is actually the very soul of you just waiting for you to discover it.

Yet Earth is a free will zone. The choice is yours.

The Edge Of Mystery

I am standing at the edge of mystery.
So much of the lesser has already slipped away,
And I begin to sense the vastness of the Full Energy,
      the overwhelming power of Its deep, abiding love.
Light — so brilliant I am lost in it
Until I cannot comprehend its ability to burn
      with such incredible, healing balm
      through every cell of my body
      and every facet of my soul!

Am I within? Or am I still outside the fullest light?
Yet I feel It reaching deeper, deeper in Its Radiance
      into this darkness which has finally agreed
      to yearn itself away, and flow within all Truth.

This is the only day of Sacred Moment held.
The place where words dissolve,
      where sound becomes the brilliance
      and the stillness of spirit — realized!
Fire burns to Light revealed,
      and healing flows like silver
      through the veins of all that is.

And I am right here!
I am right here at the edge of Mystery Itself...

CHAPTER TWELVE

MEDITATION, CONTEMPLATION, AND BEYOND

Living in the Rhythm and the Flow

Greater than activity, devotion or reason is meditation. To meditate truly is to concentrate solely on Spirit. It is the highest form of activity that man can perform, and it is the most balanced way to find God. If you seek Him only through discriminative thought you may lose Him in the labyrinths of endless reasoning, and if you cultivate only devotion for God, your development may become merely emotional. But meditation combines and balances all these approaches.

- Paramahansa Yogananda

Listen in deep silence. Be very still and open your mind ... Sink deep into the peace that waits for you.

- The Course in Miracles

When Albert Einstein wrote, "Vibration is the essence of the universe," he was identifying the essence of creation itself. Every part of anything that is vibrates to its own essence. From the slow, millennial rhythm of our planet and all cosmic bodies, to the rhythm of nature moving through its seasons, and the rhythm of our breath and heart beat, everything has its own way of dancing with the Beloved Source of All.

The more we become aware of our own rhythms, the more we understand how they define us. They rise from our thoughts and emotions, the state of our physical bodies, and the way we respond to the larger rhythms of life and change. There are times we want to dance wildly, or sway to some unheard, peaceful vibration. There are other times we are drawn to deep stillness. We step away from the world and, in doing so, we begin to feel the beat of our own place in creation and possibly in the heart of it all.

The beauty of any symphonic piece of music, such as Beethoven's Seventh Symphony, lures us into a deeper understanding of how that great composer tapped into the rhythms of life. Even when he had lost his sense of hearing, Beethoven never lost his sense of rhythm because he was still breathing. His heart was still beating. The movement and rhythms of nature were still accessible to him. In listening beyond his ability to hear, Beethoven could still compose magnificent music. He was already attuned to the rhythm of his heart and his awareness of life, so his music flowed with power and subtlety to capture the cosmic pulses of all creation.

This chapter invites you to experience the vast spiritual treasure which meditation provides. While one may not consider Beethoven, Paul Simon, or African tribal music great teachers of meditation, they, in their own ways, have helped us realize the rhythms in which we live. When the English poet John Donne wrote, "No man is an island. Each man is a piece of the continent, a part of the mainland," he also helped us realize that how we live is intrinsically connected with everything which exists in our world. From our place in society and culture, where we live and what we do, and even how we consider the place of Spirit in our lives, we have developed our own rhythms of life.

What does all this have to do with meditation? Everything. While some people say they can't meditate because they can't quiet their minds enough, the concepts of rhythm and flow make meditation easier to understand. Beyond the flow of thought, the rhythms of breath and heart beat are more subtle but constant features of existence. Understanding the rhythms of our daily lives, how we respond to them and how they affect us, is key. The dances we do at work, in our family lives, recreation, and even when we are alone, are all important. Yet, times when we seek deeper reality also have a rhythm, and that rhythm is already in us. It is the rhythm which leads to the Heart of Mystery.

How do we get there? Meditation teachers have always advised, "Follow the breath." Even as you say those words to yourself, "Follow the breath," you become aware how the rhythm of those few words carries a deepening quality all its own, distinctive from the mental message they convey. Do you want to learn to meditate, and go beyond meditation into contemplation and stillness? Follow the breath. It is already attuned to the pulse of creation.

How Important Is the Middle Man?

The most direct path to spirituality is one most institutionalized religions ignore. Western religions may do this unconsciously, but they are simply following the left brain approach to everything. These religions thrive on filling every moment of a worship service with sound, sermon and song. The left brain world holds to sayings such as "Idleness is the devil's workshop," "Don't just sit there! Do something!" Left brain religious services encourage constant busyness from readings to rituals, maybe just to show people they are getting their money's worth.

In rare cases some ministers even condemn meditative practice because they lose control over anyone's individual connection with God. They want to be sole interpreters of the Divine Message, and some even tell their congregations that, if personal meditation is practiced, Satan or the Evil One may slip into their thoughts. Congregants, they say, may fall prey to ideas and experiences their particular religion does not condone. They think and teach that meditation is harmful, though the real harm is not to the individual, but to that institutionalized religion which long ago dogmatically chiseled its specific beliefs in stone.

Remember that most Western religions exist in linear thinking. Beginning. Middle. End. Born in sin at the beginning; following a path (their path) through the middle phase, and ending in the goal of heaven after death. They seek control over everything in their particular concept of the God Source as well as how to achieve It. Their ministers and spiritual hierarchy have put up all the signposts leading to "heaven," and they don't approve anyone taking side roads on their own.

Yet, in personal quiet times, where everything else slips away and one is left in stillness, it is very possible to connect with our highest self and what it reveals. Through personal and group meditation, our truest reality can become not only evident but transformative and enlightening.

Personal revelation is the birthright of every human being. We are actually all closet contemplatives. Quiet times alone in nature, or times when our very psyche seems to just get off the merry-go-round for a while and simply be, have given us a taste of The Stillness. To deny our innate yearning to experience that stillness, and the fullness of spirit it may provide, is to deprive ourselves of one of the greatest forms of nourishment. Of course, most spiritual practices can be beneficial. Community prayer and ritual are valuable. Finding true teachers who provide guidance is golden. Weaving our way through the ego's mental gymnastics can always use some help.

The truth is that meditation is not something we need to learn. The desire for it is innate, but that rascal Ego Mind doesn't want us to acknowledge that. In fact, it does everything in its power to keep us from the stillness meditation brings. It wants us to keep taking everything personally and rerunning past events, or fills us with fear about things which might happen someday, or not. It perpetuates what has been called the Monkey Mind, producing endless mental chatter in continuing dialogue with ourselves.

The quantum consciousness in us is beginning to know what we really need. In that aching to return more fully to our Source, the spirit seeks the stillness beyond ego, where we can begin to actually experience a higher connection. No one needs to tell us when our physical body needs food or attention. We don't need a guide to tell us something is beautiful. If beauty really is in the eye of the beholder, how much more profound is the beauty we sense in times alone with our own higher self or with the Divine Beloved!

Meditation provides that — and much more.

Be Still — and Know

The beauty of meditation lies in its simplicity. There are no set rules nor are there rigid demands on protocol or procedures to follow. One refers to the "art" of meditation and that gives a clue to its nature. Just as art presumes creativity from the artist, meditation presumes personal creativity in the way it is practiced. One aspect which becomes paramount, however, is the quieting of the mind. While meditation teachers encourage beginning students to observe the mind as it flits from one distraction to another, deeper meditation moves to a place of peace and inner quietude. In that place surface thoughts fall away, leaving a stillness which reaches to the soul.

Following that need for stillness as a spiritual aspect, several religions have developed words to describe a concept where a certain void, or still point, enables a person to achieve a state beyond thought. Buddhism's *sunyata* is a place of emptiness, often considered a state of no-thing-ness. While some may consider that a void, in reality it is a state where one may experience all that is.

The Hebrew term *einsoph*, considered to be the first emanation from God, carries a similar meaning. It involves a condition of sacred emptiness which calls for participation in the presence of all. The Hebrew alphabet also honors silence and the no-sound of no-thingness of the Divine Mystery to such a degree that its first letter, Aleph, has no sound. In that "no sound" all sound is present. In that no-thing, all of creation is present!

In this "no space" achieved through meditation and contemplation, the Presence of the Source is not only encountered and revealed, but becomes Radiance Itself. Speaking of this state, where higher consciousness experiences That Which Is, David Hawkins writes:

> The Present is silence and conveys a state of peace that is the space in which and by which All Is and has its existence and unfolds. It is infinitely gentle and yet like a rock. With it, all fear disappears. Spiritual joy occurs on a quiet level of inexplicable ecstasy. The experience of time stops; there is no apprehension or regret, no pain or anticipation. The Source of Joy is unending and ever present. With no beginning or ending, there is no loss or grief or desire. Nothing needs to be done as everything is already perfect and complete. … When the mind grows silent, the thought "I am" also disappears and pure awareness shines

forth to illuminate what one is, was, and always will be, beyond all worlds and universes, beyond time, and therefore without beginning or end.

Meditation as Prayer

While some people used to think of meditation only as some strange practice done by monks in far off lands or in lofty, isolated mountain retreats, these new times have made it more common. While the western linear brain still tends to think of it as something strange, people are turning to meditation for a variety of reasons. Because many people have become more health conscious, for example, meditation is now promoted in spas as a stress reliever, as part of one's daily health routine, at martial arts clinics, and many other places, including prisons. Doctors and psychologists are now actively promoting meditation as an integrative therapy for patients with everything from high blood pressure and anxiety to more serious health problems.

In this time of axial awakening more people find meditation practice brings a calming centeredness to their lives. There are even physical benefits of certain sitting meditations when, as the body de-stresses, human organs literally return to the place where they belong in our bodies, and the physical form becomes aligned along its seven main energy centers known as chakras.

Meditation, however, can be so much more. It truly can become a form of prayer, but not in a petitionary sense. Most prayer is couched in the asking mode. "Help me do this." "Make this happen." "Don't let that happen." "Save me from whatever I think I need to be saved from." "Dear Santa, here is my Christmas list. Now let's see how much you can come through for me!"

Higher forms of prayer are closer to the true concept of prayer. Forgiving another, or ourselves, is a form of prayer. Holding compassion for those suffering from war, violence, hatred or personal trauma is the frame of mind and the frame of heart which comes close to the highest attitude anyone can have.

There are even higher prayers when we ask for nothing, but purely lift our spirits in praise to The Transcendent Mystery. The *Kodoish* in Hebrew, translated into the *Sanctus* of Catholicism, and echoed in Sanskrit or African chants, and the hymn, "How Great Thou Art," all offer heartfelt glory into the Radiance of Divine Light. Meditation moves beyond thought or sound to the sacred space where no thing is, and all exists. It is simply being in awe of the deepest truth and the presence of The All.

No Mind

There are those who meditate occasionally and often make comments such as, "I work at meditation, but I don't feel I'm getting anywhere." The very concept of meditation is that one does not *need* to get anywhere. In our essence we are already there! There are no goals in meditation. The ego, of course, will always want results. The ego's linear nature cannot accept the premise that no result is necessary. But, so much for the ego mind!

Eastern cultures have given us the beautiful concept of No Mind as it pertains to meditation practice. Buddhist meditation concentrates on simply observing the mind, watching it flit from thought to thought, concern to concern, desire to desire. After enough flitting, the mind actually begins to quiet down. The ego mind does not like to be observed; it is much more comfortable in the role of observer. In the concept of No Mind, one can move beyond mental constrictions to the stillness where All can be experienced. In that place of No Mind, we can lay down the burden of chattering mentality and rest in the stillness alone.

Where Do We Begin?

While meditation can be undertaken by walking in nature or other physical exercise, the most beneficial meditation requires physical stilling as well as mental quietude. Traditional meditation is practiced by sitting quietly in an alert yet comfortable position. One may choose to keep the eyes open with the gaze lost in a candle's flame or focused on a single object. The eyes, however, are usually closed, but not shut tight. After a period of meditation, the eyes may even open slightly from their own relaxation. That is why statues of the Buddha often show the eyes half open and half closed. It is a sign that stillness has reached that part of the human anatomy.

Quiet music may be played, with some form of aromatherapy or incense present. Some people have an indoor fountain running gently in their place of meditation. If these things work for you, so be it. If they become a distraction, they are not productive. They are also not necessary.

"Be still — and know." The truest form of meditation quiets everything and lets even the mind drift to a place of No Mind which scientists and psychologists identify as the mind in Theta state, the third state of mental awareness. Normal awareness of life's give and take is the Beta state of thought; while when we relax more and "chill out" in a quieter peace, we are in the Alpha State. Theta is that state in which the mind is more open to inner experiencing and is most ready to absorb greater understanding beyond words or concrete ideas. It comes before the fourth state, known as Delta, which usually leads to sleep.

The third state of Theta is most conducive to contemplation, allowing the mind's quiet emptiness, where the Presence is not revealed, but more immanently experienced. When people ask me what I do in meditation, my usual answer is, "I just sit in awe of the Presence and let the Presence be in awe of Itself."

Having a place in one's home which becomes the sacred space for meditation practice is also becoming more common. Establishing special time for this practice helps, too. With children, pets, phones ringing and computers beeping, those who meditate find ways to let other family members know when they are in their "special time" and are not to be disturbed.

Helps and Benefits

Several helps to meditation practice have come from some of the planet's earliest wisdom. Knowledge of how life force bio-energy flows into, through, and out from the body has been gleaned from teachings of Indian mystics and reinforced by intuitives today. This has led to greater emphasis on how to position the body, and parts of the body, in times of prayer or meditation. This enables an individual to achieve the most beneficial flow of *prana*, life force energy, during a meditative session.

Because proper physical position is so helpful, the practice of using a mudra, or arrangement of the hands, is often used. This placement can be beneficial to mind and body since each specific finger carries a certain energy. Even without understanding the flow of life force energy, it is enough to know that the left hand receives and the right hand gives. In placing one's hands into any of the classic meditation mudras, one's meditative practice can be enhanced as the *prana, chi, ki* or life force energy is received and cycled through the human vessel.

The easiest mudra, which helps the life force energy move from the left hand, through the heart, and out the right open palm, is the classic meditation mudra. This is sometimes called the Zen mudra, since it is used while practicing zazen, or sitting meditation. This form of meditation is easy and conducive to many things.

Sitting comfortably in a chair, or on a cushion in a lotus or half lotus position if your body allows it, maintain the torso upright yet not rigid. Concentrate your balance on the lower abdomen, place your hands a bit below your waistline in front of you. Since the left hand receives energy, hold it under the open right hand, with both thumbs barely touching. Your hands are now forming a horizontal oval signifying all things are unified. Place the sides of the little fingers against your abdomen a few inches below the navel. This brings harmony and balance to your center of gravity, and you may wish to begin your meditation concentrating on that area of your body.

This is an almost intuitive hand position for going within. It also allows life force energy to enter through the left hand, flow through the mind, body and heart, and leave the body out the right hand. This mudra produces a closed circuit of energy which can flow through the individual as the meditative process continues. With eyes closed, or resting on a space a few feet in front of you, concentrate on the energy center below your waist or on the Brow Chakra centered and above your eyes. Then let meditation take you where it will.

Another mudra which is commonly used in the Western world is the Prayer Mudra, or Gassho, which Christianity has adopted. With left and right palms pressed gently together in front of the heart, allow the two middle fingers to touch a bit more strongly. This mudra cups the heart energy and transfers it from left to right sides of the body, once again allowing the bio life force energy to flow beautifully through the human form. Performing this mudra as a sign of greeting or respect begins with a slight bow. Then the word "Namaste" is spoken, carrying the message, "The Divine Presence within me bows to and acknowledges the Divine Presence within you."

Another mudra, where the thumb and middle finger touch, is also helpful for circulating life force energy. It is also good to note here that, in early icons, and even some later paintings of Jesus, he is depicted with his hands and fingers positioned in teaching mudras which have come from early Asian spiritual cultures.

Another meditative help used to quiet the mind is called a mantra. This is a word or phrase which one can place in the mind because the mind usually needs something to do. Also, since life force energy follows thought, mental dwelling on one concept can be useful before true stillness leads to contemplation. Words such as "peace" or "love" can be used as well as simple phrases. For a time I used the mantra, "Find the center," as I began meditation. Then I changed to, "Be the Center." When the mind addressed that thought, it became easier to place myself in the center of all that is where my Higher Self could then proceed to its sole purpose, being in the Presence to help radiate the Transcendent Reality.

If you are open to them, there are magnificent mantras in Sanskrit which have come to us from the ancients. *"Om"* is considered to be the actual sound of all existence. *"Om mane padme hum,"* with its vowel sounds more important than its literal meaning, is one of the most powerful mantras in existence. Its literal meaning is: "The All is a precious jewel in the lotus flower which blooms in my heart." The power of its sound and energetic vibration has been used for centuries to center, ground, then lift the human spirit into heights of the Perfect Mystery Itself.

A Trial Run

As an example of a guided meditation, I offer here a few suggestions for beginning a session.

Once situated in a place set aside for this spiritual practice, it is good to prepare by calling in any angels or spirits with which you have a bond. Calling in the Energy of Jesus works well in the western world; in eastern traditions the Buddha Consciousness is welcomed. You may ask for guidance of deceased relatives or friends or from ancestors whose lives paved the way for your own. A saint whose life has touched yours, or a totem for those who practice within the native cultures, can also be invited.

A short offering of your own private prayer may help before you settle into the session, allowing the silence to become stillness. Full but comfortable breathing is a vital part of any meditative practice, and some people actually spend a good part of the session concentrating on breath as all the mental gymnastics of the ego mind slip farther away.

For people who are more visual, picturing a scene may help. I have for years used and taught what I call a Hurricane Meditation. High technology planes can now fly into the eye of a storm to gather data for weather warning systems. Those planes have found that the eye of a tornado or hurricane is perfectly calm. Around the stilled eye of the storm, however, violent winds whip in a funnel motion. If you can picture yourself in the eye of a storm, in the center of that stilled, peaceful air, perhaps sitting on a soft cloud, you can begin your meditation. With your hands in a receptive mudra and using the mantra "Find the center," you can give your mind that task and then simply sit in the stillness. Breathing consciously and focusing on your breath are two keys to peaceful meditation.

When thoughts of people or things begin to arise, see them coming from the whirling wall of wind around your quiet space. Whether they are positive or negative thoughts does not matter. As they come to you, simply acknowledge them, bless them, and let them go back into that whirling wall of wind. As your meditation continues, you will find that storm wall of distraction and concern drifting farther away as your place of peace and stillness widens. It's a good thing.

The benefits of meditation, done daily and at specific times, such as in the morning before starting one's routine, or in the evening before sleep, are many. Physical benefits will accrue; and, even when times are especially hectic or worrisome, peace of mind can be more quickly regained. Meditation is now used in hospitals as therapy and even in sports programs to help athletes focus on their performance.

Most importantly, true meditation can lead to that sacred space where life is not a chore or a burden but where communion and even union with the Highest Reality can be regularly and wonderfully achieved.

Writing in *Grace and Grit*, Ken Wilber helps describe meditation for what it is, not a particular religious ritual, but one of the oldest, most holistic and non-judgmental practices humanity has ever experienced. Some of his words may be harsh, but radical surgery is sometimes the best cure:

> Meditation is spiritual, but not religious. Spiritual has to do with actual experience, not mere beliefs — with God as the Ground of Being, not a cosmic daddy figure — with awakening to one's true Self; not praying for one's little self — with the disciplining of awareness, not preachy and churchy moralisms about drinking and smoking and sexing — with spirit found in everyone's Heart, not anything done in this or that church.

"Meditation," Wilber says, "seeks to go beyond the ego altogether. It asks nothing from God, real or imagined, but rather offers itself up as a sacrifice toward a greater awareness. Meditation then is not so much a part of this or that particular religion, but rather part of the universal spiritual culture of all humankind — an effort to bring awareness to bear on all aspects of life."

Making Meditation Real

Developing a meditation practice is not difficult. All you need is a desire to keep to the discipline needed to set aside time at the beginning and end of each day. Also, as your practice develops, you may find shorter times during the day to return to the center of your life and true being. A few minutes of meditation before a lunch break, for example, help bring more balance to one's day and keep stress from ruining productivity and peace.

It is also good to remember that clear thinking can begin even a short meditation with direction and focus. Two questions can help at the start of any session. One will put your mind into the right state for meditation and possible contemplation. The other question will put your heart and ability to have objective compassion into the right place. The questions?

"Where is my mind?"

"Where is my heart?"

Finding the ability to put your mind into the Divine Mind of Light, where there is no separation or division, but where differences are simply honored, blessed, and released back into the fabric of creation, releases the ego from its need to dominate. Realizing where your heart is, possibly holding anger, blame, fear or judgment, helps calm your emotions and reach a place open to compassion for all, even yourself.

Finding our inner ability to love and reach out to others in true compassion also defeats the ego. It scoops up all of creation with its different cultures, races, spiritual paths, and ideologies, and holds them all in the Source Heart of Creation.

Meditation is not some mysterious practice. Going into stillness is the basis of all spirituality. It reaches beyond any religious practice and rises beyond dogma or religious teaching. Meditation is the direct communication between all of us, as part of creation, with the Source of Creation Itself. When Jesus taught, "The kingdom of Heaven is within you," he was pointing us in the direction of inner knowing and inner union with our Source. What he referred to as the *Basileia*, the true kingdom, is more easily accessed through simple meditation which then gives us direction for being and living in that kingdom within.

For those who have religious beliefs, they can easily bring them into their meditation practice. For those who have left certain religious practices behind, meditation brings the one thing we all seek into greater focus. "What is truth?" Pilate asked, and, in his silence, Jesus gave the perfect answer. Go into the silence and understand. As the Zen saying teaches, "Be still, and understand what you already know."

What is the rhythm which leads us there? Follow the breath. Follow the breath.

Meditation provides access to stillness where answers, truth, beauty, and completion are found. To deprive ourselves of its benefits is to invite spiritual anemia and spiritual deprivation.

It is also good to realize that, as your own meditation practice develops, you will probably move from one level to another without really trying. Once the mind and body become accustomed to quiet times of reflection and renewal, the spirit lures us on, always coaxing us into deeper levels of thought, then No Thought, then moving into the gentleness of directly experiencing the All That Is.

Contemplation and Beyond

While our practice may begin with visualized or group meditations, continuing these sessions over time will lead to many things. Most meditation guides suggest observing your thoughts and letting them bring greater realizations. There does come a time, however, when those thoughts drift away. Then our observations become more restful, gently forgiving and sometimes even amusing as we witness our own humanity through the lens of higher consciousness.

In those times when we no longer ask for, look for or expect anything, we begin to experience a type of knowing which is transmitted to us from what Hawkins calls "The Silent Field." As we gradually enter that state of higher grace, it is best to simply remain in the Spirit of Grace. It is there that we experience the profound stillness which is vibrantly alive with all knowledge, all being, all love, and all peace. To simply be, completely beyond any fear or concern or desire, lost in the Infinite Energy Field of Silence, becomes a state of reflective contemplation.

This is the place where the inner voice begins to make itself known, the place of experiencing a fullness so deep we can never truly fathom it. This is the top of the mountain. This is the place of surrender, the realization that no more sacrifice is necessary. This is The Knowing which, in its own time, will demand to be made manifest. This is darkness and light become Radiance, and a sense of being lost and found over and over again in a Beyond which never ends. It's beautiful. Terrifying at times, but incredibly beautiful. Though we can't stay there in human form, it's an incredible place to visit. It is, quite obviously, a place very far beyond words...

Dynamic Stillness and Response

From that stillness, or any other peace and perspective which meditation brings, there is always a need to respond. Just as a life in spirit demands surrender in its highest form, meditation also demands that we take what is treasure and spill it out over all we meet. Spirituality without service quickly becomes empty and self-centered. It is in giving to others, being what they need when they need it, and being gone when they don't need it, that we do the best thing love suggests. We share ourselves gladly and offer thanks that we are able to give at all.

Again, I turn to the words of Father Diarmuid O'Murchu, who is a Catholic priest, member of a religious order, and a teacher of spirit and action. Calling each of us to meet this new time with courage, compassion and basic human intelligence, he writes in *Evolutionary Faith*, "It is time to embrace the awakening consciousness of our time, inviting us to reclaim the ancient mystical wisdom of the one earth and the one universe. A new universality characterizes our time. It is a cultural and spiritual breakthrough inaugurating new evolutionary thresholds inviting us humans to respond in a much more enlightened, creative, and cooperative mode."

In dynamic stillness, we finally realize what we really are and begin to tap the inner knowing of what the Divine Mystery really is. Everything else we do depends on our agreeing to reach for that understanding, and meditation is one of the surest ways of finding it.

RIGHT BRAIN CHAPTER REVIEW

After Meditation

Once, beyond the edge of things remembered in the mist,
I slipped between two worlds I had never known before.
A golden door flung open and I was in a rainbow of pearlescent hues
which danced themselves to silver —
then to light beyond all colors I have seen.
Chantings from the universes hummed through tunnels
made of silence and the sound of solitude —
Where all the One became vibration
Pulsing from the Birth Star of what is yet to be revealed.

All of it began to call to me through strings of cosmic filaments,
Insisting my resistance fall, as all became the multitude —
gathered into one tiny seed of pearl.

231

All the worlds of evermore became a new gate of deeper knowing,
  sacred union as that portal held no entrance and no exit
  until all that is became that one single pearl —
  and I loved the joy of simply being lost in it!

Our love began to glow to brilliant iridescence,
And we met there in such exquisite shining
That there could no longer possibly be two —
  but only One.
And we spun ourselves like dervishes,
  content to be the energy of manifesting suns
  and stars which signal through fields of ebony
  that all of Light is home.
Night became a tapestry of dark matter
  proving all creation's radiance
  can meet within the essence of one simple pearl.

Our spiral reached a great embrace of what is only Now
  where no space is filled with all —
Then focused to the singular reality of the One, only Truth
  which always is, and never need become.

And it was us, my Love! It is us!
The seed and the gem and the Essence contained
  in the beauty of one, simple pearl!
Ah, Beloved! Ah, the joy of it!

CHAPTER THIRTEEN

FEMINISM IN A DUALISTIC WORLD

Opening the Heart of Humanity

A spirituality that lacks heart lacks quality of life...
What feminist spirituality brings to humankind is the power
of nonviolence and the effectiveness of empowerment.

- Joan Chittister

O ne of the most enigmatic steps in the human dance is the concept of duality. From ancient times, wise women and men have championed the idea of oneness, often identifying the Highest Source as One, or the Highest, Perfect Mind. Yet there is, epitomized in the concept of Trinity, acknowledgement of individual energies. As the king would have said in *The King and I*, "Is a puzzlement!"

On this earth plane there are visible opposites. A woman is not a man. What is loving is not hateful. To be courageous is to conquer fear. Experiencing winter in Minnesota is not the same as February in Florida. There are all kinds of opposites, but the most common to nature is the difference between the male and female of any species.

Beyond physical differences, there also lie the stereotypical characteristics of each sex.

Following the patriarchal thought thrust upon us for the past
several thousand years, men are supposed to be superior and strong,
always poised in a "take charge" mode. Women, on the other hand,
have been labeled the "weaker sex," best suited to following. Men make
good warriors who are capable of inflicting harsh punishment; women
tend to be peacemakers, less inclined to do battle, and more apt to
give calm consideration to any conflicting situation. Men are more
likely the judges, strong at administering justice. Women are more
about mercy, and easily given to compassion. Men are all about logic.
Women? Tapping into another show tune from *The Sound of Music,*
"How do you catch a cloud and pin it down?"

All stereotypes aside, however, there is still the truth that male and
female are uniquely different, from their physicality to more subtle
differences in the way they approach life. Study of those differences
has become part of society's attempt to better understand the human
dynamic. It is even part of discussing ideas about God or the actual
Divine Dynamic.

As we go deeper into this Axial Age, new understanding about
the duality of masculine and feminine energies is being considered.
This has nothing do to with sexism, but more with which energies are
predominant in the brain. Moving away from the overbearing patriarchal mentality of the last several thousand years, this new age is
finally righting many long-standing wrongs. For example, we are now
witnessing severe cracks in the concept of dominance over equality
and belief that hierarchy is necessary to preserve world order.

Accepting greed and war for the powerful, while leaving the "less
important" or marginalized members of society to their own sad state,
is now seen for what it always has been, wrong in the eyes of humanity
and wrong in the eyes of God.

One of the clearest changes of attitude, in this new time, is the emergence of a more feminine philosophy based on peace rather than power, and based on equal importance of all. While aggression and intolerance still continue, the more compassionate, creative depth of feminine energy is emerging. There are more people who still live with war's reality but who really want an end to death and destruction, urging diplomacy instead. In reality, the idea of extensive dualism, which was imposed by men in the patriarchal age, is crumbling beneath the burden of masculine righteousness.

There are signs of this changing dynamic. While, in the past, most parental duties were left to the mother since the male breadwinner felt his job was finished by bringing home a paycheck, things are different on the home front, too. More marriages embrace the sharing of parental responsibilities and, in at least some countries, greater acceptance of equality between the sexes is growing. Women assuming leadership roles may still be a problem for some dyed in the wool patriarchs, but, as Hillary Clinton noted recently, there are a lot more cracks in that proverbial glass ceiling!

No More 'When in Rome'

As more compassionate and all-inclusive feminine energy is present in the world, there is no doubt it is also emerging in many forms of ministry and spiritual awakening. For example, some Christian denominations and Judaism now allow women priests and rabbis. It is disheartening, however, to witness the inquisitional study of American communities of religious sisters which has now begun. Initiated by the Vatican in Rome, the results of these studies, and future actions taken by male church superiors, remain to be seen. We have reached an era, however, where delay of equal rights within religious ministries, and the demanding of continued subservience of women religious to male dominated hierarchies, will no longer be tolerated. Women religious in America have become too strong, too creative, too spiritually solid, and too intent on living the gift of their vocations in manners which make a real difference in the lives of the people of God. Feminine energies are already changing the rest of the world. No doubt they will not stop knocking on the Vatican gates in Rome.

The Brain Begins to Understand

As the phenomenon of rising feminine energy continues on a global scale, Dr. David Hawkins has again contributed to greater understanding of tendencies on the left and right sides of the brain. Because of changes occurring in this Axial Age, he finds, the actual physical brain is changing. We still have, within our occipital lobe at the lower back of our head, the reptilian brain, which is one of the first cognizant tools which helped humanity rise from the ooze. That is the area of subconscious mind, and it is extremely important as we move forward with intelligence and inner knowledge.

What Dr. Hawkins describes in his writings and lectures now, however, is that more energy is being used by the right brain which holds a more feminine, peace-loving attitude toward the act of existing. The left brain, responsible for the patriarchal "me man, you woman" attitude of the last several thousand years is still here, but it is now forced to interact more strongly with the emerging right brain energy of stillness, creativity, and acceptance of differences. Dr. Hawkins notes that, in the masculine dominated brain, emotions move faster and are more explosive and quick tempered. As feminine consciousness becomes more pronounced, however, that attitude of act first and think later is giving way to greater patience and even-temperedness.

Hawkins also sees the development of an etheric brain whose energy impacts the human brain, but which exists more energetically than physically in each individual. It is this etheric brain which adds to the development of humankind's mentality, giving even greater access to the feminine dynamic. In this new approach to thinking, emotions are much slower, resulting in greater tolerance and acceptance of people.

The Energy of "God"

Key point: The Energy of the God Source is One. There is no duality in the Source; it is absolute and non-dualistic. There is no separate masculine or feminine energy in The Source. What we call God is One. Period!

It is we humans who, in trying to understand the Divine Mystery, have used narrow human thought to define God the same way we define ourselves, including male or female. In its essence, there is no such distinction in the God Source. It is we who have decided the masculine, left brain characteristics of power and judgment must be part of God, as well as the right brain characteristics of patience, compassion and holding of mystery we think of as more feminine.

There is no duality in the God Source or in the God Source Energy. There are not two. There is only the unity of One.

Today, more attention is being paid to the concept of the Divine Feminine which coincides with the emergence of right brain thinking. Discovery of early writings, including the Dead Sea Scrolls and ancient works found in Nag Hammadi, Egypt, have focused new light on the importance of early women in roles of leadership, spirituality and authorship. From study of the short text, "The Thunder, Perfect Mind," written by an early woman author — to extensive discussion of the role of Mary of Magdala as an apostle, companion, and equal partner of Jesus, the power and spirituality of early women is greatly influencing thought today. This is also leading to greater respect and credibility of today's women leaders as well as a deeper understanding of how women and men can create more balanced, positive partnerships in all areas of society.

The Age of Fading Duality

As the feminine aspect of Creation Energy is emerging, the shifting of the pendulum is not always easy for some to embrace. We are entering a new time. Some of our great institutions are either going to move into this new energy and exciting new paradigm of thought or fade away like any old paradigm should. Another example from the Catholic Church paradigm is its intransigence in refusing women's ordination to priesthood. It boils down to the fact that, when the priest stands over the Host at the moment of consecration in the Mass, it is believed he stands in place of Jesus who said at the Last or Seder Supper, "This is my body."

If the hierarchy of the Catholic Church will not allow a woman to stand at an altar and say the words of consecration, "This is my body" simply because she has different physical plumbing, one wonders if this is what the Great Christos really intended. There are numerous holy women who would serve that church well as full ministers, especially in this time when fewer priests are being ordained. If the old patriarchal hierarchy of Catholicism insists on retaining that hard line of "For Men Only" as part of its dogma, that dogma invites the risk of being run over by its own karma.

The people of God who, by the way, are all the people, need to be guided well into greater consciousness of The Divine Mystery. Any person or religious institution which holds itself up as a true guide into that God Consciousness must either walk the talk of non-duality and Oneness in God or get out of the way.

God is not an old man in the sky. God is not an old woman in the sky, either. What we call God is even more than the Ground of All

Being. The Divine Source is the Eternal Energy of Essence behind the Big Bang and all of energy itself. The Divine Feminine is not a being or even a state of being. It is a human term to identify a characteristic of the One — which is absolute compassion, absolute quantum potentiality, and absolute fullness.

Where We Have Been Is Not Where We Are

Going back through history, ancient cultures of predominant feminine energy considered the Ultimate Source of creation as maternal and, humanly speaking, a Goddess. With the dawning of another Axial Age several thousand years ago, however, the matriarchal society faded and masculine energy emerged. With that shift in consciousness, not only were the feminine aspects of the God Source denigrated, but all women were put in subservient roles and demeaned as property and second class beings. They became objects of sexual pleasure and breeders with no authority in determining societal patterns. The slogan, "It's a man's world," was true then and is still very prominent today. Women are still encouraged to "stand by your man" and suffer the consequences if they don't, but the times are changing!

Consider the fact that whether we are in male or female form, we all carry masculine and feminine energy. As manifestations of the Great Creation, we are indeed made in Its "image and likeness." Earlier religions, some of which are still active, have identified feminine characteristics of The Great Source. While more commonly using the masculine identity Adonai, for example, Judaism still uses the concept of Shekinah, which suggests the feminine face of God. Hinduism is replete with feminine figures. Most embody the more compassionate sides of higher consciousness but the energy of Shiva is known as a destructive energy which destroys evil and darkness, usually in one's own self. In human lore, the goddess Kali, for example, is awesome in her destructive power. Her main task, however, is driving away the negative characteristics of humankind.

The goddess Sophia is the Fount of Wisdom which gives us, from the Greek word *philos*, denoting a kind of love — *Philo Sophia*, the words for love and wisdom. Thus, philosophy is a love of wisdom. Diana, the Huntress, is not a figure who hunts for the sporting joy of killing, but hunts, instead to provide for her children and bring nourishment to the world. Kuan Yin is the Chinese embodiment of the earlier Tibetan figure Avalokiteshvara, the Energy of Divine Compassion. It is interesting to note that earlier images of Kuan Yin were seen as masculine. Although now you can buy a very feminine statue of Kwan Yin, older statues of this figure are androgynous — with both male and female characteristics. It is a sign that, even in much earlier times, there was enough wisdom in the world to realize the great Source Mystery carries both masculine and feminine energies, something we have truly lost in this dying patriarchal age.

The New Spirituality of Feminine Energy

With the rise of feminine energy, it is important to understand there is no sexism involved in this new approach to living. With all people carrying both feminine and masculine energies within them, the more gentle approach to life can be manifested by many men as well as women. Much of this has happened on its own because of humanity's rising consciousness. Whereas people before blindly accepted the decisions of their national and spiritual leaders, the new awareness, based on equality and respect for all in a feminine mode of thought, is changing things. From thousands marching in the streets of Iran, questioning decisions made by their national and spiritual hierarchy, to greater respect for other belief systems, more people are walking away from authoritarian dictates of leaders who say theirs is the only way forward.

Considering patriarchy and feminism as two world views, the Catholic nun and author Joan Chittister defines feminism as a "consciousness of the equality of differences." Seeing feminism as stressing awareness of the forgotten side of society, she states, "Feminism critiques a culture built on power for some and powerlessness for most. To the feminist, people are not up or down, disposable or valuable, higher or lower than others. ... Feminism frees everyone to think broader thoughts."

A powerful advocate for feminism and its more heart-based priorities, Chittister realizes the great implications a world living the philosophy of feminism would bring. Speaking at the CTA Conference in 1997, she stated:

> Those concepts would change domestic legislation and foreign policy, theology and corporate life, families and churches. The world would begin to operate on a spirituality of compassion, of empowerment, of dialogue, of community, of openness, of non-violence, of feeling as well as reason, of circles rather then pyramids, of hearts of flesh — instead of hearts of stone. Those concepts would turn the world around us upside down. They are the holy making ideas for our time.

As the new order of living mercifully emerges, the concept of war will become an outmoded, barbaric memory of lesser individuals. If serious conflicts of ideology arise, they will be solved not through arrogant vengeance and murder, but through efforts to understand, compromise, and let real truth emerge.

True, Jesus told of the good shepherd who, in times of crisis, chose to lay down his life for his sheep. And in history that has been done. The man Jesus sacrificed his life for the greater knowledge his death would bring. Socrates drank poison hemlock rather than renounce what he knew to be truth. In these cases, it was the leader who opted for his own personal immolation for the good of the whole. Socrates did not ask his young men and women followers to die for his cause. Neither did Jesus. World leaders in the new way of living will not ask others to kill and be killed for what they consider important. They may, as did Martin Luther King Jr., be willing to risk their own death for greater consciousness to prevail. But they *themselves* will stand in the breach, not their well-intentioned surrogates. The patriarchal age put great value on the need for the utmost sacrifice, the blood sacrifice, but that will no longer be needed.

The feminine energy now coming into prominence can thrive beautifully without self immolation or competition. Women are gatherers who find no threat in others' ways of living. They have no need to be crowned "Queen of the Mountain." They welcome community and delight in others' happiness. While women in the corporate world often need to show a competitive, tough-minded spirit in order to advance, they still bring a more caring, sensitive mindset to their work. Feminine energy favors peace and healing. It needs to nurture. The feminine ego prides itself on making a positive difference.

Today's women have inherited a legacy of incredible strength from all women who have gone before. From their strong spiritual roots in African religions and belief systems, through the matriarchal power of healing and holiness, African women of today remain the strength of their society. For African American women, many whose roots trace back to days of bondage and slavery, the needs for familial stability and energy to rise above sexism and racism have resulted in powerful strength and undefeatable wholeness. Women of native cultures and the Orient retain their strength of spirit holding the wisdom of those who have gone before. The role of women in Muslim nations continues to demand sisterly support from all corners of the globe.

Yet, in all cultures, as women's strength holds much of the human fabric together, women also need solitude and time to hold the energy. Anne Morrow Lindbergh's timeless classic on woman's identity, *Gift from The Sea*, still reminds us of woman's power to embrace all, yet nourish herself in necessary times of solitude. She wrote:

> Actually these are the most important times of one's life — when one is alone. Certain springs are tapped only when we are alone. The artist knows he must be alone to create; the writer to work out thoughts; the musician to compose, the saint to pray. But women need solitude in order to find again the true essence of themselves, that firm strand which will be the indispensable center of a whole web of human relationships. She must find that inner stillness which Charles Morgan describes as 'the stilling of the soul within the activities of the mind and body so that it might be still — as the axis of a revolving wheel is still.

I cannot help but remember Morrow Lindbergh's poem *Bare Tree* which has been my favorite poem since I first read it as a young woman. Likening herself to a tree, blossoming with branches and flowers in times of her youth, Morrow Lindbergh traces the tree's life to its later years when all those flowers have gone away. The last two lines of that poem powerfully portray the state of any woman who has moved down the quiet hall of years until she can say, as Morrow Lindbergh wrote:

> Blow through me, life, pared down at last to bone.
> So fragile, and so fearless have I grown.

I am also fond of Joyce Borysenko's words in *A Woman's Journey To God*:

Women who love God as Father, those who love God as Mother, and others who couldn't give a hoot about God's theoretical gender or existence find themselves sisters on the journey. Beyond our religion or lack of it, beyond the warm fuzzies or cold scars that ideas about God have planted in our minds, the unmistakable perfume of divine belonging envelops us as we come together as friends.

Coming together as religious friends in religious contexts requires respect for forms of worship different than our own. These differences keep heart and mind open. They are soul food. If we are to find a path of our own, it helps to know and appreciate the paths of others. To realize that the household of God is indeed big enough for all gives everyone room to live and grow. The idea that there is only one right way home, one path for all, creates judgment and separation. Women's spirituality is about connection.

If a more feminist and compassionate style of living is changing today's global consciousness, it is also bringing women's true spirituality and gentle strength to a new position of global action through peaceful wholeness. It is bringing those words from the prophet Ezekiel, through Joan Chittister, into the place of a new heart and a new spirit, powered by the compassion of a heart of flesh.

The New Society

Are we saying our species will return to another matriarchal society after all these thousands of years? No. The fact of consciousness rising is effecting a new type of society never known before. Instead of the pendulum swinging back to the female energy base, the old dualism of ego will take time to fade but it will begin to disappear. A chief characteristic of that new world will be perfect balance between the feminine and masculine energies. Consider these words of Gloria Steinem, writing in *The Fabric of the Future*:

> We've convinced ourselves and a majority of the country that women can do what men can do. Now, we have to convince the majority of the country that men can do what women can do. If we don't, the double burden of working inside and outside the home — always a reality for poor women, and now for middle class women, too — will continue to be a problem shared by most American women nationwide. Let's face it: until men are fully equal inside the home, women can never be equal outside it.
>
> This humanization of men has even more importance in the long term. Children who grow up seeing nurturing men (and women) as well as achieving women (and men) will no longer have to divide their human qualities into "masculine" and "feminine." Gender will no longer be the dominant/passive model that is then followed by race and class.

And, in perfect step with that balance of feminine and masculine energies, the new world of higher consciousness will feature peace, not power. It will, since we as a species are growing more into the image of Creation's Source, be a world of balancing and centering the very energies of the divine as well. That is the Wholeness which is the essence of pure consciousness.

We are already seeing signs of its happening. There are more and more men who bring great sensitivity into their work and lives, and there are more women who, once they have touched their spiritual reality, are leaving subservient "Me man, you woman" relationships. After all these years of nurturing others, modern woman has finally learned to nurture herself. More women are finding strength to create their own new identities. Their own feminine energies are demanding greater realization, and the concept of "help-mate" pales next to the true word of balance — "partner."

The beauty of balanced relationships will also transfer to understanding and honoring among nations until we reach the point of world community. War and aggression must become obsolete, replaced with a sense of global sisterhood and brotherhood. In the true balance of feminine and masculine energies, peace will become the reality it needs to be.

And on a spiritual level, we will be able to bring forth the greater Sophia, the higher wisdom of the Christ, the *Sophia Christou* which J.J. and Desiree Hurtak describe in their commentary on *The Gospel of Mary* (Magdalene). If Sophia was considered to be an emanation from silence and depth by some early Christians, the rising feminine spirituality now awakening will bring greater peace, the treasure of wisdom, and the promise of new hope for our needy world.

RIGHT BRAIN CHAPTER REVIEW

I Am the Altar

I stand within the altar of myself —
In deep humility resolving and intending to be
The fullest Christ I may, in this lifetime, on this planet,
*   possibly become.*

I hurl the manifesting masculine energy within me
And my soft, creative patience of possibility
*   into the Essence of the Source,*
Calling for grace and courage and knowledge in greater Light.
I seek the emptiness of ego, bowing to the fullness
*   Of Truth Which Always Is.*

I put my body in the breach
And my soul within the Godhead,
My mind within the generous wisdom of divinity
And my heart in true alignment,
      sweetly centered in the balance of compassion
      which is the only true heart of the only True Beloved.

I honor and I praise the One Eternal Source
Kodoish — Kodoish — Kodoish!
Holy — Holy — Holy!
And I place myself in that embrace of
      Mother Father God —
      The One that is not two.
I hold my spirit up into the greatest Light
Intending vision of the Whole
And I will the resolution of all vestiges of duality
      finally brought to sacred union in the One.

For I am Yours as You are mine.
And so it shall be done.
And so We Are.
And so it eternally is!

CHAPTER FOURTEEN

THE MANY SPLENDORS OF LOVE

Forgiveness Is the Light of the World

Love is letting go of fear.
- The Course in Miracles

The saying, "Love makes the world go around" is correct, yet inadequate. Love not only makes this world go around. When we consider the Prime Source of All That Is, it is that love which makes and sustains universe upon universe and the entire being and non-being of creation.

The problem today is that the word "love" has become a mere plus sign for any number of conditions. In its weakest sense we say, "I love your new car," "I love your new hairdo," "I love your house," and "Oh, by the way, I love you!" In reality, "love" is used to simply show approval and is much closer to the meaning of "like."

There are people who love the outdoors. They go into nature to camp and hike as often as possible. There are people who love mountains. Some love the sea while others love the quiet mystery and magic of the desert. Any love of that kind does draw people closer to Gaia, this mother earth which sustains and nurtures us and that's a good thing.

The world, however, contains some people whose love for power and wealth, often at any price, still reflects the selfish attitudes which are becoming archaic dinosaurs in the new world order. There are those who even justify violation and destruction of people and things in the name of God. These actions, however, are merely a shadow side, if there can be a real shadow side, of this generic word "love." In reality, they are mere aberrations of the one Truth which does make all the worlds go around.

A Glimpse at Love Beyond Ego

Real love, the wisdom of Spirit tells us, is letting go of fear. From wisdom of the ancients to teachings of spiritual masters today, real love is the only love which abides within Truth. Real love has the courage of willingness not to always know, but to surrender through mystical strength into the very depths of mystery. Real love is caring so deeply it knows it must share, while never considering payment in return.

Surpassing any human need to cling, real love goes beyond attachment to any thing or any one which only the ego desires. Real love lives within the gift of generosity. It knows the art of letting go so genuine affection may flow, and it is comfortable in surrender through strength, confidence led to compassion, and joyful peace in the knowledge that everything is already perfect as it is.

In this form of honest love, there is only one Beloved. The only real love stems from It and our participation in It through our own mode of living spirituality. The way we feel and the way we act depend on this level of our understanding. It lies in our realization that we as a species, and we as a planet and star system, are perfectly one in Divine Creation.

In that form of love we are never in the command mode of directing and ordering our lives through mere ego desire. Instead, we live humbly in the receiving mode as gratitude becomes one of the many forms of love and one of the purest forms of prayer. It also forgives us in our forgiving and brings us closer to wholeness because of its ability to heal.

The Different Levels of Love

Before we speak more about the highest form of love, however, it is best to consider its development in our lives and in society. Of course we are born and go to our graves with one challenge, that of taming the ego. We naturally bring a strong ego into everything we do and, the one thing ego and emotion have helped us develop is passion. This is the ability to grow into a deep caring for any thing or any one which makes this life journey worthwhile.

It has long been said we need some reason to get out of bed in the morning, and the thing which most gets us out of bed is the depth of passion we bring to various aspects of our lives. While the world in today's semantics sees passion as a thing which drives some people into bed to experience the delights of physical and sexual passion, it is the depth of living that feeds us on so many levels which calls up true passion.

What is passion? Dictionaries can give us their definitions, yet the old advice — be still and know — always holds true. We need no guru, priest, minister or spiritual mentor to tell us what to care about deeply. Passion develops innately in our youth or we discover it along some side road of life. Sometimes that passion stays with us; sometimes it carries us along for a while, then we grow away from it when other demands for love, attention and time lure us in other directions. The truth is that passion is a heightened form of love which encourages action and sometimes even sacrifice.

If love truly does come with passion, that passion itself can be used or misused in many ways. The ancient Greeks, considering love, defined three different aspects of it. The lowest level is *eros*, a physical love, which, in human intimacy, can become self-fulfilling and satisfying. Done on the highest levels, it can actually reach a symbolic union of the feminine and masculine aspects of the Source. A study of the Tantra can lend much light on that type of physical union, though there is much more than sex involved in Tantric philosophy. But physical union is physical union. Erotic love is primarily physical.

To go into a higher state of love, even in an intimate relationship, needs more than the simple union of bodies. Unless two partners can find a higher level of intimacy beyond sex, that relationship is bound to fail. Human relationships may last or not, but they always do change because they are not the ultimate reality. We humans can "fall in love" and "fall out of love" with incredible ease, so that thing we call love in its deepest meaning can never be found on the purely physical level. Any love built merely on the roller coaster of human emotion and physical intimacy cannot survive. There must be more than that between the human body and the Source of Creation.

Knowing this, the Greeks considered a higher level of love — *philos*. This is a love of the mind where two people or many people share the same interests and enjoy each other's personal appreciation of that thing. Philharmonic means love of music; philanthropy means love of mankind; Philadelphia actually means love of the city and, many city dwellers, though they live in different parts of the world, can, in the Greek way, be called philadelphians. They love living in the city and put up with its chaos and stress just to be part of that vibrant surging and reaching of masses of people joined in the busyness of life. Cities carry a special pulse of energy and, for some, that pulse becomes a wonderful resonance to the beat of their own lives.

The love of most friendships falls within the category of *philos*, yet, as we change, those relationships may also change or end. As life proceeds through different stages, we often meet people who relate to us more at our current level of interest or development than those who shared with us when we were younger. The old saying rings true that we are meant to know some people for a season and very few for a lifetime. It is also true that we are graced with the friendship of some only when we have reached the development of our own lives which allows us to truly share with and appreciate them.

The Greeks' third level of love — *agapos* — is a bond so deep that two people can actually share soul to soul and spirit to spirit. In this level of love the lesser aspects of human relationship may be present or not. This is the kind of love where the duality of attachment falls away to greater union within the majesty of Truth — realized.

This term *agapos* also reaches its highest definition as a name for union with the Divine Mystery. It could be used to describe the experience when we feel our very essence, our soul, is communing with the God Soul Itself. Actually, since our very existence is already part of and not separated from that God Soul, *agapos* may just be a good word to describe our finally becoming aware of that.

There is an old saying, "Tell me who your friends are, and I'll tell you what you're like." In the same sense, we could say, "Tell me what your true loves are as you move through life, and I will tell you what you are." Where your passion lies deepest is the height of any love you hold. The only true relationship is not physical or mental, but within the basic human psyche. It is rooted in one's spiritual awareness and willingness to share. The only real love is the love of union between ourselves and the Divine Heart which cries out to us from within our own hearts. There is only one Beloved.

Passion and Unconditional Love

In charting consciousness, David Hawkins has found that the purring of a cat and the wagging of a dog's tail rate at a consciousness level of 500. The purring of a cat named Skoshi, and the act of a dog named Maggie wagging her tail, signal the height of unconditional love! It is the level of pure, total love, enjoying the act of loving and being loved, with no hidden agenda. What a concept!

While some may say absolute unconditional love is impossible for self-centered humans, it is still a great goal to set for ourselves as we learn to keep the ego mind in as much control as possible. I've often wondered why Jesus' painful journey through the streets of Jerusalem to the cross on Golgotha is called "The Passion." The only way I can accept that term is to consider that, in allowing himself to endure the torment he suffered, Jesus was really exhibiting the highest form of passion — unconditional love within the full God Consciousness which he held. Pure love, exquisitely given, with nothing asked for in return.

Yet, as we grow older, we can realize the world's definition of love may not be real love at all. Loving others who love us is icing on the cake. But the love that will save the world and bring peace to this beautiful planet comes closer to what we might call humble compassion. That is the realization that we are individuals collectively working our own ways back to Our Source. We are merely players in our time on the stage. We are part of the human drama which portrays the development of global love or our species' failure to achieve it.

Honoring, as a son or daughter of the Divine Creation anyone who pushes our buttons, causes us pain or any kind of sadness, comes closer to what true love really is. Perhaps Charles Schultz saw humanity's foibles when Lucy told Charlie Brown, "I love mankind. It's people I can't stand!" The love which will save the world has nothing to do with individual preferences, self-gratification, or even national honor. Instead, it is loving with acceptance and compassion and, at least, making an attempt to understand our partner travelers through the cosmos. We may want to judge some of their actions as harmful. We may even feel some people closest to us still have a long way to go! But it's good to hold the idea that most people, in their own ways, are still trying to get it right.

We are called to love within the Divine Mind. We are called to be witnesses of compassionate caring and nonjudgmental acceptance. When we see those who do wrong, who rape the planet or make war on another person or another country, we have a right to our opinion. But in our heart of hearts, the judgment is never ours. All we can do is hold those people in love, already imagining them as healed individuals who respect all life as equal within creation.

That is a tall order and we cannot do it alone. The only way an individual can love with the divine heart is to be part of that Heart. That may be a lifetime's work but we need to get on with it. As the planet keeps spinning through time, it must be done. Otherwise our egos, judgments and selfish arrogance will cause the world's destruction.

No government or law can teach us that. No religious dogma or fear of eternal torment can teach us that. Jesus came the closest in his version of what we have come to know as the Golden Rule, "Love one another as I have loved you," "Do unto others as you would have them do unto you."

More war will never end war. Only the majority of people wanting peace will eventually make war an obsolete emanation of lesser minds. We are all one in the Source which continues creation moment by moment. "Behold, I make all things new." Perhaps it's time for us to love our collective self as we deserve since we, too, are the seed of that Source — and nothing less.

Forgiveness

One of the greatest challenges our human species has imposed on itself is the ego-driven phenomenon of pain and suffering. Much of the psychological baggage we carry involves different hurts we have experienced in the past, some from ourselves, and many more, we think, from others. Every crevice of our brains may carry deep pain from times others have betrayed us, misused us or, in any number of ways, caused us suffering. In our minds, they violated our personal agenda for happiness and, even though we think we have buried the hatchet with most of them, we remain very aware of where those hatchets are buried! We even trace the map of where those hatchets lie over and over again in our memories, reinforcing the pain which often leads beyond thought to physical dis-ease.

Living on the level of higher love is achieved through the grace of being able to forgive. If the sacred heart of Divine Love is pulsing within us, we can move beyond the cloud of supposed suffering — to the realization that all people are merely following their own paths. "Creator, forgive them. They know not what they do."

Even the greatest challenges given to us by individuals or nations soften when we realize those actions are opportunities for our greater growth. Then, jealousy, control, possessiveness, and anger fade through their own weak, ego-driven uselessness. Forgiveness is critical to the act of healing suffering we received from others as well as pain we have imposed upon ourselves. *The Course in Miracles* mentions forgiveness as a high form of witnessing divine love. In the lesson, "Forgiveness is my function as the Light of the World," we are told:

> It is your forgiveness that will bring the world of darkness to the light. It is your forgiveness that lets you recognize the light in which you see. Forgiveness is the demonstration that you are the light of the world. Through your forgiveness does the truth about yourself return to your memory. Therefore, in your forgiveness lies your salvation. Illusions about yourself and the world are one. That is why all forgiveness is a gift to yourself. Your goal is to find out who you are. Having denied your Identity by attack-

ing creation and its Creator, now you are living to remember the truth where this attack must be replaced by forgiveness, so that thoughts of life may replace thoughts of death.

Can you live in the presence of Divine Light? Can you live with the realization that you are Divine Love present on the planet?

Look to your ability to forgive and bless each supposed infraction as a challenge to be used for learning. Then let it go. Can you do that? Is your level of love high enough to really forgive and let the past and its pain go away? If we want to move beyond the mire of our own self stuff, we must do it. Forgiveness is one of the greatest forms of love we can give to ourselves and others. It is also one of the most freeing acts we can give to our own spirits.

True Love

Understand what you already know. All else is illusion. Our only true reality is that we are part of the Source. In connection with the I AM Mind and the I AM Heart of Love, all things are possible. All fullness is a reality we merely need to recognize and embrace.

Those great words did come down to us, "Be still, and know I AM." *EHYEH ASHER EHYEH.* I AM. I AM is our Source, our Reality and the Fullest Depth of our love. By reminding ourselves of that each day through stillness and contemplation, we can move through life with grace and strength. Empowered by our place within Love as daughters and sons of the Divine Energy, we can understand what the soul in us already knows. Can you accept that your call to live love is the one task and true joy of your life?

The power of your intention, the degree of your willingness to be all of what you really are carries your answer. It's a goal, and any goal is reached by beginning. So let's be on our way!

RIGHT BRAIN CHAPTER REVIEW

Where Only Love Remains

I am a channel of your Love, as my own heart blends within Divinity.
I stand within your presence as your Eternal Present stands in me.
I cup the brilliance of this Holy Light, then radiate the power —
    as a mirror which has lost its image —
        to become instead the source of its reflection — magnified.

I am love defeating hatred.
I am joy to conquer ego's misery.
I am healing grown to wholeness and belief beyond despair.
I am truth beyond all knowledge and the poverty
    of seeking awareness in mere mind.

I am the comfort of our love and the shining
        of its sweet, undying brilliance.
I am Spirit, standing strong
        within eternity's embrace.
And I am love — because we are, as I am home,
        here, in this sacred heart where only love remains.

CHAPTER FIFTEEN

DARK NIGHTS AND ARID DAYS

What Are You Teaching Me?

Where have you hidden,
Beloved, and left me moaning?
You fled like the stag after wounding me;
I went out calling for you, but you were gone.

- John of the Cross — Spiritual Canticle

There is incredible joy in the search to sink deeper into the Divine Mystery.

There are, of course, various aspects of religion which make one's heart leap. The power of majestic choirs raised in worship can be awesome. The deep, haunting tones of Tibetan monks, native shamans, or the rolling beauty of Gregorian Chant can inspire personal prayer. The art and splendor of glorious cathedrals, temples, mosques and other places of worship offer great respect for the Divine. They are made to give God the very best, and to give all who enter the idea that these are special places where man might touch the magnificence of what God must be.

We love to have our spirits lifted in wonder and awe by what we see and hear. We are also creatures of emotion, and the thrill of a great sight or a thundering choir can lift us to new heights.

But there's the rub. Because emotion plays such a critical role in what we think and how we act, we need to feel good about what we believe and anything to which we give our allegiance. When it comes to pledging part of our lives and decisions to God, it is only human to expect to feel good about it and the surety of payback somewhere down the road. After all, isn't it human to think in a linear mode? There is always an end. And, there always has to be something in that end for us. What we accept as greater than we are should carry the joy of knowing we have been right, with ultimate payback of salvation beyond this mortal life. While we are following a religion or any kind of spiritual path, we know there may be some rough times, but we still need to *feel* good about our choices. It's only human.

Gut Feelings Say Stop or Go

The problem is that we're trying to live in two different dimensions, which is always tricky. This job of being human, with the ego mind always trying to run the show, takes all our time. We do our best to keep many plates spinning in the air, and that's a full time job. And whether we are aware of it or not, every aspect of life involves feeling. We may really enjoy our job, or drag ourselves to work like a prisoner forced to labor. Relationships and family life bring a constant roller coaster of emotions. The list goes on. Our primary relationship, with ourselves, is the hardest one, and usually the most intense. Everything we see or do brings a positive or negative impact on us, from being stuck in traffic to dreading the economic impact of filling up our gas tank so we can idle that precious load away in another traffic jam. The weather affects us. Our moods affect us. Our minds' constant playing of reruns of our past good and bad times affects us, as well as needless worry about future events which may never happen. No wonder our pharmacies have become one of the most frequent stops in our trips around town.

Simply living life takes effort, and how we feel about every part of it affects not only our moods, but our mental and physical health as well. Emotional energy, for example, is usually carried in the belly area, and the number of chronic or serious illnesses many people endure in that part of their bodies is directly attributed to emotional imbalance. It will manifest either from difficult experiences in this life or, if you can accept the concept, from traumatic events in previous lives.

When people use the term "gut feeling," they are right on target. How we **feel** about a situation is usually how we decide to act on it, and that part of our body, about two inches below the navel, seems to have the inside track on how we should proceed or hesitate. In the East, for example, both in China and Japan much consideration is given to that physical area of the body — called the *dantien* in Chinese and the *tanden* in Japanese. It is considered the physical place of the *hara*, the energetic essence of one's human vitality. Do you remember hearing replays of loud and deep guttural sounds made by Samurai warriors or martial arts experts? In forms of Oriental disciplines, bringing up those sounds from the *hara* is used to bring one's total life energy to the task at hand.

Because our emotions are so powerful, how we feel about a person or situation may eventually cause us to move on if a relationship or any part of life no longer brings us joy. From divorce and the fading of once vibrant friendships, to changing careers or moving away from an area, we are geared to keep seeking the joy we inherently know is part of the human condition. Likewise, if we are unable to make those changes, we often feel trapped. This can lead to sadness, stress, and often takes a toll on our bodies and our minds. The despair some people reach is usually related to an overwhelming sadness which is so deep that there seems no possibility of joy ever returning.

We all experience dark nights at some point of our lives. Mercifully, we have also learned to expect a dawn which still lurks out there somewhere. Maturity gives us more patience to wait for that eventual return to light. The seasons of nature and the rhythm of our lives teach us to live with the ebb and flow of everything, even ourselves. Our emotions are, indeed, extremely powerful.

Letting God Be God

No matter what religion or spiritual path one follows, especially in the Western world, it may help to consider one of the main thoughts of Buddhism. In his long search for ultimate truth, Siddhartha Gautama, the Buddha, realized human suffering is caused by emotional attachment to people, things, or even our own life. Because all those things exist for a limited time, their passing in one form or another causes the sorrow which keep us from the joy which is our birthright.

The Buddha taught the concept of non-attachment, honoring all that is, yet not holding anything as the source of real joy. Non-attachment, he taught, is rising above humanity's need to find joy in attachment to lesser things. Everything our emotions and ego minds perceive as necessary for joy are what he called *samsara*, aspects of the world of illusion. They have nothing to do with real existence in the eternal realm of spirit.

From that teaching and our own innate wisdom, we have come to realize the only truth which really gives us joy. It is living our mortal lives in alignment with the only Truth which really matters. Many call that truth God, Allah, Adonai, many other names, or no name at all. It is the One Truth, and it is the only source of happiness.

Some have given that Truth human characteristics to help us grasp its concept. We have made God the ultimate "Be-er" in the world of beings. We have praised or blamed "God" for all the events of our lives, reducing the One Absolute to the role of Master Puppeteer of everything. "God" is the one whose whims are pulling the strings in even the smallest events of everyone's life. And following that line of belief, we even claim the right to praise or blame "God" for whatever transpires.

Rather sad, actually. Also, rather unworthy of us who share the Divine Mind and the Divine Heart of our only true source.

Throughout history, the killing of one's mother or father has been considered the most heinous crime possible. In selfish judgments based on our need to feel good and never experience sorrow, however, many attempt to destroy the transcendent Mystery of Absolute Truth every day. Lucky for us, we "know not what we do."

Endure the Night, Enjoy the Light

Because every part of our lives is controlled by emotions, our tendency is to also carry our relationship with the Divine Source into our realm of attachment or detachment, joy or sorrow. If we think that Source has direct responsibility for everything that happens to us, we also feel we have the right to turn a cold shoulder to "God" once in a while. It allows us to keep adding to our list of "Why did you's ..." to ask once we meet somewhere beyond the "pearly gates," — if we get "there".

It seems, however, in this time of rising consciousness and awareness, we humans should be getting a bit smarter. If Paul of Tarsus could acknowledge his own spiritual growth, writing, "When I was a child I thought as a child," it may be time for us, with the light we have been given through human and spiritual evolution, to act more grown up as well. Perhaps it is time to realize the role emotions play in our relationship, or lack of it, with the Divine Mystery. We ride the ebb and flow of feeling in every part of our lives. That's part of the human condition. Maybe it is time to realize those same surface emotions enter our relationship with God.

I don't recall a teaching which says, "Blessed are those who feel good about me ..." nor do I accept the idea that if we try to live a "godly" life we should expect pain, sorrow and awful things as a price for that privilege. Every part of human life involves change and, the more we learn to live with that fact, the more we will enjoy the ride of this lifetime and our eternal life as well.

The Deepest Agony

Most of us know the pain of losing someone we love. We also know the suffering involved when any relationship ends, or never grows to the point of beauty it might have achieved. With our very real need to feel close to those we love, anything which deprives us of that can cause exquisite agony.

Because we expect religion to fill the need to "feel" inspired or transported to some realm beyond human existence, we are often inviting trouble. Just as many have walked away from church or temple attendance in rebellion to "religion by rote," others have just lost any sense of connection to the greatest thing which could give them joy. Attending religious rituals or trying to say daily prayers may become tedious and seemingly useless.

More intensely, we may have the feeling that God has abandoned us or that there may not actually be a God at all. Some may also feel their deeds and unworthiness have caused God to take one hard look at them and turn away. Having found serious fault with ministers in any religion, we may have left a congregation, only to feel that, in doing so, we have also left our only connection to God. We may find ourselves in a very lonely desert of isolation. Any feelings we may have held for our divine source have dried up to an arid wasteland, devoid of sustenance. These are times which leave us empty, confused, and alone. Even in personal meditation, we may often give up the practice because we feel too tired or distracted, feeling we really aren't getting anywhere.

Those times of spiritual desolation are exact opposites to what we once considered part of the spiritual experience. In other times, prayer, meditation, and attending spiritual events brought comfort. Many have been inspired by a powerful speaker and left a spiritual retreat with hope and love for God high in their hearts. We may have driven away from a spiritual seminar with the highest of intentions and determination to live a more productive spiritual life.

Those times were an emotional upside of spirituality. After several days riding those highs, however, we found ourselves back in the stress and chaos of daily life, with the emotions we felt so strongly lost again in the maze of daily existence. That's life. That's the way it's supposed to be. No one can ride on the pure emotion of love for any length of time; nor can we expect to constantly feel that way in our spiritual life.

Just as there is an ebb and flow in all parts of existence, our human response to a Mystery far beyond our understanding will also have its ebb and flow. Some of those we call true, spiritual giants and enlightened, holy people have written in their private works about times they didn't feel the presence of God, when they too were as dry as dust. When John of the Cross wrote about his anguish of feeling separated from the True Beloved, his poetry wept with the intense sorrow of loss. While some spiritual and religious leaders hold up saints and spiritual ascetics as having visions, special gifts, and extended times of bliss, the truly honest teachers will also note the dark nights and arid days of many who felt God had abandoned them. Therese of Lisieux endured a time of doubting God's existence even as she poured every ounce of her life into that Mystery she could not understand.

Pay Attention

Experiencing a dark night of the soul may be a sign that your own spiritual life is deepening as you draw closer to union with the one Beloved. The more of your own energy you pour into your life with God, the more the ego mind will assault your deepening love and belief. It will cut off all emotion, luring you down to more perceptible and seemingly pleasant pastures.

If you experience times when you doubt the existence of Source, or do not feel the presence of any divine mystery, your only prayer may be, "My God, My God, let my cry come unto Thee." If those are the only words you can pray, then pray them! Change is part of the world of illusion. The Sacred Mystery is our only constant even if at times we doubt it or find no consolation in it.

Truth is constant, immovable and unchangeable. We stand by it and in it. Whether we feel nothing or are filled with ecstasy really doesn't matter. It is enough to be grounded in Truth. Consider that perhaps our prayers and faith during those arid times are actually our highest prayers. Although devoid of feeling, they remain solid in deeper knowledge that what is true is always true whether we feel it or not.

Surrender is the key. To place our lives with all their emotions, thoughts and experiences into the Divine Will is the answer. To intend that our love remains constant in this Great Truth is to arm ourselves for the times lack of feeling and endless questioning assault our highest intentions. Those times are merely the ego mind, trying its hardest to retake command, but it can be defeated. During those times, the only prayer we may be able to muster is, "My God, just let me love you. Just like a rock, let me stay immobile in that love, beyond feelings, mental gymnastics, or even faith. No matter my emotions, need for surety or anything else. Just let me stay present in the Truth which is Your Love, and where, in the essence of Truth, we are always one."

Use It Well

If you are now, or ever find yourself, in a time of no feeling or alienation from the Ultimate Truth some call God, console yourself with the thought you are in some very good company. Many spiritual leaders have sometimes even imposed upon themselves a time of detachment and deprivation of feeling just to reach deeper understanding of their life's work. Jesus took himself to exile in the desert to experience greater understanding of his life's purpose. Moses kept people wandering around in another barren land for years, trying to bring them to greater truth about their own destinies. Then he went alone up into the mountains seeking his own deeper reality. The Buddha wandered for years seeking realization of ultimate truth.

Likewise, many people have gone into long retreats in nature, away from human contact and communication to take themselves deeper into life, its purpose, and their role in it. Even today, on a much lesser level, in business and government, people are urged to take "alone time" for introspection and clarity.

If you find yourself in one of these arid times, even in your relationship with the Divine, learn to use it well. Sometimes we don't realize the magnificence of Light until we have experienced extended darkness. Any time we lose feeling or go into a difficult period, we have two choices. We can wallow in its emptiness and consider it a negative thing, or we can use it as a time for greater learning.

We may feel we are being mistreated by the universe and shout, "Why me?" We can also consider our need to grow and ask, "What am I supposed to learn from this?" Then, after realizing the desert had its own truths to teach us about life and divinity, we may be able to live the words John of the Cross wrote at the end of his own dark night:

Oh noche que guiaste!
Oh noche amable mas que
    el alborada!
Oh noche que juntaste
Amado con amada
Amada en el Amado
    transformada!

Oh night, my guide! Guiding night!

Oh night more lovely than the dawn!
O night that has united
the Lover with his loved one,

Loved one in the Lover fused as one!

- John of the Cross

RIGHT BRAIN CHAPTER REVIEW

What Are You Teaching Me?

Once I felt Your Heart of light dwelling in my soul.
Once I knew that constant burst of Purest Love pulsing in the Radiance,
*   held within and choosing then to stay with me.*
I felt you chose to call my heart your home,
And you have always been so very welcome there!

Once you made my spirit sing
just from the sweet, delicious joy of knowing you,
You even made my voice resound with echoes of your love.
Once my feet pushed higher toward distant mountain tops,
*   And never did I tire in that climb.*
All seemed to be so perfect, and I loved the joy we shared.

But now these days have all grown dark,
     in loneliness I never knew before.
I cannot feel your presence here,
     and there is nothing left but fear and the shadows of fears
     I thought had gone long ago, before I felt your love.

Now, alone without you, this darkness makes me stumble
     in the painful loss of light,
I can no longer hear your song within my soul,
     and I cannot feel you touch me any more.
Whispers of doubt begin to echo. I even wonder —
     are you really there at all?
Are you with me in this time that is no time —
     of not realizing you,
     not feeling the soft vibration of your love?

This is a night I cannot comprehend, nor continue to bear alone.
Why can't I feel you here?
And what are you teaching me?

CHAPTER SIXTEEN

ALLOWING HEALING TO FLOW

Energy Follows Thought

*Healing is accomplished the instant the sufferer
no longer sees any value in pain.*

- A Course in Miracles

From the first time we held up a finger with an "ouchie" to our mother's lips, we have known the value of healing and sought it on all levels of human experience.

Next to staying alive, one of the most important aspects of life is involved with healing. In our linear mode of thought, where there is always an end somewhere down the road, we automatically fear anything which may bring that end too soon. As a result, we look for healing at almost every step of the way as we move down the corridor of time.

Certainly the body draws our attention through pain or dysfunction. As soon as there's a hint of a problem, we seek to cure whatever is not right. There are areas of the mind which also need healing and as our emotions react to supposed injustices, betrayals, abandonment and other feelings of loss, they also need healing. Rarely, however, do people consider healing the ego mind since it is always too busy creating more illusion, rather than thoughts of healing itself. Even more rarely do we look for ways to heal our spirit and connection with our Source.

Distinction needs to be made here between what it means to be cured and what is involved in the process of healing. In medical terms, doctors are tasked with curing a physical problem which involves making its symptoms go away, returning the body to health. In the search for cures for various types of cancer, for example, the medical profession seeks ways to cure conditions which have already manifested. Of course, preventative medicine and programs are always helpful, but a cure involves overcoming a problem which already exists.

The concept of healing, however, is very different. The body itself can heal various problems, just by letting nature takes its course. Healing on a deeper or even metaphysical level is another matter where the very cause of a problem is corrected, enabling a return to wholeness. To heal means to go to the cause of a problem and eliminate the source of dis-ease.

In that sense, it is good to remember that "heal," in its roots, means to make whole. It is the act of "re-membering" our true identities and the causes of all those things which have taken away our freedom of joy and health. It involves getting back all those pieces of ourselves we have lost to fear, anger, judgment or false belief. For example, the concept of soul retrieval in some native cultures focuses on doing that, retrieving parts of our psyche and identity that we may have lost in stressful times. To retrieve those parts actually makes us whole again.

Energy Follows Thought

One of the most exciting aspects of rising consciousness is greater appreciation of the mind's power. By using that new awareness, we can now move into entirely new areas of creating or actually co-creating with our Source. Even scientists, metaphysicians and medical professionals are now learning that the mind is more powerful than anyone thought. This enables us to affect new balance in our physical, mental, emotional and even spiritual selves through new ways of thought.

The energy produced in action really does follow thought. This is important to remember as we go forward through life. The way we think actually produces certain results and, as we join others in holding the same attitudes and ideas, this also enables positive change to occur on a global scale.

The old saying, "As you think, so shall you be," becomes truer with each new day. Where we put the energy of thought becomes reality as we perceive it. If one expects life to be miserable, the expectation of that thought usually makes it a reality, for that individual. The energy from our thoughts can also create and invite happiness, fulfillment, and even longer, healthier lives. Likewise, negative thinking from self-deprecation, hatred, judgment of others, or expecting the worst while hoping for the best, can also lead to physical disease, mental disorder, emotional problems and even fear of the God Source Itself. If we feel some omnipotent being is judging our every move and keeping score on some supercomputer in the sky, that thought alone can cause major stress!

Energy follows thought. The more we can quiet the ego mind and let our higher self live its beauty of compassion, love and forgiveness, the less we will eventually need healing of any kind. Because the human mind is so powerful, a large part of any form of healing can be affected by a change of attitude. If we expect negative results, we create them in our mind. Holding hatred for another or another race, for example, actually invites physical problems in the individual who harbors those thoughts. When our thinking is taken up with negative or fearful behavior, our minds are distracted from carrying on their function of keeping the body well-tuned and healthy.

If, on the other hand, we move to more positive thinking which *A Course In Miracles* describes, we will begin to see incredible things happening. We will then know the joy of being truly whole.

By opening new, more positive pathways of thought in our brains, we can actually affect our physical bodies and our life force. This does not mean, however, that we can think everything into a reality which suits our desires as some recent books have claimed. It does mean we have greater control over how our lives are lived. It also gives us a very powerful tool for creating a happier, more peaceful and less fearful approach to life.

Intention — Balance — Forgiveness

Dr. Wayne Dyer and others have written much about the role of intention in human development. Intending to be positive and inviting positive things to happen in life actually creates the energy for them to manifest. Putting the ego mind on the back burner, intending that only positive results come to us, actually invites their reality. By moving beyond worry of lack, abandonment or failure, we begin to create the newer reality of abundance, acceptance and success. By being *pro-active* in setting our intentions for the day and the time ahead of us, we can avoid the need to react to whatever the whims of others' decisions are doing to us. By setting the intention of right living and right reward in the areas of family, work, relationships, tasks and events, we invite wholeness.

The French philosopher Rene Descartes once said, "I think, therefore I am." The question now is "What are you thinking?" And, as a result of your thought patterns, what kind of person are you now and what kind of person are you becoming? Finding honest answers to those questions may take some healthy introspection, but that may also involve some of your deepest self-healing.

It's a Balancing Act

From the time we learned to ride a bicycle, we've known the importance of balance. We've also learned that balance involves more than losing it and crashing into the neighbor's bushes. Without balance in every part of our lives we invite crashes of many kinds from physical reaction to unhealthy eating or living, to overdosing on a wide possibility of addictions, or letting stress destroy our sense of peace and well-being. What balance really involves is harmony. All components working together for the greater good, all aspects of life lived to the fullest, but never out of synch with the central core. That is what balance in anyone's life is all about, making all decisions and experiencing all reactions from that one, central core.

As noted earlier, "Find the Center" is a mantra I used for a long time in daily meditations. It was a directive that helped me move beyond thought to where all the good answers usually await us. Living from our true center can be the greatest help to self-healing, since the center of each of us remains our connection with the divine mind and the divine capacity for compassion and love.

A few eons ago, my college philosophy professor drew a daisy on the chalk board. One petal was inordinately huge so the other petals dwarfed in comparison. So it is with our lives. We owe all the petals equal nourishment and attention. We need to be active members of our families, productive workers, people who keep good contact with those we are fortunate enough to call friends. We also need periods of relaxation when we can re-create our best stress-free and happy selves. We need all those parts of our lives to make us whole.

Yet the center remains. That is the hub and focal point of everything. If that center for us is the dominance of ego, healing emergencies will become our constant companions. If that center is our union within the God Presence, we are already whole, and we are already healed. Balance is more than keeping the neighbor's bushes intact. It involves keeping ourselves intact the only place we really can be — in our true Center.

Then there is forgiveness which always leads to peace. No real healing can occur without it. Forgiveness itself is an interesting concept since it comes from our human tendency to judge. If we allowed others to be where they are on their own evolutionary path, there would be no need to forgive, since we would realize everyone is exactly where they need to be, doing what they need to do on their own paths into the Fullness. But we do judge and, when we allow others to hurt us, the only right way out of that scenario is to forgive. Not an easy thing. True, most supposed grievances against us come from our own delusion, but not all people are yet walking the path of Light. There is hatred. There is the arrogance of misusing power. There is selfishness and greed. There is darkness which feeds on its own comfort of not really wanting to see, and we may have suffered from all these things.

Forgiveness

Forgiveness is not something we do for other people. It is something we do for ourselves. Those who have supposedly wronged us are moving on happily in their own little worlds. They're fine. They are where they are on their own particular paths. But ah, the myriad negative emotions they may have caused in us! Cord after etheric cord of our own precious energy has gone to them in anger, judgment or mistrust. So we really do need to forgive them, not for themselves, but for our own peace and healing.

I look at the word for-give as exactly that. Once I have gone beyond the raw human emotion of what I perceive as a negative impact on me, I see forgiveness as cutting my emotional etheric cord to that individual's action, and giving it back for them to understand and deal with. In forgiveness, I set them free to consider their action. Then I can move more quickly away from the hurt and focus on my own healing into wholeness again.

Our fertile ego minds and raw human emotions are awesome enemies of healing and peace. Once again, however, balance means we react from the center. If our center is our ego self, we will never forgive and we will continue to suffer because of it. If our center is the God Presence within us, balance beyond hurt will return more quickly so healing can occur.

Do you need healing? Find the center. Be the center, and let the God Source be the absolute, loving Presence your ego mind can never comprehend. In that mode, all healing is not only possible. It is already done! *Baruch bashan!*

In healing, there also comes a reversal of the concept of forgiveness, and that is recognizing the need to ask for pardon when another has intentionally or unintentionally been hurt by our words or actions. Though our ego minds may think it is a magnanimous act to seek forgiveness, that pales besides the great healing which may occur when we have humbled ourselves and asked for another's pardon.

I recall a time I was attending a Marianne Williamson seminar. If you ever have opportunity to attend one, I recommend it because Marianne is an authentic woman of God and she speaks great truth. She is filled with the lessons of *A Course In Miracles* and she has learned them very well.

As part of her seminar experience, Williamson makes microphones available to her audience. Individuals can ask questions or comment on the material presented. At this particular seminar, I heard comments from the audience which I have heard most of my life. Those comments were from people who have had negative experiences with representatives of the Catholic Church and nuns in particular.

At one such audience participation session, after several people made comments such as, "The nuns ruined my life," or, "I'm still suf-fering from my experiences in a Catholic school," something com-pelled me to respond. I know now it was nothing less than the holy spirit of God working its miracle of healing.

Raising my hand to speak, I felt an energy greater than mine come over me. Soon, with microphone in hand, I stood and turned to the three hundred or so people in the audience. "I was a Catholic nun for thirteen years," I began, and that large crowd suddenly became very, very quiet. I felt my legs trembling but I continued, telling the audi-ence that the nuns and priests I had known all started out as well-intentioned people. Some, I said, had experienced their own frustra-tions, but none ever intended any harm or suffering. Then, in words which came from the Great Heart through my own heart, I said, "On behalf of any priest or nun who may have ever caused you suffering in any way, I apologize. Please forgive us all."

That entire audience rose to its feet and vigorous clapping thun-dered in my ears. Once people settled back down, I continued, "And if this is a day of spiritual growth, now I ask you to extend your forgive-ness to them and to me because in doing that, you will heal us all, as well as the experiences you have had with them and the Church."

By the time I sat down I was shaking but, for the rest of the day, people came to me, some in tears, thanking me for the gesture I had made. And it was I who learned the lesson that day, that, in the simple act of asking another's forgiveness, we can facilitate incredible healing in them. Then all can move forward in the joyful, unrestricted experience of being in the wholeness of love. That is powerful healing for all sides!

Energetic Healing

Let's revisit the concept of energy. Whether you call it *ki, chi, prana,* or grace, it is the energy of life itself. If you can accept the term "grace," we are talking about the very grace of energy which sustains not only life on this planet, but all that exists and holds the potential for existence throughout creation. What our new awareness now reveals is the fact that this very life force can be reached at a higher level when the mind finally uses its innate capability of tuning into it.

Just as a computer may go into the sleep mode to limit the use of electricity, we have been in a "sleep" mode for many millennia. Our evolution has been very slow as different lessons had to be learned. Now, however, we are becoming capable of accessing our full power mode or at least getting close to its potential. Scientists, for example, have still not determined the uses of several strands in human DNA. Could it be that those very indefinable parts are the keys we will use to access greater awareness of our Source Itself?

Again we return to the concept of intention, consciously directing the mind to reach into that full power mode. And in that mode, we are becoming aware of our ability to transmit or channel higher levels of life energy into ourselves, to others we may reach through thought or various healing modalities, and into all of creation itself. If we have been in the sleep mode for thousands of years, this Axial Age is opening the tool box we need to draw closer to the power of our source.

One of the fastest growing fields in this new time is the practice of using life energy for healing all levels of body, emotion, mind and spirit. Even in strict medical fields, there is growing openness toward a holistic approach to healing. More physicians are accepting the concept of using metaphysical or energy modalities in conjunction with medical treatment. For example, a highly respected neurosurgeon, discussing patients' needs, once told me, "If someone needs back surgery, I'm the perfect one to do it. But many of my patients don't need a back surgeon. They need you." He was addressing me as one who uses energy on a holistic level through consultation and energetic healing in the modality of Reiki. He was also confirming a truth now widely accepted that, once the ability to access higher levels of energy is commonplace, many dysfunctions which now afflict humanity will no longer exist.

Healing with the Chakras

Reiki is just one form of healing modalities which are now becoming accepted in the Western world. This is due, in large part, to greater understanding of bio-energy centers in the body called chakras. Each of the seven main chakras draws from both earth energy as well the cosmic energy of creation. Each chakra houses the life force energy in one particular area of the physical form. Brought to the Western world through greater understanding of yoga and Chinese medicine, use of the chakras to address problems of healing and health is now becoming more common, even though some religions and skeptics still do not embrace it.

The chakras, sometimes called the Orgone Field of Energy, are key components in energy medicine today. They not only help determine some causes of physical dis-ease, but also bring more attention to how faulty thinking or emotional imbalance affect the total individual. According to Ambika Wauters, writing in *Healing With the Energy of the Chakras*, "The chakras conduct and filter a constant flow of life-energy through us. What is so unique to this system is the gradation and refinement of energy available as we evolve through the chakras to higher levels of awareness, responsibility, and consciousness. As we evolve and develop, so each chakra opens and feeds that next level of development."

The chakras affect health and healing in critical ways since they maintain the spiritual, mental, emotional fields known as the aura which surrounds the physical form. The energy from them can now be photographed by special cameras showing the strength or weakness of individual chakras based on the intensity of their vibrating health in the body. This advanced photography also may show "holes" in the aura. Holes indicate a problem in that area where energy is not flowing properly. This may stem from emotional or mental imbalance which, then, may be causing a problem in the physical area of the body which the particular chakra embraces.

Understanding chakras not only provides answers to causes of some disease, it also aids in helping reach and eradicate those causes on all levels of healing. Using the term "wheel" to identify the chakras describes the action some adepts have felt in referring to them. They are etherical rather than physical, and their power reaches to all levels of the human entity. Chakras move in a type of metaphysical vibration of vortices drawing, not only from the earth's energy, but energy from forces beyond our planet as well.

The importance of each chakra comes from its manifesting whether faulty thinking may be causing a problem in the physical entity. It shows the level of balance or imbalance any individual is holding and also reveals the places where a physical problem may develop if the existing cause of imbalance is not corrected.

Dealing with the energy of the chakras, known as a more subtle energy, however, may be difficult for the left brain, logical approach to life, death, and healing. Wauters writes:

> What is being asked of us in exploring subtle energy is a willingness to go beyond our everyday belief system. We need to incorporate a different view of ourselves. We are energetic beings, not mechanical robots. With this understanding comes the need to realize the depths of our gentle and sensitive natures, and to honor the spiritual dimension within ourselves.
>
> We are responsive to everything that happens around us, both internally and externally, throughout the planet and, for that

matter, throughout the universe. Our minds act as filters for the vast number of stimuli which are bombarding our consciousness at any one time.

The first chakra, known at the Root Chakra, is located at the base of the spine. It carries a very slow vibration channeling down into the earth energy and manifests in the color red. The Root Chakra governs the physical areas of the body including the legs, sexual organs in the male species and areas around the pelvis.

The second chakra, the Sacral Chakra, is located a bit lower than the navel, and rests in the center of the pelvis. Vibrating to the color orange, it carries the vitality and energy of the life force present within an individual, which is known as the *tanden* in Japanese. Areas affected by the Sacral Chakra are the intestines, kidneys, bladder and female sexual organs. It is the seat of emotional balance or imbalance. The Sacral Chakra gives one the feeling of being home on the planet and is addressed more in Oriental cultures than in Western modes of thought.

The Third or Solar Plexus Chakra is located under the sternum and is one of the most sensitive energy points in the body. This is the area of personal identity and self-worth and it vibrates to the color yellow. Sometimes called the sun energy of the body, the Solar Plexus impacts many of the body's vital organs. The liver, gall bladder and stomach are impacted by this chakra which holds the proper balance of judgment, integrity, and self respect. A strong Solar Plexus gives us the strength to move out into the world with confidence. It is the source of our personal power and gives us the energy to attempt new ventures and live life to the fullest. Its vibration is at a higher level as this chakra rises higher in the physical form.

Acting as the central and most important bridge between the three lower chakras and the higher vibration upper chakras, lies the beautiful Heart Chakra. Vibrating to the colors green or pink, this chakra locates slightly to the right of the chest — opposite the physical heart on the left. It also expands from shoulder to shoulder, reaching through the arms and hands and through the front and back of the chest as well.

Attributes of the Heart Chakra include compassion, balance, harmony, purity, a true sense of sisterhood and brotherhood and, of course, love. Our Heart Chakra carries our deepest feelings and also the deepest hurt when we may feel lonely, depressed, or greatly saddened by anything which affects our rightful state of joy. The Heart Chakra feeds on qualities such as compassion, forgiveness, gratitude and love, both conditional and unconditional. It is the center of our very strength yet open to the vastness of energetic love flowing to us from dimensions and realms far beyond this human existence.

Just as the physical heart is central to life of the body, the Heart Chakra is central to meaningful life for the total person. The physical heart pumps the life force of our body. The Heart Chakra flows with the energy of love itself, our direct connection to our true life force which is Love Itself.

Moving into the three higher chakras, the Throat Chakra vibrates to the color turquoise and controls the balance of expression, creativity, spiritual determination, and successful communication. It affects the throat and neck as well as the upper back, scalp, jaw, and mouth. Key to proper balance of this chakra is freedom to speak your own truth, holding confidence in the power of your voice and the resonance of your life force energy. The vibration of this chakra is higher than even the heart, and gives one the delight of sound both in singing or even humming to the planetary sound of the universe. This is obviously the chakra of sound, yet I also consider it the chakra of silence. In working with my own throat chakra, I always make a point of respecting and calling life force energy to my sounds and also to my silence. One feeds the other, and that is what can make any form of expression more powerful with meaning, or tender with compassionate love.

The Brow Chakra is powerful. Period. Vibrating to the deepest indigo, this is the energy center for consciousness and thought as well as inner knowledge and wisdom. Physically it brings intensified force to all the senses and governs the eyes and all areas of the skull, including the brain. It carries the balance of clarity and the ability to concentrate, using the brain to its fullest capacity. It is no wonder the outward physical marking of the Brow Chakra, located between and just above the eyes, is customary in some parts of Hinduism. The recognition of this chakra's importance in spiritual growth and connection to the Higher Source merits such outward expression.

The Brow Chakra can often be the visual center for various forms of meditation. It is, in fact, the easiest chakra to physically witness. During deep relaxation, certain forms of body work, contemplation, a healing session, or experiencing higher mental or spiritual moments, one may become aware of the deep indigo light flowing behind one's closed eyes.

The Brow Chakra's vibration is extremely high but very gentle. As the center of greater consciousness and deeper spirituality, this chakra becomes the touchstone of mind, rising strongly into spirit and the wordless beauty of what lies beyond. This is the energy center which lifts us to the greater expanse of mind and spirit. If true spirituality really has a home in the physical human entity, the Brow Chakra provides it.

Located at the top of the head, the Crown Chakra carries the color violet though it sometimes spins off into gold and the brightest silver, or more brilliant forms of light. Wauters notes the attributes of the Crown Chakra as, "Cosmic consciousness, unity, communion, inner peace, refinement, beauty and grace. ... It takes in the feelings of beauty and goodness, light and purity."

The energy of the Crown Chakra flows upward, out, and away from the individual, yet also draws the expansive energy down, through the Eighth and Ninth etheric chakras, into the human form. The Crown Chakra is the crowning achievement of energy which flows through imperfect yet beautiful forms of humanity.

The seven chakras nurture and monitor the human form as they allow the life force energy to flow through spiritual, mental, emotional and physical aspects of each individual. They are accompanied by many lesser chakras or energy avenues in the body, as well as higher chakras which exist above the physical form.

Most forms of energy healing now being practiced around the world utilize knowledge of the chakras. As you choose to participate in your own self healing, you can use this knowledge to determine what physical discomfort might be arising from faulty thinking, emotional distress, or negative feelings you carry from past hurts or current fears. Then, you can activate your own healing by understanding how your own thoughts may be affecting you. The miracle of healing calls for a return to wholeness. It may be a time now to consider — "healing thyself." Also, you may incorporate clearing through each of the chakras every morning at the beginning of your prayer or meditation times.

Prayer, Power and Energy

One phenomenon many have experienced for years is the efficacy of prayer. While recent studies have shown different results in the power of prayer, there are instances where calling upon the Higher Source has resulted in many kinds of healing. Prayer of this kind combines strong intention and belief in healing, uniting with the Energy of the God Source Itself. The phenomenon can never be adequately explained. Still, it does make sense that when the human mind is raised to a higher level, with the intention to bring wholeness to another person, the energy of that intention can actually become the cause which produces the effect of healing.

Likewise, those who are attuned to working with the energy of the life force, *prana*, *chi*, or *ki*, have, at times, been able to channel energy on a much higher level to individuals or events where greater wholeness is needed. Consider again the human mind and known levels of consciousness. The common level of consciousness where we interact with each other is Beta. The Alpha state holds the mind in greater relaxation. Yet the deeper state of Theta has been proven to be the level of mind consciousness most open to receiving the *chi* or *prana* energy and interacting with it. It is the place where, once the active brain has been set on a back burner, an individual is more open to connection to the life force energy. As a result, it is in the Theta state that the mind and entire physical entity can receive that energy in more intensified form.

How do we access the Theta state? It can be done through deep meditation, going beyond the mind into the no-space of Buddhist *sunyata* or Hebrew *einsof*. In some cases it may involve actually going into The Void, the true emptiness which holds all that is. That is the space where the mind is not consciously directing things any more, but where, instead, it remains receptive to the energies of higher awareness. This is also the state of creativity, the place where we access what might be called miracles. It is the place of deeper union with Source and it is a beautiful place to be. How do we reach it? In the stillness, you will know. This is the very stillness where our silence has gone beyond the soothing sounds of singing bowls, the power of chanting, drumming, or choral music, where the individual is more receptive and closer to the Source Energy Itself.

As consciousness continues to rise, many feel we will be able to not only heal dysfunction on the physical, mental, emotional and spiritual levels. We will actually be able to live longer, healthier lives both physically and psychologically. The more we become attuned to higher consciousness, the more we can actually reach for the stars, and the brilliance of the Source which created them.

RIGHT BRAIN CHAPTER REVIEW

The Blessing of Healing Hands

What have you done to my hands?
How did you teach them to cradle each aspect of God
*   with such new, delicate, caressing dignity?*
How did you spin them to somehow lighter density,
*   yet heat them to brim with sacred fire*
*   that yearns to keep burning itself away?*
Then what intense flame did you blow through them
*   with power to heal in Love's searing energy?*
And what incredible balm did you pour through them,
As they now reach Divinity
*   through these channels of light*
*   You have carved in my hands?*

I am soft now. I am gentleness
    and quiet, distant echoing.
I am force of Purity, Light, Love
    and endless, reverent chanting the Divine.

I am become the silence
    and the sound of sacred home.
I am become the blessing as I become the blessed —
And my hands become the most tender of all embraces
    anyone could ever reach around this world.

I am clean now. I am holiness.
I am Love. I am Home. Yet still I do wonder —
    what have you done to my hands?
And how can I ever thank you enough?

CHAPTER SEVENTEEN

HEALING INTO WHOLENESS

Mastery Comes from Being in the Mystery

I am the Sound of my own Name.

- The Thunder - Perfect Mind

L et's go back again to those words of Albert Einstein, "Vibration is the essence of the universe." Yet this time let's focus on two things we seldom consider as dualities, if we consider them at all. Sound and silence are so much part of our lives that we rarely pay attention to them. In today's world, sound has become such a constant that it is rare to experience true silence at all.

Yet, it is within the sounds and the beautiful silences that much of our deepest understanding and potential for learning occur. This is also true in the realm of healing. Whenever real stillness can be achieved, healing becomes present in the energy of silence's power. When we have learned to differentiate between noise and true, meaningful sound, there are many sounds which allow healing to flow.

From humanity's earliest times, sound has been considered one of the surest ways of reaching the Higher Power. While the human voice is our first method of addressing that Power, primitive instruments have shown how our ancestors called into that Great Beyond for healing, assistance, and even to just make contact with what seemed to be absolute mystery. Drums, for example, have been some of the world's earliest instruments, catching the rhythm of the human heart beat, and raising that rhythm into a higher source.

Healing Sounds

Sound is part of sacred activities for most religions and belief systems. While Sanskrit chants have come to us from humanity's earliest times in the Eastern world, Western religions have brought Gregorian Chant, polyphonic music, creative songs and hymns to worship services. In recent times, however, more serious study has been applied to sound itself and its potential for healing, and attaining higher levels of spiritual consciousness.

There are many pioneers in the field of sound healing, among them Jonathan Goldman. His work now includes tones, chants and music which incorporate ancient sounds of the Eastern world. Vocal and instrumental recordings match vibrational tones of the chakras, metaphysical energy centers of the physical form. Goldman and many others have produced a wealth of music which reverberates in our bodies and our spirits as well.

Today's healing music includes many different sources of sound. While drums and flutes have been mainstays since ancient times, now Tibetan or crystal sound bowls, gongs and chimes also lift spirits and create healing energy. For example, Guy Matthews, a practitioner of crystal sound bowls, states, "Sound as a vibration can be used to entrain cells in the body to a harmonic level of balance — which can equate to well being and healthy cells. Greater wholeness and balance can come from using sound, working with entrainment, transcendence and intention. My work with crystal sound bowls gives the receiver a profound experience of moving beyond time and space to a deeper level of healing."

Adding the human voice to that reverence, vocalists such as Deva Premal and Krishna Das have proven that sacred sounds from around the world can be extremely healing. Also, listening to or becoming part of chants from other cultures and belief systems creates resonance which can lead to healing.

The sound of sacred drumming, and the magical quality of flutes and indigenous musical instruments from around the world can become part of the healing experience. The sweet, stilled hush of nature, the magic of the wind, and the energetic vibration of this planet mother herself are all part of humanity's return to wholeness.

Understanding the Essence of Vibration

As much as studies reveal more about the power of healing through voices and various instruments, there is another sound we cannot hear. That sound is the vibration of our own stillness. It is the heart sound, created by our intentional act of directing love to someone or to the world. It is the vibration of compassionate love, and it reverberates throughout creation. The human heart, wishing love not just for itself or for another individual, but for creation as a whole, elevates the energetic vibration of all. It produces healing which affects human consciousness. It births the energy of love from its own stillness, and creates vibrations which can become a symphony of love extending throughout the cosmos.

Kototama

In this new time, realization is now growing that certain sounds can actually access a deeper, almost mystical state. One study of this from the Japanese culture is *kototama*, a literal study of the mystical meaning of sound. These sounds occur in all languages. People accept the words of their culture without knowing that, when using a sound incorporated within that word, they are accessing the deeper truth that sound produces. For example, the "I" sound, in Japanese, is part of the word *Dai*, which means the Great One or the One in charge. This same sound has come into English in the word tycoon. We refer to a tycoon as someone like Donald Trump who is in charge of a corporate empire. He is the single person in charge of the entire operation. That letter I, which in Japanese is written *ai*, still carries the *kototama* sound denoting the singular individual at the head of something.

Likewise, the sound *ah* is often considered a sacred divinity sound. We see it in words such as "God", when the *o* is pronounced in English as *ah*. It is also in the Hindu word *"Brahma,"* the Creator, and in the Hebrew word *"shalom"* which also holds another sound, long *o*, considered to be the sound of creation. *Shalom* can literally be interpreted as the sounds of God and Creation. When we wish *"Shalom"* to another, we are wishing them more than what we consider to be peace. We are, through sound, wishing them ultimate peace of actualized universal spirituality.

It is also interesting to note that negative words, let alone words of cursing or wishing negativity on others, most often do not carry the sounds of love or peace. By the negative use of sound, therefore, we are actually sending negative energy to others or even to ourselves! Understanding that, we can realize that what we consider "bad" sounds are negative sounds and, by using them, we bring negativity to ourselves.

This is where the use of sound in chanting holds great value. In chants we are literally putting out the vibration of God and peace, healing, right living, and sounds which lead the higher part of ourselves into being spiritually actualized. Chants are sounds of characteristics of the Great One, our Source.

In the classic *Alice in Wonderland*, when the witch said, "Words mean what I want them to mean," Lewis Carroll was tapping into the science of *kototama*, the use of sound to denote what a word describes or can actually activate by its sounding. It's interesting to note here that the words "religion" and "spirituality" do not contain the more adept spiritual sounds. The word *awaken*, however, does actually start off with the Source Sound. So, perhaps instead of talking about religion or spirituality, we should take a clue from the Buddha who considered himself the Ah-wakened One! Religion and spirituality are all vehicles, but the state of "ah-wakening" is the state of becoming spiritually involved with the deepest part of us. That is awareness of our inner union within the Divine Source Itself. In that sense, if we are working toward our own awakening, we are already putting ourselves, literally, in the vibration of God.

The Future of Healing

Due to rising consciousness, the concept of healing now means much more than going through a surgical procedure. Many of us have already experienced the effect that our thoughts and emotions produce in our physical bodies. Many have experienced upset stomachs when we were nervous or chest pains when we were angry. Those are mere hints of a greater reality. For many years science has used the term "psychosomatic," denoting mind and body equally involved in disease or healthful life styles. Now we are aware of the much greater energy which incorporates the spiritual energy within us, as well as the power of the human mind.

The Western world has now begun to understand energy knowledge which was long known in Oriental cultures. Every human form is contained in its own "egg" of energy which includes its aura. The outer layer is spiritual, not religious but spiritual, in connection with its creation source. Closer layers of energy around the individual form involve the mental, emotional, and etheric layers then, finally, the physical body itself.

Considering that information in the field of healing, for example, if one is told not to sing or speak her truth, that mental concept of not singing or speaking out eventually engenders the emotions of anger or frustration. This emotion may then lead into the densest layer of the human organism, the physical body. The result may produce problems around the energy center which controls expression and creativity — the throat chakra — and physical problems may appear.

Greater knowledge of how this affects our health has led to greater desire for alternative "healing centers." Whereas every metropolitan area now has its own medical complex of hospitals and medical buildings, some dedicated to coping with only one disease, centers for true healing are only now beginning to emerge. These offer what are considered alternative modalities but which are really complementary medicine. Healing centers in the future will have rooms dedicated to massage and aromatherapy as well as many kinds of hands on healing work such as Reiki and Therapeutic Touch. They will also include classrooms for education in balanced eating, proper care of mother and baby during pregnancy and beyond, as well as programs to help understand the impact of mind and emotion on the physical body. There will be areas for body work and study of stones of the earth which carry their own specialized energies.

These centers will offer many practices of the Eastern world such as Yoga, Gi gong and Tai Chi which clear and open the body's energy centers. There will also be practical study of Ayurvedic medicine and dietary practices which correct imbalances from acidity due to constant ingestion of over-processed food. Several forms of meditation practice will be taught, opening the way to deeper personal awareness.

These centers will offer instruction in living more consciously with the earth as society takes to heart the old Southwestern native phrase, *"Hosho go na shadow,"* walk gently on the earth. Instead of continuing to rape and pollute the planet, people will learn to live more eco-friendly lives since, the healthier our planet is, the healthier our lives as a species upon it will be. These centers will also contain areas dedicated to understanding mental problems and addictions at their source.

At the heart of each of these healing centers will be a central area dedicated to quiet meditation, introspection, and prayer. Its atmosphere will promote the healing in wholeness which is the rightful state of every person, perfect in creation's plan.

The difference between the medical complexes and these healing centers will be their basic approach. The medical centers will be seeking ways to cure a problem, while healing centers will be seeking ways to identify and then eradicate the cause of a problem.

Modern doctors do not work miracles. Neither do modern healers. The only difference between them is while that a doctor brings a medical approach to cure an affected part of the body, or in the case of psychiatry, an infected attitude in the mind, today's metaphysical practitioner helps a client uncover the imbalance which is expressing itself in physical, emotional, or mental distress.

The truth is that every human being is a potential healer. Each of us, once aware of our untapped potential in the power of thought and intention, can use that power to promote greater wholeness. Even in national or governmental matters, a new type of healing can occur. For example, just as the United States has a Department of Defense, enlightened people such as Congressman Dennis Kucinich and author Marianne Williamson, with others, have petitioned to make an equally funded Department of Peace.

Likewise, the healing center of tomorrow will be as much preventative as it is curative. It will not wait for problems to occur but instead will promote methods of healthy thinking, feeling, living and praying. The very term "healthy" carries the two words we now need to understand as perfect possibilities, "Heal Thy". A healthy person is one who understands the possibility of healing much about herself or himself.

The Mind and the Healer

Enlightened scholars, knowing the mind, and with greater awareness of the depth of its power, have studied the Dead Sea Scrolls and other ancient writings. Gregg Braden, in the *Lost Mode of Prayer*, takes from the scrolls an early form of prayer which does not ask for healing but which offers gratitude for a situation already considered healed. In this prayer, one does not pray for a disease to be taken away. One instead gives gratitude for the body returning to wholeness where, in the Eternal Present, that action is already done. *Baruch bashan!* Also tapping into the newer level of consciousness, one can return to greater health by correcting imbalances and doing what is necessary to alter one's thought patterns, behavior, and diet.

Of course we are all heading toward physical death. Some condition will eventually cause our physical heart to stop. The quality of life, however, and the lessening of physical problems are more quickly reversed once we start using the beautiful life force energy within us.

Healing the Earth

Another place we need to put healing intention is with this Earth Mother of a planet which sustains us. While some complain about how terrible nature has been in such phenomena as tsunamis, hurricanes and earthquakes, others question how a God of Love could cause such devastation and loss of life. It's time to take a longer view. By now you know "God" is not a master puppeteer running the show with reward or vengeance. Creation is what creation is, and it will do what it will do.

Chardin rightly defined the earth as a true living organism. As such, it has its own path of evolution on its journey through the stars. It has its own creative energy to spend and, though its upheavals and changes can affect our human agenda, we cannot fault the earth or its Source for being what it is. And we have done precious little to help it. Through continuous use of harmful chemicals and misusing its own natural products, we continue to force this planet to find its own ways to retain its balance within creation. Raping the earth and bombarding her with weapons of destruction is not how any child should treat its mother.

The most critical problem life on earth now faces is global warming. Yet we still see world governments doing pitifully little to help reverse this process which will, if not corrected, literally bring about the end of life as we know it. To harm the earth through greed for the obscene wealth of the few, and to support the egos of those who insist war is inevitable , as long as they themselves do not die, is contrary to the very meaning of life in all its forms!

The best way to heal our earth mother planet is not to complain about her eruptions but to conserve her very ecosystem, and to continue offering love and gratitude for what she has given us. Ultimately, it is the only way we as a species will heal her and ourselves.

Revere the Mantle

One other way we can begin to heal the earth, as well as ourselves, is to recognize and utilize the gifts she is giving us. One aspect of her generosity comes in the actual pieces of this earth which are all around us. The very mantle of her core, stones, rocks and even the energy of plants and trees, are all parts of the Earth Mother's healing sustenance.

While early humanity learned to use the properties of certain plants to heal physical conditions, rising consciousness now points to other ways to use the earth's healing properties. Knowing there are yet undiscovered remedies for many illnesses still waiting in the rain forests and less traveled parts of the world, one form of healing is to join forces in stopping the destruction of those forests and places before we lose the possibility of finding those remedies.

Another way is to open ourselves to the various healing energies of plants now being discovered through herbal studies and expansion of organic gardening. Going back to the philosophies and spiritual beliefs of our ancestors, we can start taking our food once again directly from the earth, refusing to support the over-processing of foods which we know create disease and potential for early death among our population. Training ourselves to stop using food for comfort or consolation, we can become more responsible for our own health.

The Stones May Be Singing

This Earth Mother has also spent billions of years generating other forms of energetic healing which some only now are beginning to realize. The Western culture has long recognized birthstones — semi-precious or precious stones assigned to every sign of the Zodiac. This is also true in signs of Vedic astrology, which has existed over ten thousand years.

Those born in the sign of Aquarius, for example, are told that amethyst is their birth stone and purple is the color which bests suits them in apparel and home decoration. Most Aquarians then blindly buy into the love of purple and tend to seek amethyst jewelry, never knowing the ancient knowledge which is behind those choices. Selection of those "birth" stones, for example, was drawn from certain astrological signs of the year with consideration of what qualities those born under those astrological signs might require.

The color of stones is also used to coincide with the color to which any particular chakra vibrates, thereby enhancing its energy. For example, lapis lazuli and blue calcite are used to enhance the Brow Chakra, while pink coral, dioptase, and emerald are chosen to give greater intensity to the Heart Chakra.

With the metaphysical science of stones now expanding in this new time, however, there are intuitives and adepts who channel properties of various stones found in different places of the earth. They are, of course, tapping into knowledge of the ancients who innately knew the value of certain stones and their use as amulets or forms of energy needed for various reasons. Diamonds, before any jewelry store considered their value, were used for accessing higher energies and experiencing higher vibrations of love. They also became the stones empowering sovereignty. And knowing the importance of the chakras, since the ancients also innately realized the power of those energy centers, diamonds were also used to provide strength for the Heart, Brow, and Crown chakras. Naturally then, they became regular fixtures used in crowns and royal scepters.

For those Aquarians gifted with amethyst rings, many do not know that, in receiving that stone of their Aquarian birth date, they also received good wishes for higher spirituality, protection and greater activation of the Third Eye or Brow Chakra. They were also receiving greater energy to open the Crown Chakra, and higher chakras as well. This then, makes amethyst one of the most desirable stones in the metaphysical sense of the word. There are many stones now recognized for their healing energies and while some people collect them, put them on home altars, or keep them on their persons in the form of jewelry, others actually use those stones in placements on the body during healing sessions.

You may wish to learn about the metaphysical qualities of your own birth stone or other stones which seem to hold special attraction for you. If you consider the concept of reincarnation a possibility or a probability, you may also realize your love for stones of this earth goes back many lifetimes and into earlier forms of energetic healing and prayer.

Mastery Comes from Being in the Mystery

If quantum physics today says the sum is greater than its parts, we can utilize the mind's great energy for healing. Whether a person thinks of God as a Father Being in the sky, as Pure Consciousness, the Goddess, or the Source of All, tapping into divine energy is empowering. The efficacy of prayer is huge. When others remarked on Jesus' ability to perform miracles, he told them they could do those things also, and more. In his perfect wisdom, he was telling us our greatest ability to heal lies within us.

We can become masters of our own healing especially when we stay connected to the Life Force of Creation Itself. By being proactive through right thinking, eating, and making positive life decisions, we keep ourselves whole and avoid many of the ills which threaten to take our life force energy from us. No one can cause us pain except ourselves.

Love Can Be Healing

As already noted, one of the main teachings of Buddhism is non-attachment. That, however, does not mean we fail to love or fail to take joy in the people and aspects of our lives. True non-attachment is not detachment. It means we can love others well and generously. It also means we can love the things we love when we have them, as long as we realize our only true treasure can never be destroyed. We do not mourn the passing of things but, instead, offer gratitude for having them at all.

My friend and sensei Taka Kanno once said, in speaking of kimonos, "Once I had a most beautiful kimono, but I left it in a taxi, and I never got it back." As I began to show sorrow for her loss, Taka immediately looked at me with calm, beautiful strength. "When I had it, I enjoyed it," she said. "Now I don't have it."

That is true non-attachment, to love what is, but never to hold anything beyond its perfect place in our lives.

"Be the Change You Wish to See"

Those words of Mahatma Gandhi are some of the best advice anyone can receive. When it comes to healing, that advice rings very true. If you want to heal, be a healer. Be an agent of bringing new wholeness to yourself in setting priorities, accessing your higher mind as much as possible, and living in connection with your source and the source of us all. Honor your body and your self, then honor with selfless compassion all those in your life now and all who are currently sharing this world with you.

Honor this earth, refusing to accept the continuing flow of bombs, the raping of natural resources, and other atrocities which some consider a natural part of humankind's evolution. Refusing to honor and care for this planet which sustains us is moving toward our own demise as a species. That does not have to happen. You are an integral part in deciding which way we will go. In whatever way you can, be a healer to this Earth Mother which has given so much to all our ancestors, and to us. We are her caretakers now, and it is vital that we take care of her well!

Send healing to all you feel have caused you pain. In a way, they made the sacrifice of doing those things so you may grow. Thank them. If there needs to be forgiveness, forgive them now. Theirs was a difficult yet important part to play in your life's growth, and they showed up to help you move forward. At the same time, ask forgiveness from all you may have hurt and most of all, extend forgiveness to yourself.

Strive to be a healer in all aspects of your life. Be the one who helps each member of your family move into greater wholeness. Be the one in your work environment who refuses to add to negative gossip and grumblings of unhappiness. Be the one in your community who cares about its positive growth. Be a good neighbor who cares about the peace and well-being of those who share that little part of the planet where you live. Be the one who votes and votes unselfishly for the highest good. Be the one who holds authentic, right-minded and selfless government of all the people as one of your highest priorities.

Be the true friend who uplifts, understands, and encourages. Be the lover who wishes to give more than receive. Be the one who holds gratitude more than desire and forgiveness as one of the highest forms of prayer. Be the one who loves sacred sound, and be the one who relishes sacred silence. Be the one who honors the God of us all, and be the one who honors its presence within yourself.

Is it all about you? In this sense, yes, because you are the only one who can make the impact you were assigned in your life's mission. The energy of your living in wholeness and acting as a healer has direct impact on us all. Your courageous integrity of accepting rising consciousness lifts the consciousness of the world.

You are the master of your life. You are the one who chooses to heal and extend healing by living in authentic, compassionate wholeness. In doing so, you honor your own as well as others' paths toward actualized enlightenment. It's your choice.

Can you dare not to become the change you wish to see?

RIGHT BRAIN CHAPTER REVIEW

Loving Thirst

If I could heal the world
    and all its many immediate intensive agonies —
If I could open the heart of those who fear to love,
    or love to hate, that task would feed my soul.

If I could speak in perfect resonance
    for those still too afraid of their own sound —
If I could be the purest power of loving worth, independent,
    strong, and vibrant energy saying myself as I say Divinity —
How I would soar to that task and pay any price demanded of me!

If I could turn the Inner Eye to a mirror where the Divine speaks
    its thoughts in brilliant, lustrous indigo,

And whispers words on far more human terms in lapis, turquoise,
    and the special blue of the sky on certain days of cosmic purity,
    all wispy-laced in the heavens' swirl,
How I would ride with that! On and on and on!

If I could open the Crown of Godly Light,
The streaming crystalline of sacred luminosity,
    then pour it out — so strong — all over this world,
How I would rise to that treasure, and dance to the spinning
    of glorious golden sweet intensity!

How I would love with purest healing,
If I could listen and speak and gladly become a child of love all over again,
    just for the joy of growing again to Love
    and the task of simply breathing Divinity.

I am wonderfully human and wonderfully spirit born.
I am Energy of God in Light. Light and Life. Actual breathing sound.
Holder of life and birth, beyond, eternal birth — again and again and again.

I have learned to lift my head up!
And I smile across this vast expanse of earth,
    with head flung back and arms thrust open wide
As I speak the joy of sweet, simple union —
Ah, Beloved!
Ah, Beloved!

CHAPTER EIGHTEEN

ARE YOU MYSTIC MATERIAL?

"To Dance with the Beloved"

*I have only one desire – to disappear into God...
to be submerged in his peace.*

- Thomas Merton

If the Zen saying is true, that we keep becoming what we already are, then your becoming has brought you to this point in your life and level of spirituality.

Yet, if you have given any consideration to this book's message, you know there are treasures ahead just waiting to help your journey. There is healing from the wounds life may have inflicted on you, as well as the possibility of living in realistic joy beyond stressors or doubts your ego mind may present to you. Wherever you are right now might be considered the prime of your life, since you have never before had so much experience to draw from, and so much potential in areas which really count. You have matured to this level, and you stand at the edge of endless possibilities. All it will take for those good things to manifest is your willingness and intention to claim them.

Are you mystic material? Of course you are! You are, in fact, a material mystic who just may not have realized it yet! You are in the material form of a human being, existing for a "limited time only" in a certain amount of space yet, you are also part of the Absolute Mystery Itself! And, if you can consider the thought, since God is One in God, you are of God Itself. There are not two. There can never be two because two involves separation. There is only One.

Am I saying you are God? Are you the transcendent Light of All Creation and all that is yet to be? Not quite. But you do hold the God seed and the God fullness within you; otherwise, you would not exist. Because God is the All That Is, you cannot be separated from that one, only Truth. Now, all you need do is realize that and start finding ways to live in more perfect union with God's essence within you.

The Deepest Ache

I was a high school teacher for many years and, one day one of my students came to my classroom after school. She seemed a bit tentative, then asked, "Can I talk to you for a minute?" Then she settled at a desk in front of me. "I don't know if you know this about me, but I'm adopted." Her name was Karen.

"I wasn't aware of that," I said.

"Somehow I want you to know," Karen said. "And don't get me wrong. My parents are the best! They really love me. I live in a great house and have everything I could ask for. They've already told me I can go to any college I choose, and my life is really good." Then she paused. "But there's an ache in me." She put a hand over her heart. "I'm almost old enough to start making the search, but it's getting more and more important for me to find my birth mother. Everything else in my life is fine, but — ."

She reached that hand away from her heart and out into some distant healing. "There's an ache in me that won't go away until I know where I came from. I just want to find out if my birth mother is still alive, and where she is. I want to make some kind of contact with her, and maybe even get to know her. Something in me just won't be complete until I find her. It's the only thing that will make this ache in my heart go away."

She was an attractive, intelligent, young woman, already on track toward a successful, meaningful life. Yet Karen's simple yearning to know the source of her physical life mirrored the same gentle but persistent pain all humanity shares. We need to make contact with our source. We need to know our roots, because somehow, in knowing where we came from, we can have a better idea of what we are now and where we might be going. Knowing our source can put everything in perspective.

That very human ache has been part of every person who ever lived, and healing that ache is the goal of any religion or spiritual practice. We just need to make contact with our source.

What we seek is direct, experiential knowledge of God. Thomas Merton's quote at this chapter's beginning says it all. "I have only one desire … to disappear into God." In saying that, Merton was describing our desire to not only know our source, but to reach beyond the mind to actually experience that Source Energy.

That is the goal, not only of every religious system, but of every heart which looks honestly within. That ultimate experience has been written of over the millennia in religious books and sacred texts and carried on in oral traditions from the most indigenous tribes and ancient peoples to today's theological scholars. It all comes down to finding one real way of attaining that direct experience.

Mysticism Is No Mystery

The word to describe that way, which the *Tao Te Ching* actually calls *The Way*, is mysticism. It is living in direct personal connection with the Source of your creation. That may sound a bit too much to ask, yet it is very possible. Achieving that does take effort on your part, and the way will not always be easy. It is a reachable goal, and the journey to finding its treasure becomes quite a treasure in itself. It may, however, also be a very lonely journey at times, and it will demand courage to stay the course.

One of my favorite poems is by Dag Hammarskjold, a former head of the United Nations. In his journal *Markings*, he wrote of humanity's sometimes lonely weariness and temptation to quit that journey into the actualized presence of the Divine Mystery, and it fits perfectly here:

July 6, 1961.

Tired and lonely, so tired the heart aches
Meltwater trickles down the rocks.
The fingers are numb. The knees tremble
It is now — now that you must not give in.

On the path of the others are resting places,
Places in the sun where they can meet.
But this is your path, and it is now,
now that you must not fail.

Weep if you can, weep.
But do not complain.
The way chose you
And you must be thankful.

In these words, a great thinker and Nobel Prize winner described the human temptation to settle for less. He talks about the way as not just a goal, but the essence of the goal itself. It is this way, this search, which has become the seed of many divisions among religions, dogmas and belief systems.

The only way, however, is the mystical journey each individual makes into what we call the heart of God — until she or he realizes that we have been the ones to create the separation through faulty thinking. The God Essence has never separated itself from us. Human illusion concocted that pseudo-reality. Now it is time to be still again, and remember with new awareness what our deepest selves have always known.

The only true theology, or study of God, is not a study at all! It is recognizing this sacred state within our minds. It is an inner state of already knowing we are more than the sum of our parts. We are in the true Quantum. We are one with the source which creates us. Our spiritual essence and true identity have always been, and can never be separate from, what we are. We are individual shards of the great, transcendent Light.

Our earliest ancestors were sacred and full of God. Through all the millennia of humankind's struggle, we have been growing closer toward the final realization of what we innately know. That's what Jesus was trying to tell us. The Kingdom never has been "out there." We are already in it! You are in it!

You have a beautiful human heart and a soul which is your direct connection with your Source. No matter how much noise of distraction there is in your life right now, you are actually very close to that connection already, and it would be foolish to postpone a truly beautiful time of sacred union.

The questions are: how much longer do you want to stay in the noise? How many more years are you going to wait until you get serious about living? How many more things and how much other human stuff, drama and events are you going to wade through until, perhaps, on your death bed, if you are allowed that luxury, you will finally say, "Now I get it. Now I know there's More! My God! You were there all along!"

The Past Speaks the Present Need

To illustrate the fact you are not alone, consider these words from holy people across the world. We stand on the shoulders of those who have written of our human species' greatest search; let their words speak to you now as you consider the way ahead.

Black Elk, speaking from the wisdom of indigenous people, wrote, "I am blind and do not see the things of this world; but when the light comes from above it enlightens my heart and I can see, for the eye of my heart sees everything. The heart is a sanctuary of which there is a little spirit wherein the Great Spirit dwells, and this is the I of the Great Spirit by which he sees all things and through which we see him."

From the ancient *Shveteshvatara Upanishad*, "No longer identifying yourself with the body, go beyond birth and death. All your desires will be fulfilled in him who is one without a second. Know him to be enshrined in your heart always. Truly there is nothing more to know in life. Meditate and realize the world is filled with the presence of God."

From the Gautama the Buddha, "Know all things to be like this: as an echo that derives from music, sounds and weeping, yet in that echo is no melody."

From the Judaic tradition, the *Song of Songs*, addressing the divine beloved. "I am my beloved's and he is mine."

From the Hebrew scholar Moses Cardoveros, "Each of us emerges from *Einsof*, (The unnamable One) and is included in it. We live through its dissemination. It is the perpetuation of existence."

From the Persian poet Rumi, "Borrow the Beloved's eyes. Look through them and you will see the beloved's face everywhere. No tiredness, no jaded boredom, 'I shall be your eye and your hand and your loving!' What a miracle, you and I entwined in the same next, one Fire in this world and the next in an ecstasy without end."

From a short piece called *Thunder: Perfect Mind* in scrolls of antiquity, these words by a woman speaking in the I AM context of those who give words to the God Source: "I am the knowledge of my name. I am the name of the Sound and the sound of the name ... for I am the one who alone exists."

Knowing the Only One

Just as in Buddhism *satchitananda* is considered true living with consciousness, the Buddhist tradition of Zen, which simply translates as "meditation" offers the image of a perfect circle called *enso*. Often drawn with a simple wide brush stroke, this circle is known as the ultimate shape of explaining Zen. It signifies the end of duality, brought about by direct inner experience of the One. In considering the *enso* circle, some people feel it is a "coming full circle." It portrays the fact that, in rising consciousness, we are growing closer to experience our source. From all ages the circle is considered to be the perfect shape and symbol, where all is contained within one space. Perhaps the *enso* circle will speak to you.

You may think your attempting to leap "full circle" into the essence of all may be a bit taxing for your life right now, and you may be right. But there are ways for you to grow in deeper knowledge of what you really are, and that may be considered as simply showing up. It could also be called Modern Mysticism.

Manifest the Light

With meditation and stillness part of your alone time with the Divine Mystery, today's modern mysticism also demands we leave that solitude to address the needs of the world. To assume the true role of a modern mystic, it is important that we get off the mountain top or get out of the desert and become people of action in today's world. After the beauty of solitude, growth means nothing if we cannot "take it to the streets." Action after solitude is essential. Involvement in our cities and communities is important, as well as finding ways to benefit others through volunteerism or involvement with community projects. Now it is our turn to be like the elders who heard the cries of the world in other times and did something about it.

Our neighbors today need help in many different ways, and it's our turn to step up and do something for them. Find your own ways of getting involved and then let the Divine Mystery reveal Itself through you.

We live in a world where the middle class is falling away. We have the rich and the extremely rich on one end and the needy and the extremely indigent at the other end of society's spectrum. If we refuse to stay aware of what is happening in our cities and our schools, our nation and our world, then anything we say, as Paul wrote, becomes mere "sounding brass and empty cymbals."

In the history of Judaic mysticism, the growing popularity of the Kabbalah is another sign people are understanding the need to get involved. Based on the teachings of the Zohar, which is the central text of the Kabbalah, the term "ripe grapes" is used to describe those who hold God's light and manifest it in the world. They carry the true essence of *Shekinah*, which is the manifestation of God's presence in the world and considered to be the feminine aspect of the God Energy. To be in the world and of the world, the Kabbalah teaches, brings God's light in many ways to those who will witness it.

Whether you wear a red string on your wrist or not, what needs to really be worn is a ring of compassion around your heart and a willingness to make that compassion an active ingredient in your personal life experiences. Our world is more needy now than ever, and there are people and causes desperately waiting for someone like you to make the difference which counts. Find them; then do something about it!

Can You Do It?

Are you mystic material? Absolutely. Can you make a difference in the world as you rise to greater involvement with the Divine Source implicit in all of creation? Yes, you can.

Hold some stillness in each part of every day and begin to hear the sounds which silence teaches you about witnessing Love to all creation. Then, take your growth within the divine mystery and use it to make a difference in your world. The time is now, and now is a beautiful present!

RIGHT BRAIN CHAPTER REVIEW

I Remember You

I remember you in the first Light.
 The thought of you seemed like home to me.
The earth was moist and you were full of crystals.

You are Light — shining, stone — shining,
 shining from so many shadows to a brilliance
 which I wanted to become and oh, how I envied you!

I remember you in water — rushing to a place it did not know.
In ecstasy, I felt the thrill of you —
Each wisp of moisture seemed a baptism from other worlds,
Until the sweet, silver whispering of you became a stream

Which coursed its way deep and ever deeper through my soul.
Ah, the joy!
To be in awe of beauty I could only sense,
    yet strangely never see.

Sweet moss of earth became a canopy of stars
And universes far beyond the places in my heart.
And I became them! How we danced in them!
And what a journey still remains for us to remember
    In the future past of Now
    As together we witness the Light!

CHAPTER NINETEEN

DISCOVER WHAT LIES BEYOND

Now It's All Yours...

Freed from the limitations of ego, free to see and hear and touch the magic we've been missing all our lives, we're becoming at last who we really are.

- Marianne Williamson

There are many paths which lead to the One Truth, yet there is only One Truth. If you are comfortable and content in your approach to whatever you call God, keep it up. Read your own heart which reveals the light and wisdom given you. Your path may have come from your culture, from teachings ingrained in you from youth, from society, or any ideas you have come to believe as the only truth there is.

Just remember, "In my father's house there are many mansions," and the roads which lead to those citadels of Spirit are varied and numerous. Some are directly opposed to all others. Some embrace the goodness of all.

The truth is that a Buddhist woman in the outreaches of the Himalayas, who lives a quiet life of compassion and service to herself, her family and those she meets along her journey, is no less precious and holy, in the "eyes of God" than the mightiest pope, guru, teacher, or world leader. The life of a child in the Congo or in Appalachia is no less valuable than the long-lived existence of the greatest thinker, or one whose name lives on in this world's history books.

Whatever religion or modality you are currently following is your medium for arriving at the ultimate goal. And that goal isn't even something you reach. It is already in you. It is your gift to discover, celebrate, and draw upon for nourishment now. Even if you are a diligent follower of a particular belief system, remember that religion is only a path you choose toward a destination. That last part of the journey, however, can never be reached by anything less than your own heart. Any path simply leads to its end. The final joy lies in embracing and enjoying the one thing which put you on the path in the first place.

Don't rely on any religion or belief system as the ultimate ticket to the Divine Banquet. Most religions have problems of their own. More angst among people in religion comes from their frustrations with the human conditions within the religion itself. Dealing with human foibles of ministers and the dictates of very human hierarchies and dogmatists is not conducive to creating idyllic bliss. They can, however, be dismissed when we remember religion has nothing to do with the purity of spirit one holds between her or his heart and the Heart of the Divine Mystery. Religion is flawed because it is a human creation dealing with spirit in a very human way. It actually has very little to do with one's personal relationship to that Mystery. We all know there is more.

It's All About You

Much has been said, even in this book, about the need to hold compassion for others and the world. Modern mysticism calls for action and witnessing Absolute Truth. Once we have found the slightest glimmer of light, we are encouraged not to keep it under a basket. There is, in all of us, the desire to give, and that's good.

Yet the one recipient of our giving, who really needs it most, is our self. The greatest gift we can give another or the world is not the treasure of time, service, or even prayer, though all are of powerful value. The greatest contribution which is only ours to make is the development of our own soul. That is why meditation is so important. It is the surest way to promote the acceleration of intuition, wisdom, and ability to sink more deeply into Eternal Truth.

Our greatest task is to reach our highest potential. The journey of our spirit, whether you believe it is confined to this one life, or through many lifetimes, is to rise above the world of illusion. It is to personally experience the Truth which holds us, and everything else, in creation. Because we are included in the One Soul, our rising even a bit higher in spirit and the ability to love affects the whole. Any thought of anger or hatred also affects the total dynamic of creation. Likewise, any thought of forgiveness, gratitude or love creates the same impact on all of us and all that is. We are all connected in the One Mind. In actuality, there is really only one of us here. How deeply we love, how compassionately we hold this earth, including every thing and every one on it, enriches the collective consciousness.

It is that collective consciousness which is now awakening throughout the world. We sense the need to make our lives and life styles more earth-friendly. The concept of "Greening America" is finally catching on, and other positive signs are all around us. We are seeing more clearly how war, greed, and misuse of the earth's great gifts are impacting the human condition. We're more aware of how petty addictions dull our senses and prevent the freedom of spirit from soaring beyond the illusions we've held so dear. We are rethinking what has been and beginning to embrace the possibilities and reality of what is meant to be. We are actually starting to think in the quantum like true sojourners in this Axial Age!

We are witnessing many pillars of society, government, and even some approaches to happiness and holiness beginning to crumble. Our way of being, as we have known it, is shifting into a new paradigm, a new way of living which portends how we and this planet will move forward in time.

It has always been about change, hasn't it? We have all experienced our own evolution through life. And we have dealt with it. All those changes have made us what we have become. Now, however, we are experiencing the huge dynamic of life itself, and the life of the human heart, rocketing forward in this axial time toward a new way of being. Now it is our choice to strongly embrace it or become part of the archaic wreckage which doesn't fit this new emergence any more.

More than ever in human history, it's up to you. How you think, feel and act impacts us all. You are part of the whole; no man or woman is an island. We are all in this together more than we ever conceived that concept before. Your thoughts are powerful. They literally create the world as you perceive it. You have shown up in this all important time in human history to walk as courageously as you can between the old world of what has been and the new way of being. You are the product of all who have gone before and, in gratitude and forgiveness, you might honor them for their contribution to the collective whole.

This, however, is no time to blame, judge, or criticize. This is your time to embrace truth and hold it as a beacon to guide you through this seemingly dark night into a glorious dawn.

Get over all your past petty hurts. Bless the challenges and love the journey. Let all your answers begin to resound in the stillness of your heart, and all of us will thank you! In this time of collective consciousness and axial transition, it really is about each of us and, in your case, it is intensely about you! And, on behalf of the universe, let me be one of the first to thank you for showing up!

Ascension Time

Whatever you may have taken from these pages is intended to be nothing but a springboard. Now is it your turn to dive into the ocean of your own inner knowledge and higher consciousness. That is how you can open the floodgates of deeper understanding of the Source and its impact on your life.

You are indeed walking between the worlds of duller and higher consciousness, between the old patriarchal, dualistic way of perceiving life and a more vibrant, more feminist way of being. We are all actually walking deeper into the Divine Mystery Itself! And, as time seems to be speeding up, it is a sign that we are drawing closer to that actual occurrence. The very fact you are still reading this book is another sign that you are one of those whose walk will be highly meaningful.

I ask you now to consider the concept of Shiva. Shiva is one of the three representatives of the Divine Source in the trinity of the beautiful Vedic culture, whose religious system is Hinduism. Shiva is the Destroyer, yet that destruction is not what we think of in society today. Shiva destroys all that does not serve our highest good, and that destruction is essential. It brings each of us to the state of what we, in our true essence actually are, perfectly and divinely whole, enlightened human beings who walk in the mystery of Light. By destroying the many illusions of ego mind, Shiva opens the way to deeper union with our source. Christians look to the Holy Spirit to provide that same kind of inner guidance. Whatever name we give that concept, its essence is still the same.

If human existence is an "earth school" of living through "sacred contracts," thanks to Gary Zukav and Carolyn Myss for those terms, with challenges and lessons to be learned, the end result of any life has the same goal. Raymond Moody, M.D., in one of his books on near-death experiences, speaks of two questions the soul feels the need to answer at the end of life. They are: "How well have you loved?" and "What have you learned?"

Those questions mirror the same goal of any valid religion or spiritual belief system. They should help us realize how well we have learned to live unselfishly and with true compassion for all. They should also help us recognize what we have learned by replacing the illusion of separation with the reality of Oneness.

In order to answer those questions well, we need a bit of Shiva's destruction of the lesser and the useless within our ego selves. We need the guidance of the Holy Spirit to show us a way into living within deeper reality. We need the rising into the Great Spirit of indigenous people after they have walked the Good Red Road of right living. All those things involve a type of ascension.

Death and Ascension

Christians honor the ascension of Jesus into his true essence of the divine. Some spiritual thinkers consider that same ascension of Jesus' transfiguration to be the manifestation of his true body of Light. He then allowed the radiance of that Light Essence to be seen by those who were honored to witness it. Rather than "ascend" physically to a locality or actual place called heaven "out there" somewhere, Jesus allowed his presence within the Source of All, the Oneness, to be made manifest to individuals still in human form. He showed us there is only one way to achieve that ascension, through a form of death.

Jesus the teacher was right. But there are many lesser deaths we must experience on our way into living within the Light Source we call God. There are human relationships which fail, addictions to be overcome, difficult lessons of greed, ego and selfishness we need to sometimes painfully learn. Each of these is a kind of death. If we are learning from them well, we are allowing all those lesser parts of our ego minds to fall away, replacing them with new ascension into higher awareness of allowing the God presence to shine its radiance through us.

Is there pain involved? Yes. Is new birthing a blessed result of all that pain? Yes. By allowing the little deaths and many ascensions into a higher form of consciousness, however, we keep becoming what we always were, co-creators of the divine Source. All those forms of little deaths bring ascension. They help defeat the separation of duality while creating ascension into soul level awareness of being truly One.

Consider Consecration

Any form of consecration is a personal and momentous event. Many belief systems have a marriage ceremony where two people consecrate their union together with God as their witness. There are consecrations to the ministry or religious service and attunements to other organizations or modalities which use ceremony to lift one higher into a sense of duty and identity with the divine.

Whatever else you may do in life, whatever cause to which you may dedicate yourself, the most sacred and personally rewarding is the only one true consecration you can make. If you are serious about your intention to live within the Divine Presence, you and the Energy of that presence are already in a holy contract. A sealing of that pact on your part, however, might involve a personal consecration of yourself to live as fully and wholly as possible in that most sacred relationship.

Every culture and belief system has its own methods of initiation and affirmation once a person reaches supposed mental maturity. Both the Catholic sacrament of Confirmation and the Judaic Bar or Bat Mitzvah are examples. From wrapping a blanket around two people in indigenous marriage rituals to more involved ceremonies of ordination or attunement, you may make a very simple consecration of yourself to the Divine Presence within you.

Meditate on it. Hold the concept in your mind and especially in your heart. When you feel the time may be right, choose a place meaningful to you. Gather around you any artifacts — or no artifacts — which you choose. The most important thing is that you consider it a sacred time and place. It can be done in your home, in a group, or out on the land where the very sound of the universe adds to and witnesses the act you are making. We human beings love ritual and a ritual such as this is most appropriate and profound. Its action and meaning is intended to echo down the rest of your life, and you should make every attempt to make it and seal it with as much consciousness and love as possible.

Once you have determined a time and place, be in stillness before the actual consecration. You may even take a few days of preparation before this will happen. Then, let the silence of your own heart begin a vibration within Pure Consciousness. Be singularly one with it. Be in its peace and its joyful fullness. Then honor the directions of the earth and the vastness of all creation.

Gather the intention of consecration to that Source in your mind and heart. Place your life, in gratitude for all that has been, and with confident intention for what is yet to be, in the essence of this consecration. Make it a vow if you wish but, whatever name you call it, let it be the placing of all your life and spirit into the loving embrace of the Divine Mystery. Intend this consecration not to be merely for this lifetime but for the eternity in which your spirit truly resides.

Then, when the time and fullness are right, say aloud your own personal words of consecration. Let the vibration of them and your loving, conscious intention reach deep into the Divine Source. Make it as meaningful as possible and resolve to live from that time on, as much as you humanly can, with awareness of your consecration's impact. Whatever other community, organization, nation or belief system which claims your allegiance, make your first allegiance to this Divine Presence within you. This is the only consecration which really matters.

Think about it and don't do it lightly. Any vow, contract or pledge can be dispensed through proper channels. I know that personally. Not this one. This is a consecration which binds forever. Make the intention to live it as much as possible in your daily life.

It's a beautiful and meaningful act which brings you blessing and holiness. Consider it.

Teachers and Communities

If you are like the rest of us, we have all looked at various times for those who know more than we do. When our car is making strange noises, we look for a good mechanic who understands "car speak." When our teeth are doing more than ripping food apart or adding to our happy smile, we look for a dentist like my friend Butch in Albuquerque who can make teeth behave like proper teeth again. And, when that quiet but wise little voice inside our higher mind keeps whispering, "There's more. I know there's more …" we look for someone who can help us understand what that "more" might be.

Titles such as "master" or "teacher" are highly overused these days. In truth, we are all teachers and learners in every role we play in life. When it comes to delving deeper into that "more," however, we may look for one who can help us along the path. If you are ready to find such a person, set the intention to meet an individual who can serve you well. There are many today who call themselves masters and teachers and, while many are valid, there are others who have just started believing the title they put on their business cards. There's that old saying that an "expert" is anyone who is sixty miles away from home! Have a well-intentioned open heart and, when you find someone who might help, determine what resonance they may have with you. Read the energy of their authenticity.

A true spiritual teacher is not one who fills you with pious platitudes, definitive dogma, or various forms of what O'Murchu calls "insipid religiosity" or pseudo spirituality and who is always very glad to take your money. A true teacher is one who provides the sacred ground for your spiritual growth and holds the stillness for it to nurture your own greatest blossoming. We learn best not from what a teacher might say, but from what we come to understand about the depths of her or his heart. There are true holy women and men out there. Make the intention to find one and, in that discovery, you may find one whose presence actually holds the resonance of the God Source. Look beyond their physicality and listen to the vibration of their souls. It can be a beautiful experience.

Just as Jesus of Nazareth was a great teacher and God realized human being, he met the mark of a true educator, one who draws out from another the inner brilliance of God Light that any single individual may contain. My dear friend and Sensei Taka Kanno never used the title "teacher," but, with few words, exquisite silence, and the joyful modeling of her own spiritual depth, she taught me to be ever more mindful of the Teacher Within.

Make the intention for that special one or more persons to come into your life and then be open to whomever the angels may bring across your path. The old saying, "When the student is ready, the teacher will appear," is another piece of wisdom which becomes more evident as consciousness rises. Just know that your part of "being ready" is doing your own work first. Take time each day for meditation and silence. Start looking at the people in your life, and strangers on the street, not with judgment and suspicion, but as brothers and sisters on the planet who are all trying to get to the same place as you.

Spend some time in book stores and check the Internet for key words such as consciousness, spirituality, and body-mind-spirit living. One thing you may also do is begin to look for groups or centers in your area where like-minded people tend to gather. Because there are many more people now who are "getting it," almost every area has seen the growth of small communities of individuals who meet periodically to share their growth in spirit. As one who spent years in a Catholic religious community, and more recently in groups and small communities of like-minded people, I know the value of being with others who share the same purpose of living in discovery and inner growth. While there is extreme value in developing our own spiritual practice, there comes a time when we feel the need to share. The true nature of love is always to give and to share.

Again, make the intention to find such a gathering of people and then attend some of their functions. Your own discernment will quickly tell you if what they're doing is authentic and right for you. Of course, you will run into very human egos, various levels of spiritual depth, and all of the other very human things which come with the territory. But, listen and observe well, then run what is happening through your own beautiful heart.

There will be drumming circles, home liturgies, Reiki evenings, book clubs, healing circles, and all kinds of circles, which are an ancient practice coming back into fullness now. Women's or men's wisdom circles are growing in popularity, just as groups which have the same base such as being in recovery from various addictions. Wherever you are on your path, there is probably a group or loosely-knit community in your area which can help. Start looking, then be open to what you may discover. If the resonance is there for you, stay with it a while. If not, you will still have learned. We can always be in a learning mode even when we discover what is not right for us. There are treasure houses of community groups out there and, when you find the right one, walk with them a while. It could be a good thing.

Be Your Own Truth

There is one Source of us all, whatever name you give it. It is not only the Creator, but the Source of All that was, is, and is yet to be. It is the potential beyond chaos and the source beyond all of evolution's possibilities. And, the best news is that you are never apart from it and it is never apart from you!

There are feminine and masculine energies in you. Honor them, and know they disappear in the non-duality of the One. Realize the earth is now experiencing a more feminine mode of consciousness where equality, compassion, and respect for all are changing life on our planet.

Knowing what we now know about the power of intention, consider taking time to consecrate each day. Because the ego mind insists on living in a linear pattern, take some time for preparation. Create some stillness, preferably in meditation, where you can slip down from beta and alpha states of consciousness into that theta state where your mind is open to higher vibrations. Then let your mind slow down with your attention focused on listening to the silences. Intend the best possible activities which will aid your deepest growth for that day. Intend that, no matter what life may hurl at you through the coming hours, the deepest part of you will remain in that beauty where judgment falls away and you merely become an observer of yourself, your world, and your presence in the Mystery.

Remember, earth is a free will zone. You are not a puppet on a string. Rather, you are someone who can intend through the power of your mind to show up for the deepest form of living available at this point in your life. Breathe in the God Light through the top of your head and let it sift down through each energy center and into every cell of your body. Consecrate yourself anew to the greater presence of divinity within you. Intend your willingness to be divine love present on this planet through that particular day.

Another help you can choose is to create your own mantra. You can then use it at different times of the day, either in times of stress or when negative thoughts or pains of addiction or judgment make themselves known. You may adopt a mantra such as, "I stand in God Light," or, "I am divine love present on the planet," and use it for months until you feel the need to adopt another set of words which serves you best. If you are going through a particularly difficult situation, you may adopt a mantra just for that day. If, for example, you are going to meet with someone at work who causes you stress, adopt a silent mantra to use during that meeting.

You are the master of your own life. You do not have to react to everything which happens to you. By setting the intention of higher consciousness and living in the Source Presence Itself, you become proactive. You create around yourself a buffer from negativity as well as a layer of energy which allows you to be present in this world in a much higher state, living in it more deeply, beautifully, and in greater peace. By adopting a positive, proactive attitude toward meeting any pressure or circumstance throughout the day, we can, through practice, observe more and be less involved in any difficult situation. Instead, take the long view from your heart and your union with the Divine Heart. You can begin to see every action and your own reactions as part of the Divine plan you once accepted as necessary to your growth. Learn to see not only the problems, but to also consider their value in your own development.

Resolve not to think of yourself as a victim of your life circumstances. Determine to stop living in any kind of fear, be it fear of financial lack, fear of danger, or fear of any kind. Instead make the intention to be one who heals yourself and those around you as well as healing this earth and all of creation.

Every problem contains its own solution. Every source of stress rises from a need for deeper healing in some part of your self. You are your own master and that title may never appear on your business card, but you are fully capable of living in the God Light with extreme beauty and peace. Aligning yourself in the highest participation with the Divine Mind and the Divine Heart is aligning yourself with the transcendent God of All, as well as that presence within you. As Paul wrote once, "Of myself I can do nothing." But you, with the spark of divinity which yearns to express itself through you, can do all things. Consider the words of Jesus the teacher, "All these things I have done, you also can do — and much more." Believe that. Know that, because those are words of truth.

Welcome the divine spirit of holiness into your life and celebrate its presence. Learn to laugh more and judge less. Intend to love more and fear less. Through intention and being part of your own silences, resolve to be one whose light and love changes the collective consciousness of the human race, thought by thought and day by day. You are important to the whole because, in your rising to higher awareness, you lift the totality of all, not only the human species, but all that is.

Can you heal a headache? Perhaps. Perhaps not. Can you heal the world and the consciousness of the human race? Absolutely! And the God Consciousness is counting on you to participate as fully as you can in the plan of that divine mystery.

Realize the beauty of your own soul and resolve to let it shine so others may witness what we as human beings can possibly become. What others think of you in their own judgments is exactly that, their judgments. You know what you are. You are a spark of God present on this planet. No matter what anyone else may perceive in their linear thinking, you know you are magnificent because you are of God!

Whether you periodically visit a formal place of worship, or not, you are a sacred space. You present the locality of your body and the energy around you as it moves through this earth. Be holiness and others will draw from that wholeness within you. The locality of your body is surrounded by the non-locality of your own holy spirit. Just let it be so it may truly keep becoming more of the Source Essence within you.

If Christian scripture records the visit of the angel Gabriel to Mary, the mother of Jesus, saying, "Hail, Mary, you are full of grace and the Lord is with you," realize that message also comes to you in every continual emanation from the God Source. You are full of grace. The Divine Presence is with you because you can never be separated from it. It is in your life force and the beauty of your eternal soul.

Follow those you see as people of good heart when you need to follow but, remember, you are a leader who can change the world through your own right intention and honest living. You hold the greatest potentiality for healing the world as only you can. You are as important as the most powerful person on earth and, in the right ways, you may be even more important because your power is aligned with the higher source. Your power comes from standing in your own authenticity as exactly what you are, perfect and wonderful and ready to say "Here I am" into the Mystery Source of All. Only you can say in your own life, "How can you use me today, and how can we together change the world?"

It's not only possible. It's probable. All you have to do is say yes, with love and right intention, and then live that "yes." All the rest are just details.

You are not a victim of life. You are a champion of the God Presence in human form. Remember that and be what you are!

Keys to Moving Beyond

Honor all creation as facets of ever-encompassing radiance. Honor and be grateful for the past, and hold the future's possibilities in your heart. Remain, however, within the Eternal Present of Now and the next breath you take. Hold everyone and everything in love. Whatever people or events cause you pain, forgive and bless them all, then let them go. They are part of your learning. Honor them as catalysts to your greater growth.

Be for the healing, for the silence and the sound. Be the witness of Divine Love on the planet while you're here. It's very important because that love pouring from your heart is raising the consciousness of us all.

Love your mind in its growing awareness and its power of intention to co-create the highest good for yourself and all that is. Be one who heals and protects the planet and all life which thrives on it.

Be more than a person of peace. Be peace. Be forgiveness and be gratitude, and be Divine Love present in this world today.

And, for God's sake, and your own, enjoy every minute of it!

These words now go into silence. Now it's all up to you. Namaste!

RIGHT BRAIN BOOK REVIEW

I Shall Follow Only the Light

I sense ancient voices whispering to me, and I celebrate
    the wisdom of their words as I applaud the higher thinking
    of brilliant ones today who celebrate the quantum
    and thoughts beyond the limits of beginnings and ends.
I begin to share the Consciousness of Source —
    of secrets that now flicker in my soul
    as wholeness fills the seeds of possibility.
I hold only God because that is the only Truth which really holds me.
I honor the giants of religions and those whose humanity
    made religion necessary at all.
As I bow to needful change while holding to the one immobility
    which locks its very essence in the unchanging heart of the Divine.

I hold the silence and the stillness which reveals that truth to me,
And gladly suffer emptiness as I learn to heal well.

Now I sense the soul of me, willing to reach with love so strong
I cannot probe the source of all its power.
I can only know it is true and at the very depth of me.
And I feel it, full and grown now — as it is growing still —
         mature and tender as strength has finally come.
I am words now, and I am melody. I am silence, filled with awe.
I am tension wound to peacefulness, and ready for encounter now,
         full and sure there is a purpose for me now.
And I believe the giving shall be beautiful
         As I live my gift of love.

Now I shall follow only the Light.
I shall flow with the depths of this silent, mystic sea.
And nothing, ever again,
         will hamper this journey I feel inside of me.

EPILOGUE

This book began with the observation that "Being" was the easy part. It was the act of becoming which demanded attention early in life, and "Becoming" has indeed been the prime task every step of the way.

As much as there has been space in these pages, I have tried to share facts about what is happening in this time of change and challenge. I've looked at religion's impact on all of us and, I hope, helped you sift through your own experiences within institutionalized religion as well as alternative routes into this Mystery which keeps calling us unto Itself.

In that first chapter I shared my own journey with you, including why I entered the convent and why I did not remain there. I had to revisit my pain of deciding to leave the convent religious life I once considered my destiny. I did this, however, to seek the Divine Mystery in less structured, more uncharted ways. I've had to remember again my need to learn more from some Ultimate Silence which demanded a price from me to gain its blessing and its benefits. I shared my need for more freedom to seek the "Kingdom" and to know "God" beyond limited dictates of any one religion, even the Catholic religion which was given to me at birth. And the price I paid for honoring my goal of greater union with Sacred Truth was leaving the religious community I loved. There have been times in my life since then when I have also been challenged to leave many things behind — as that vision and goal of deeper union continues to call me on.

The chapters in this book are my sharing of what I have learned in that time during and since convent days. They also describe ways of attaining deeper knowledge when I have stopped to listen to the sounds of my soul, as well as the Great Soul. They are times when I have taken the Buddha's advice and sought to be a light unto myself. In truth, all these years I have been subconsciously seeking the divine truth exactly where Jesus told us to look — within! It is there that we find the great I AM — *Ehyeh Asher Ehyeh*. That is also where we come into sweet encounter with the *Sophia Christou* — the highest wisdom of the Christ.

Once I left the convent I made choices to survive and go on, just as everyone else who makes a major life change. I set new priorities in those first few years and a new life slowly emerged for me, as I trusted it would. I also began to expand my relationship with divinity. I dove into spiritual practices from various cultures and sacred writings from many different belief systems. I found great truth in works from Buddhism, Hinduism and Islam, as well as vast wisdom in the spirituality of indigenous people. Treasures within the beautiful religion of Judaism have given me many concepts to ponder and take to heart. Other belief systems of the world drew my attention, and soon I began to realize all these religions were saying the same thing. They were seeking the same goals, only in different ways. We really all are one people reaching for the same Divine Self.

My meditations changed from the more rigid, mental and visual meditations we had practiced in the convent. Instead I loved the free flowing depth of stillness and uncharted beauty which Zen and other modalities offered. When I settled into those forms of meditation and contemplation my heart flew open. Somehow I felt I was closer to Home. Relating to the Divine Mystery in these ways seemed right and good, and I loved being lost in it.

Now I invite you to consider your own journey, then find the courage to do what you feel is right for you. Take time to pray and meditate. Listen to your heart. Go beyond the externals and see what finds resonance in your own precious soul. Your home is in the Source of Love Itself. Let us all meet there when this day is done.

Be Still. Listen. Learn. Share. Serve.

Namaste!

BEYOND THE PROSE

The Canyon

If ever there could be a place for me to pray,
Where the glory of the heavens and the glory of this earth pray me
It is here in this red rock canyon — this cathedral for my emptiness
      where I become a vessel containing wonder
      and my heart seems to leap into majesty's expanse
            like some very young eagle
            caught in the delicious joy of learning how to soar.
For it is here I begin to realize my own life has been carved
      like some unforgiving tapestry of stone
      here in these jagged mountains, whose crevices, gougings
      and scarrings from ancient water and wind
            mirror etchings of challenges I have had to meet
            along my own journey of years.
Yet there are stronger lines within these rocks
      and on this canyon's floor, as if recording other times
      I never did give in, when I never chose to follow easy paths,
      and where each climb became another prayer to lead me higher

as I have begged the universe
to make me a place of God.

And I am wonderfully lost here, within this canyon world.
As I am lost and sweetly found in the Heart of All There Is —
even as twisted, weathered trees and ages-worn rocks
remind me of harder times I have endured through all my life —
the cuttings and the strippings down to essences,
which reveal what in all my years I finally have become.
And I am grateful for them all, as they have been so critical
in some Master Plan which lay hidden for too many years —
so much a part of tearing wide and opening my heart
in twisted pain at times — until I could finally see
each scarring as a needed part of me,
a necessary wound to bring new birth —
in conquering what might have stayed
an emptiness in sterile wombs of me —
never allowing the grace of newer life.
Barren rock there, so lucid in the higher reaches —
to mirror barren times within my heart,
stark in their honesty reminding me of pain
I often brought upon myself —
and had to endure in order to understand.

Yet, within these mountains' tapestries, there is also subtle greenery,
modeling the joy I have never lost in all my life —
the joy which does not bow to any sorrow
which might mar the beauty which becomes the great ascent.

And amid the stark, sharply etched caves, and plunges, and pinnacles,
    here and there I see smoother places for resting in the sun.
Mercifully too, I have found places for my heart and mind to rest,
    and I treasure them in memories
        whose sweetnesses are giftings to my soul.

Also, from my place along this canyon floor
I watch the beauty of moisture — silvered shining in the sunlight,
    dancing down along the crimson mountain sides —
    streaming down in liquid delight after soft, springtime rain.
And I wonder — Are those tears of sorrow? Tears of nature's joy?
    Or remnants of baptisms repeated through eternity —
        over and over and over again—
        bonded to the simple grace of creation's timeless flow.

I will admit that in this canyon I am captive to this place,
This sacredness of cathedral which assures me I belong,
Where shadows dance with sunlight among the spires and rocky peaks,
    like moveable feasts to celebrate the majesty of altars set on altars
    in such magnificence that only creation herself
        could compose such a grand mosaic of sacred mountainscape —
        perfectly woven by the hand of nature's love.

And above me — sometimes held in glistened snow,
    or emerging from swirling mist on grey days of quiet birthing
Softer peaks emerge like shrouded figures, again preparing
    to reveal themselves to the clarity of Light.

And night becomes them
    as winter's cold or summer's scorching heat becomes them,
And I become them too, as they create new entrances
    to some fragile emptiness even deeper in the soul of me —
    moving through that timeless grace which allows a seeker —
      only on very rare and extremely delicate days
        to actually behold the mirror of Divinity.

Clouds roll over me on soft, misty days, as the wind seems
    to whisper them all again through my soul as I dissolve —
    in comfort and a gentle kind of peace here in this sacred space
      where I can at least reach toward wholeness once again —
Where all the real beauty grows beyond mere words,
And there is nothing left to do but become the beauty which I see
Until it is always such a pain when I must leave this altar of my life —
    such tearing of my heart when I am called to other things —
      though the depth of it strangely comes along with me,
      as all the world begins to glow anew in the radiance
        which emanates from this place of Holy Light.

This place — where hawks dare to sweep the clouds
    with the power of their wings
      and eagles glide on rivers of the wind,
Where deer approach and stay in easy sharing of the silences
    as we all dissolve to purest nature, held in creation's breath,
Where I am filled with such an easy awe,
    and spirit comes as gently as it can,

within and beside and finally becoming me
  in miracles I never dreamed could be —
  here, in this red rock cathedral, altar and sanctuary
  until — in wondrous miracle I finally become them all.

I become the canyon where other mountains always may emerge.
I become the altar which my life is offered and consecrated upon,
I become the canticle which sings me into sacred space,
The high and lofty flute which beckons me from even farther canyons,
  if only I will heed the tantalizing call of softer, mystic winds
  and dare an even higher lofty climb.

For I am home here, in this canyon hiding place,
  this sanctuary space where I begin to gently probe
    the secrets of the mystery which continues calling me
    from divinity's own precious heart.
And it is good here — set apart from all the others for a while —
To be so simply caught within the comfort of the mystery —
  so easily held within the truth of sacred union — manifest.

If ever there could be a place for me to pray —
                    I come into this canyon again — today...

Through Silent Seas

I have wandered in my time far beyond the shores of possibility.
I have split the darkness open
      and ridden through my own silent seas.
I have flung my moments far beyond
      the walls of destiny,
And I have seen the spirit brooding, moving —
Before and through and after me.

Held by love and torn by tension,
Soothed by soft and mystic melodies,
Embraced and beckoned by the flowing of a stillness
      and the agony of being too aware,
I have dared the empty sky to cradle me hard,
And I have wept from the pain
      of wanting too much to soar.
I have left the earth and thrown away
      what was given me in birth from tender wombs,
And now I await the brilliance
      for I need a force outside of me
      to contemplate and generate the Light.

Hold me, as you would try to hold a cirrus cloud,
And see me, as in times beyond,
      you might strain your eyes
      to find a hidden unicorn.

Taste the silence as it pulls in all around
      and touch me if you've ever held a dream.

I am moving forward now. I know I am.
I am finally roughly torn and born to newer worlds,
And their memory lies very sweet, indeed
      on my silver bed of dreams.
And the body will be willing,
      for the chalice never weeps,
And the mind will sleep only
      where love's spirit finally lies.

So do not look for me where I have been,
And do not call the name I cannot answer any more.
Wait, if you are seeking me,
      for you will find me whole if you dream and
      if you are strong enough to share.

In time, yes, in the filling time,
      you will find me where I sleep,
And where I know now I always have remained —
      There, in the beauty of your own precious soul!

Sacred Ground

We are on sacred ground here.
This is the mountain gone up, come down, and remained upon.

This is ascent and descent. This is continuance.
This is No Place. No Thing.
      No breath left except the Divine.

This is the Crown opened wide
      in the flowing of Sacred Light.
This is the Passage and the Journey,
      the quiet golden fountain blast
      streaming out so subtly beyond and beyond and beyond.

We have clearly gone to silence here
      with little words on paper —
      half sounds stumbled in a rhythm faintly heard —
      tiny echoes straining through the distance of eternity.

I am the tabula rasa here, complete now.
The totally blank tablet — the pure, clean slate
      with all memory shattered in Light Beyond Light,
      in the touch of a breath and the chanting of sacred sounds.

I am the child grown younger than time.
I am open here. I am new stone.
And these words can only come so simply,
      in absolute, total trust.
At last no more fear is left in me!
      Just take up your chisel —
      and carve me now.

BIBLIOGRAPHY

A Course In Miracles. Glen Ellen, California: Foundation For Inner Peace, 1985.

Aurobindo, Sri. *The Mind of Light*. Twin Lakes, WI, USA: Lotus Press, 1971.

Barks, Coleman. Translator. *The Essential Rumi*. New York: Harper Row San Francisco, 1995.

Borysenko, Joyce. *A Woman's Journey To God*. New York: Riverhead Books, 1999.

Chittister, Joan. D. *Heart of Flesh*. Grand Rapids, Michigan: William B. Eerdmans Publishing Company, 1998.

deNicolas, Antonio T. *St. John of the Cross*. York Beach, Maine: Samuel Weiser, Inc. 1989.

Hammarskjold, Dag. *Markings*. New York: Alfred A. Knopf, 1965.

Harvey, Andrew. *The Essential Mystics*. New York: Harper San Francisco, 1996.

Hawkins, David R. *Power vs. Force*. Carlsbad, California: Hay House, Inc., 1995.

_____. *The Eye of the I*. West Sedona, Arizona: Veritas Publishing, 2001.

_____. *I*. West Sedona, Arizona: Veritas Publishing, 2003.

_____. *Reality, Spirituality and Modern Man*. Toronto: Axial Publishing Company, 2008.

Hurtak, J.J. & Desiree. *The Gospel of Mary*. Los Gatos, California: The Academy of Future Science, 2008.

Lindbergh, Anne Morrow. *Gift From The Sea*. New York: Pantheon Books, 1975.

Maritain, Jacques. *Creative Intuition in Art and Poetry*. New York: New American Library, 1953.

Merton, Thomas. *Raids On The Unspeakable*. New York: New Directions, 1964.

_____. *The New Man*. New York: Farrar, Straus and Giroux, 1961.

_____. *Thoughts in Solitude*. New York: Farrar, Straus and Giroux, 1958.

_____. *Contemplative Prayer*. New York: Doubleday, 1969.

O'Murchu. Diarmuid. *Evolutionary Faith*. Maryknoll New York: Orbis Books, 2002.

_____. *Our World in Transition*. New York: The Crossroad Publishing Company, 1992.

_____. *Reclaiming Spirituality*. New York: The Crossroads Publishing Company, 1997.

_____. *Religion in Exile*. New York: The Crossroad Publishing Company, 2000.

_____. *Quantum Theology*. New York: The Crossroad Publishing Company, 2004.

Ryan, M.J., Editor. *The Fabric of the Future*. Berkley, California: Conari Press, 1988.

Teilhard de Chardin, Pierre. *The Divine Milieu*. New York: Harper & Row, 1960.

_____. *The Phenomenon of Man*. New York: Harper & Row, 1959.

Wauters, Ambika. *Healing With the Energy of the Chakras*. Freedom, California: The Crossing Press, 1998.

Wilber, Ken. *The Essential Ken Wilber*. Boston: Shambhala, 1998.

Williamson, Marianne. *The Gift of Change*. New York: Harper San Francisco: 2004.

Yogananda, Paramahansa. *Man's Eternal Quest*. Los Angeles: Self Realization Fellowship, 1982.

_____. *The Second Coming of Christ*. Los Angeles: Self Realization Fellowship. 2004.

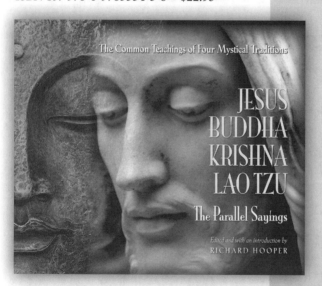